CONTENTS

CONSCRIPTS *of* MIGRATION

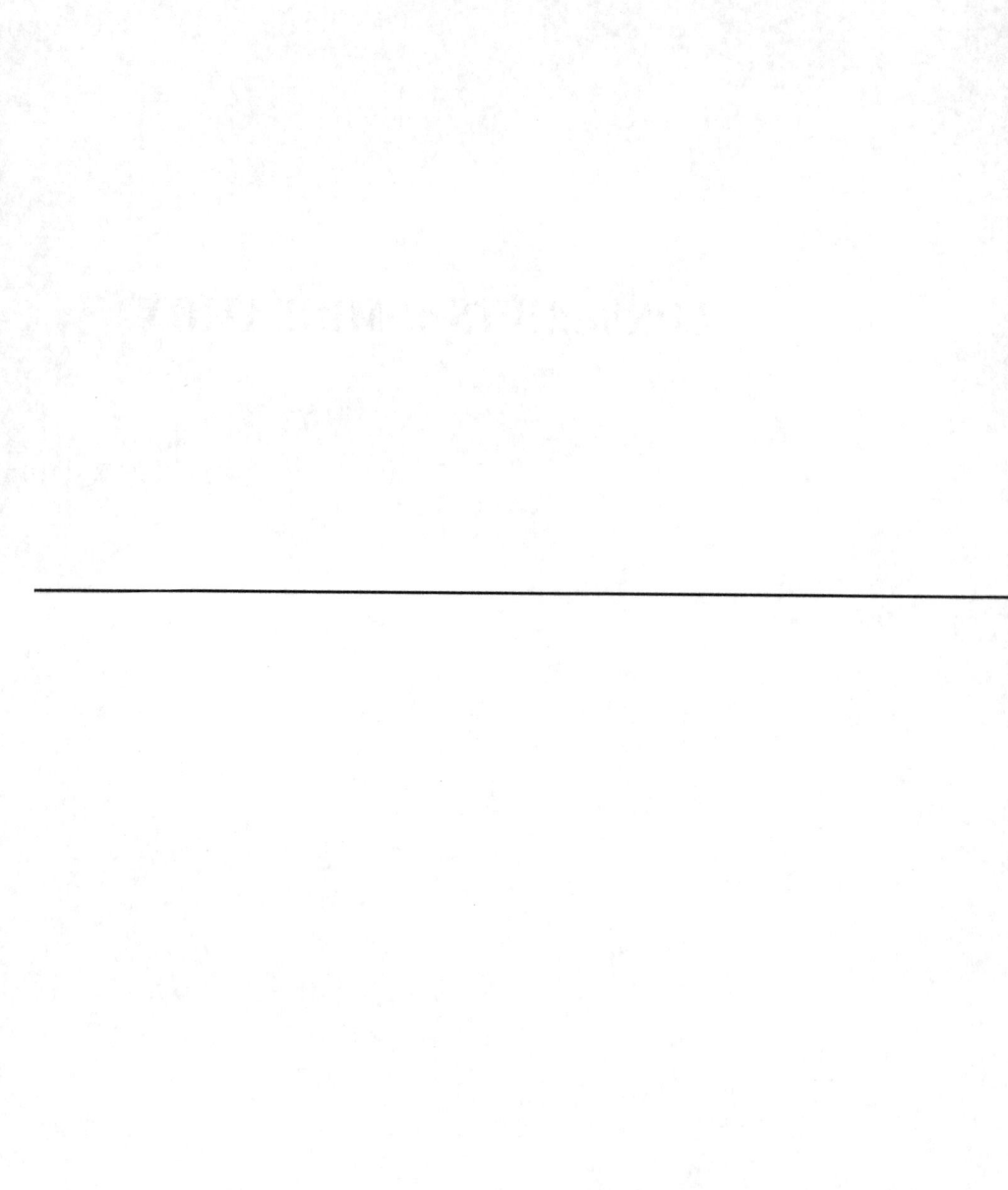

CONSCRIPTS
of MIGRATION

Neoliberal Globalization, Nationalism,
and the Literature of New African Diasporas

CHRISTOPHER IAN FOSTER

University Press of Mississippi / Jackson

The University Press of Mississippi is the scholarly publishing agency of
the Mississippi Institutions of Higher Learning: Alcorn State University,
Delta State University, Jackson State University, Mississippi State University,
Mississippi University for Women, Mississippi Valley State University,
University of Mississippi, and University of Southern Mississippi.

www.upress.state.ms.us

The University Press of Mississippi is a member of
the Association of University Presses.

First printing 2019

∞

Library of Congress Cataloging-in-Publication Data

Names: Foster, Christopher Ian, author.
Title: Conscripts of migration: neoliberal globalization, nationalism, and
   the literature of new African diasporas / Christopher Ian Foster.
Description: Jackson: University Press of Mississippi, [2019] | Includes
   bibliographical references and index. |
Identifiers: LCCN 2019002929 (print) | LCCN 2019010903 (ebook) | ISBN
   9781496824233 (epub single) | ISBN 9781496824240 (epub institutional) |
   ISBN 9781496824257 (pdf single) | ISBN 9781496824264 (pdf institutional)
   | ISBN 9781496824219 (cloth) | ISBN 9781496824226 (pbk.)
Subjects: LCSH: African diaspora in literature. | Literature and
   globalization. | Blacks in literature—21st century. | LCGFT: Literary criticism.
Classification: LCC PN56.G55 (ebook) | LCC PN56.G55 F67 2019 (print) | DDC
   809/.896—dc23
LC record available at https://lccn.loc.gov/2019002929

British Library Cataloging-in-Publication Data available

ACKNOWLEDGMENTS

If, as the cliché goes, it takes a village to raise a child, then it can take a city to write a book. The bulk of the early research for and writing of *Conscripts of Migration: Neoliberal Globalization, Nationalism, and the Literature of New African Diasporas* took place in New York City, and it was reared across and by institutions of higher learning, communities, workshops, events, and most importantly, people. I am deeply grateful for the generous institutional support provided by the Institute for Research on the African Diaspora in the Americas and Caribbean at the Graduate Center of the City University of New York and the Graduate Center's English Department. I am also indebted to the Committee on Globalization and Social Change for their fellowship, writing and reading workshops, and great events. This institutional support allowed me the space and time away from teaching (my other passion), to write, revise, and write again. To Robert Reid-Pharr, whose guidance and wit were inimitable, and to my committee members Meena Alexander and Ashley Dawson: a huge thank you. For without your many insights, challenges, and encouragement, this project would not have come to fruition. I heartily thank the student-run Postcolonial Studies Group at the Graduate Center, which was something like a home away from home. Tracy Riley, Lily Saint, Sonali Perera, Debarati Biswas, Alison Klein, Velina Manolova, Margaret Galvan, Ashna Ali who is my co-conspirator in all things migritude and an inspiration, and others provided invaluable support, friendship, and insightful comments on various drafts and projects. To Rahul K. Gairola, whose early mentorship at the University of Washington catalyzed my graduate career and whose friendship traveled from Seattle to Oxford to New York and beyond: thank you. I thank the following distinguished and brilliant readers of more recent drafts of the book: Laura Westengard at City College of Technology, CUNY, Tomaz Cunningham at Jackson State University, and Eleanor Paynter at the Ohio State University. Your comments made the book that much stronger and I garnered something of an education through them. Supriya Nair's support came at the perfect moment, when the perils of the job market weighed heavily upon me. Your collegiality and friendship mean so much. Thank you to my friends and former colleagues at James Madison University, Brooks Hefner, John Ott, Besi Muhonja, as well as the myriad folks that have helped me in one way or another along the way. I would be remiss not to thank the team at University Press of Mississippi for your sustained support and hard work on this project. Activism and thought are deeply connected for me and so I want to express gratitude for the many movements that I have taken a small part in and the organizers who have inspired me: the Movement for Black Lives, those in support of LGBTQ and immigrant rights, the tireless supporters of justice in Palestine like Boycott, Divest, and Sanction, as well as the great work in Mississippi by organizations like Cooperation Jackson. Finally, a very deep and heartfelt thank you to my family: mom, dad, and sis (Teresa Robertson, Chris Foster, and Hannah Foster), and to my life partner Erin Friedmann Foster. This would not have been possible without you. Maisha Marefu!

CONSCRIPTS *of* MIGRATION

Chapter 1

CONSCRIPTS OF MIGRATION IN THE ERA OF GLOBALIZATION

The twenty-first century has appropriately been described as "the age of migration."[1] Yet the fundamental character of migration has been, and continues to be, one of crisis. The decades-long crisis in the Mediterranean for African immigrants and refugees—a disaster that alone has claimed thirty thousand lives or more in the past few decades—the Syrian refugee crisis, the volatile United States–Mexico border, humanitarian crises in Haiti and elsewhere precipitating displacement, the apartheid-like criminalization of Palestinian movement by the Israeli government, and many other such crises, define our moment. The situation has worsened in the Trump era, an epoch that has seen the rise of overt xenophobia, racism, and anti-immigrant nativism. In early 2017, for example, United States president Donald Trump signed into law a "Muslim ban" preventing immigrants and refugees from seven Muslim-majority nations (Iran, Iraq, Libya, Somalia, Sudan, Syria, and Yemen) from entering the country to, as the Trump administration stated, keep out "radical Islamic terrorism," despite, as the US Ninth Circuit Court of Appeals would argue, no evidence of impending attacks.[2] PhD student Saira Rafiee, studying at the City University of New York (my alma mater), was forbidden from re-entering the United States after visiting her family in Iran and was detained for eighteen hours; Nisrin Elamin, a Sudanese PhD student at Stanford University, was also detained arriving in the United States after having completed fieldwork in Sudan for her degree; and, as the American Civil Liberties Union notes, among the many "barred from entering the United States [was] Hameed Khalid Darweesh, an Iraqi man who worked as an interpreter for the US Army's 101st Airborne Division who 'spent years keeping US soldiers alive in combat in Iraq.'"[3] He was detained at JFK as well. Just days after Trump's Muslim ban, radical white nationalist Alexandre Bissonnette murdered six worshippers at a mosque in Canada.[4] Trump's Muslim ban, his administration's 2018 "no tolerance" policy rending thousands of children from their parents at the US-Mexico border, the Quebec City massacre, as well as the precipitous spike in hate crimes since Trump's inauguration represent an extreme expression of anti-immigrant, Islamophobic, and white supremacist policy, practice, and rhetoric *already* in place in the United States and Europe. How did this come about? How is it connected to the myriad crises characterizing immigration in the late twentieth and twenty-first centuries? How might a study of immigration from an anti-nationalist and African diasporic perspective crystallize our otherwise muddied conceptions and understandings of our contemporary global climate?

This study explores a characteristically Western contradiction regarding immigration and the incisive body of global African literature challenging it. The United Kingdom, France, Italy, the United States, and other powers actually produced the migration that they attempt to police at their borders. Through global economic, political, and cultural processes from the era of high imperialism, decolonization, the cold war, to contemporary neoliberal globalization (neocolonialism), they have devastated nations in the Global South, creating instability and displacement. The Global North's own implication in the migration they helped create, and the violent processes that catalyze it, are often obscured by draconian immigration regimes and the anti-immigrant and racist discourses that subtend these practices and ideas. In fact, even the way we talk about immigration in the twenty-first century, whether on the right or left—from fear and hatred to benevolent tolerance—hides the plain fact of a deeply asymmetrical world shaped by imperialism, globalization, and nationalism.

Edward Said begins his groundbreaking *Culture and Imperialism* with an important point about imperialism and ends his book with one regarding immigration. On the substantially global nature of imperialism, he states:

> Consider that in 1800 Western powers claimed 55 percent but actually held approximately 35 percent of the earth's surface, and that by 1878 the proportion was 67 percent. . . . By 1914 . . . Europe held a grand total of roughly 85 percent of the earth as colonies, protectorates, dependencies, dominions, and commonwealths. No other associated set of colonies in history was as large, none so totally dominated, none so unequal in power to the Western metropolis. As a result, says William McNeill in The Pursuit of Power, "the world was united into a single interacting whole as never before."[5]

Eric J. Hobsbawm, echoing Marx, would confirm not only the totalizing nature of imperialism but its connection to racial capitalism as a world-colonizing economic system. In addition to partitioning the entire world, imperialism would transform it "into a complex of colonial and semi-colonial territories which increasingly evolved into specialized producers of one or two primary products for export to the world market."[6] Building upon Said and Hobsbawm, I argue that the management of the movement (and categorization) of populations in the world is not only a by-product of this Western partitioning of the world, but actually shapes it. This is why Edward Said's second point, ending his book, is so important. He implies that empire and migration are deeply connected:

> Imperialism did not end, however. It did not suddenly become "past," once decolonization had set in motion the dismantling of the classical empires. A legacy of connections still binds countries like Algeria and India to France and Britain respectively. A vast new population of Muslims, Africans, and West Indians from former colonial territories now reside in metropolitan Europe; even Italy, Germany, and Scandinavia today must deal with these dislocations, which are to a large degree the result of imperialism and decolonization. (Said, 282)

Said uses the term *dislocation* precisely because modern empires created migration in their former colonies, like Algeria or India, through colonization and then police those dislocated populations at home. They punish black and brown people deemed "outsiders" or "foreign" despite the intimate relationship of conquest, while creating and reproducing the myth of Europe or the United States as a whites-only enclave, which of course is historically inaccurate.[7] In this book, when I refer to empires I include not solely the imperial period but the epoch of neoliberal globalization as well, from about the 1970s to the present.[8] I follow Quinn Slobodian's theorization of neoliberalism not as a set of economic and political theories and practices that would create a borderless or stateless world governed by market forces, but as an "extra-economic framework that would secure the continued existence of capitalism" on a global scale and keep it safe by "redesigning states, laws, and other institutions to protect the market . . . from mass demands for social justice and redistribution equality."[9] Neoliberals, he continues, "sought neither the disappearance of the state nor the disappearance of borders" (Slobodian, 2). Furthermore, in *Conscripts of Migration* I show how neoliberal globalization represented a new way of colonizing the Global South by utilizing both economic and political exploitation via global institutions like the World Trade Organization, the World Bank, the International Monetary Funds (based in and benefiting the Global North), nation-states, and militaries. Senegalese-French writer Fatou Diome would call these new neoliberal weapons "economic bazookas."[10] The wholly negative effects of these policies in the Global South continue to be discursively explained away as random side effects of the "free hand of the market" or by racist characterizations of so-called "shit-hole" countries in the Global South, as Donald Trump would openly parrot and others with more decorum would quietly hold to be true. These colonial and neoliberal empires, roughly making up what we might call the Global North, created an entire complex of discourses around migration, often shoring up political and economic projects from imperialism to the present, that, in every case, erase the glaring fact of their own complicity in creating the very dislocations that Said points out above.

Given these histories and our contemporary global configuration, I analyze immigration neither in terms of invasion or free movement but in terms of *conscription*—and in two ways, the first more general and the second immediate. First, imperialism set the global conditions that dictate how and where one moves, while neoliberal capital continues to destabilize the Global South for the direct benefit of the North. This creates, shapes, and interdicts movement. Second, immigration regimes conscript people via apparatuses like passport hierarchies, checkpoints, borders, documentation, and the legalization of dehumanizing identity categories like "illegal alien," "*sans papier*," and so on. By definition, "conscription" describes the act of forcing a person or people, under duress, to join an army. And indeed colonial powers used forced African conscription to bolster its ranks in both world wars and dating as far back as 1857, which I discuss in more detail in chapters 3 and 6.[11] Nearly half a million Africans were conscripted into European armies, for example, in World War I alone.[12] For their service they were met with death, abhorrent racist treatment, and discrimination, and were denied citizenship and equal rights—a chilling parallel to the ways in which immigrants and refugees are treated today. Gebreyesus Hailu's *The Conscript: A Novel of Libya's Anticolonial War*, which was written in his native language Tigrinya in 1927 but not published until 1950, represents an early Africa-centered narrative of conscription on the continent.[13]

In addition to its literal sense, the term *conscript* has also been used more broadly by Stanley Diamond, Talal Asad, and David Scott, who describe the violence (both negative and productive) and reach of Western civilization and modernity. I discuss these incisive uses of the term in this introduction.

In my title, "conscripts" initially seems an incongruous object to the subject of "migration" since our dominant conception privileges individual choice and agency—one can, ostensibly, freely move or not move. Yet, I want to press against this dominant neoliberal viewpoint on immigration as private and personal—both figurations are variously marketable and reaffirming of "Western democracy"—to suggest that peoples from the Global South, the formerly colonized, and people of color, are already *caught up* in modern conditions that shape decisions to move or not move. These conditions then continue to catalyze, manage, and organize movement while producing discursive and legal categories that constitute diasporic existence. *Conscripts of Migration* in its entirety provides evidence to this claim and provides a literary, political, and phenomenological understanding of the literature of contemporary African diasporas, focusing on "migritude" writing and its antecedents in particular, while necessarily attending to various localized and global contours.

To understand immigration, we must take seriously the following two facts: the violence of colonialism created migration and catalyzed displacement, and northern policies of both neoliberal globalization and nationalism in the late twentieth and twenty-first centuries continue that trend. Immigrant bans ironically attempt to keep out the baleful effects of the Global North's own policies while externalizing blame via white supremacist rhetoric. As a young college student in Seattle in 1999, I joined forty thousand other protesters who assembled to challenge the policies of neoliberal globalization at the meeting of the World Trade Organization. Before the worldwide protests of Trump's Muslim ban in 2017, protesters gathered around the world to oppose America's imperial invasion of Iraq in 2002–2003 and its history of neocolonial machinations in the region. These movements and complementary global cultural production can be studied via immigration. The literature of new African diasporas, for example, phenomenologically reveal, historicize, and challenge the very nationalist and yet global policies and ideologies of Europe and the United States by focusing on migrant experiences. As I show in chapter 6, Nadifa Mohamed's first novel *Black Mamba Boy* shows us how we got to this point by narrativizing migration in the high-imperial era—an important key to understanding our present.

Twenty-first-century African literature increasingly figures immigration as a conscripting force in terms of race, gender, and sexuality. It also lays bare the relationship between migration and empire. Fatou Diome and Shailja Patel indeed connect the disciplining of movement in the twenty-first century with colonialism (see chapters 3 and 2 respectively). Nearing the end of Diome's novel *The Belly of the Atlantic*, protagonist Salie reflects on her experience at immigration control upon arrival in France in the late twentieth century, having come from Dakar. She describes it as humiliating, racializing, and biopolitical—she must pay for her own medical exam and give endless accounts of herself. As Salie moves through the liminal space of France's immigration control, she connects her own and other migrants' treatment to imperial pasts. "So illness is considered an unacceptable defect that bars access to French territory . . . in the colonies, for a long time the natives believed that the master never fell ill, so cleverly did everything conspire to maintain the myth of his superiority" (153). The colonial-era management of populations and in particular, their movement, is mirrored in contemporary immigration regimes. Salie parses her experience by writing a poem based on the traditional laments of her village: *"Passports, permits, visas / And endless red tape / The new chains of slavery / Bank branch, account number / Address, ethnic origin / The fabric of modern apartheid"* (Diome, 154; emphasis in original). I read the migrant of Salie's poem as being conscripted in two ways. First, the endless red tape shapes the movement of emigrants from formerly colonized places, those apparatuses used to control and document that movement—passports, permits, visas. These are, from the perspective of African migrants, the "new chains of slavery." Second, Salie refers to a more general condition in which the migrant is, via these apparatuses and their histories, already conscripted, indeed she is woven into the "fabric" of modern apartheid, into late twentieth- and twenty-first-century neoliberal globalization.

In a collection of essays titled *Beyond Walls and Cages: Prisons, Borders, and Global Crisis*, Jenna Loyd, Matt Mitchelson, and Andrew Burridge argue that "borders and prisons—walls and cages—*are* global crises. Walls and cages are fundamental to managing the wealth, social inequalities, and opposition to these harms created by capitalism and the present round of neocolonial dispossession."[14] This contributes to what Loyd calls global apartheid—"a condition in which the wealthiest regions of the world erect physical and bureaucratic barriers against the movement of people from poorer regions of the world" (Loyd et al.). These barriers and attendant identity categories that shape movement combine to make manifest the condition of global or modern apartheid; they suggest that, when we think about movement, immigration, and the world, we should consider the violent expropriation of free movement from the majority of the world's travelers, issues that contemporary African diasporic literature often engages.

This new literature figures immigration as individual and yet systemic and as integrated into larger global processes as authors are increasingly concerned with African mobility and the forces that animate or deter that mobility. *Conscripts of Migration* studies the diasporic literature of African women and queer migrants to argue that immigration in the era of neoliberal globalization is transnationally constituted, institutional, and historical. African migrants and the actors narrated in the literature of new African diasporas are conscripted by the conditions that produce them; their movement is catalyzed, shaped, and managed. The script has already been prepared for them. "Long before the ticket is purchased to come to the promised land of Europe," Donald Carter notes, "this 'other world' has insinuated itself into the very fabric of everyday life in the future migrants' homeland."[15] Writers like Cristina Ali Farah and Igiaba Scego, for example, address both the dehumanizing identity categories from the perspective of the African migrant or traveler, and the larger structures that weave subjects and movement into the fabric of an increasingly neoliberal globalization.

The relatively understudied migritude literature is critically attentive to contemporary immigration regimes and addresses globalization precisely as inextricable from its imperial pasts. Migritude indicates the work and ideas of a disparate yet distinct group of younger African authors born after independence in the 1960s. Most often they have lived both in and outside Africa and narrate the world of the migrant within the context of globalization, yet they emphasize that the "past" of immigration and conceptions of the immigrant are irreducibly entangled with the history of colonialism. Fatou Diome, Calixthe Beyala, Shailja Patel, Abdourahman Waberi, and other authors confront issues of migrancy (forced or not), diaspora (forced or not), errantry, departure, return, racism against immigrants, identity, gender, sexuality, and postcoloniality.

Migritude takes its suffix from the term *Négritude*, a black anti-racist and anti-colonialist literary and activist movement that would have a profound impact not just in Africa or Paris, where it originated in the 1930s, but throughout the world and in many languages. Thus migritude also brings black antiracist and anticolonial literary genealogies to bear upon the present. This transnational cohort of African migrant writers and artists phenomenologically image checkpoints, passports, and even borders as symptomatic of larger institutions like the European Union or American immigration control that, de jure or de facto, racialize, gender, and heteronormativize nonwhite bodies. Through the study of African women and queer migrant writers like Cristina Ali Farah and Diriye Osman, I argue against dominant conceptions of migration framed solely as private, choice-based, and often ahistorical; rather, *Conscripts of Migration* tracks immigration as a system developed along with the modern nation-state and with European imperial projects by the late nineteenth century, and as evolving into the present era of global capitalism as an international network of technologies, law, and infrastructure.

The contemporary world literature market has seen a wonderful explosion of African women authors in the past few decades like Chimamanda Ngozi Adichie, Taiye Selasie, and newcomers like Imbolo Mbue and Yaa Gyasi. Many of these authors and other young African authors living in various diasporas have been described as Afropolitan or as subscribing to the ideals or aesthetics of Afropolitanism, which I do not discuss at length in this book. Why not? And why not include these authors in this study? They are indeed global or diasporic in many ways, yet I do not include these authors in this book because they describe immigration in a manner very different from that of the group of authors I assess, and therefore do not answer the guiding questions of *Conscripts of Migration*. They often describe and approach immigration from an upper-middle-class perspective and do not, as a consequence, paint a picture of the kind of immigration that the majority of the world's travelers face, or trace the history of why that is. The authors I study here imagine immigration from the perspective of economic migrants, refugees, working-class immigrants, "illegals," non-elite migrants, and the undocumented. These latter perspectives effectively clarify or bring into focus the underlying causes, present and historical, of immigration and their global and underlying structures. Migritude literature indeed narrates the experiences of working-class or economic migrants, refugees, and those who move without the resources wealth provides. And, although Imolo Mbue's timely *Behold the Dreamers* does in fact deftly narrate the experiences of an economically struggling family from Cameroon in the United States, she does not pause on immigration itself for any great length.

A second question might arise: why the focus on women writers? How is the perspective of diasporic African women writers different from that of their male counterparts? I clarify this throughout the book, but suffice it to say now that, because the historical and contemporary management of movement is normative, gender, like race, intersects with immigration. Therefore, the experiences of women in migration will often differ from those of their male counterparts in various ways. These unique experiences both in transit and in various diasporas are understudied, and, importantly, provide new and exciting understandings of immigration itself. It is for these reasons and others that I focus, with some exceptions (including Abu Bakr Khaal, who I discuss in this introduction, and queer British-Somali writer Diriye Osman near the end of the book), on narratives of contemporary African women and immigration.

What are the stakes of approaching "immigration" as a network of structures and practices instituted by the imperial powers of the Global North precisely as a means to control the effects of its own policies and actions in the Global South? Simply put, these disparate colonial technologies and their scions in globalization both destabilized and displaced; they created movement and then managed it. Contemporary European and American policy on immigration attempts to keep out not just postcolonial "foreigners," but *a fortiori*, to prevent calls for social and redistributive justice because they take no responsibility for designed underdevelopment, military intervention, aid, and other means of indirect or direct control. Consider the squashing of the New International Economic Order (NIEO), which was the postcolonial "trade Union of the poor nations" launched in 1974 as a network of countries in the Global South and which criticized continued neocolonial inequality and economic exploitation after formal independence (Slobodian, 219). According to Slobodian, the Volcker Shock and Washington Consensus effectively crushed the NIEO movement by the early 1980s (222). He notes that, "given the patent refusal of the Global North to live up to its own liberal principles by practicing actual free trade in key sectors such as agriculture, further deviations from the liberal principles themselves were necessary to account for path-dependent inequality" (219). In this sense, postcolonial immigration is a symptom of the liberal northern countries' fascist policies in the South and therefore migrants cannot be welcomed as such, for the truth of their policies, inscribed upon the bodies and memories of the dislocated, would undermine the very narratives upon which the nations of the civilized world were built.

Is immigration in this context less the action of moving to another country, more the aggregate systems and politics that manage, produce, or interdict movement (particularly with regard to people from the Global South or nonwhite persons in Europe or the United States)? And how does diasporic African cultural production challenge, illustrate, or otherwise redress immigration, and by extension, an increasingly apartheid-like globality? These are the guiding questions and issues that *Conscripts of Migration* takes up. This book can be read in two ways:

1) As inaugurating a theory of conscription under neoliberal globalization, which I outline in this introduction and chapter 2, via the
study of movement and immigration in the twentieth and twenty-
first centuries from a particularly postcolonial and Africa-centered
perspective. The term conscription offers a better way of understanding the political and economic systems that undergird immigration,
and therefore, an alternative paradigm to intentional misunderstand-
ings, mystifications, and blindness regarding immigration in our contemporary moment.

2) the book can be read as an introduction to, and survey of, migritude literature. Although there are a handful of articles and chapters
on this relatively new body of literature, there are no full-length man-
uscripts on this subject, and I depart from Jacques Chevrier's brief
but founding theory of migritude by emphasizing diasporic African
authors' engagement with the materiality of immigration, rather than
focusing solely on identity.

In the past few decades scholars have published an exciting array of texts
located at the interstices of black Atlantic and postcolonial studies that mobilize a rigorously global analytical framework.[16] *Conscripts of Migration*
practices a similar kind of critical globality attendant to the importance of
both black and Asian diasporas, and espouses a rigorously transnational
politics. However, texts circulating within black diaspora and black Atlantic
scholarship, often focus on late eighteenth- and nineteenth-century black
Atlantic and more recently, Indian Ocean worlds. Although important works
in postcolonial anthropology like Laura Ann Stoler's *Imperial Debris: On
Ruins and Ruination* do dissect imperial pasts that haunt the twenty-first
century, they focus neither on contemporary African or global literature.
While owing a great debt to these works, my book corrects against the dearth
of studies on twenty-first-century global African literature and the neoliberal
processes these texts engage with. It is necessary to reconceptualize immigration through the study of African narratives of migration in the twenty-first
century and therefore to suggest new pathways for black diaspora studies and
the growing field of global Anglophone and Francophone literary studies.

Conscripts of Migration also owes a great debt to, and utilizes, queer theory.
Developing a theory of conscription, this project argues that immigration
in the era of neoliberal globalization is transnationally constituted, institutional, and historical. The construction of immigrants as such, or refugees

or "illegals," is predicated upon a national normativity striated by received perceptions of race, gender, and sexuality.[17] It is important then, in the study of transnational migration, to utilize the tools of queer diaspora studies to theorize, for example, the intersection of racial and sexual normativity. In his oft-cited article "Transnational Adoption and Queer Diasporas," David Eng argues that queer diaspora emerges as a concept that provides "new methods of contesting traditional family and kinship structures—of reorganizing national and transnational communities based not on origin, filiation, and genetics but on destination, affiliation, and the assumption of a common set of social practices or political commitments."[18] Queer diaspora importantly denaturalizes normative structures, from biological notions of filiation, "the family" or "the race," to stable notions of the nation often mobilized in the service of a problematic ethnic nationalism, all of which are tied to hetero-sexist reproductive frameworks. However, queer diaspora studies has not generally examined African literature. *Conscripts of Migration* investigates the work of African women and queer migrant writers like Cristina Ali Farah and Diriye Osman (see chapters 4 and 5) to redress normative technologies managing the movement of peoples and their experiences in various new black diasporas while articulating the history of immigration as it relates to the nation and imperialism.

~

I begin with two literary vignettes that illustrate my choice of the word *conscript* in a book about migration. In 2010 Somali writer Nadifa Mohamed published what I describe as a migritude novel. Set during World War II in the Horn of Africa, North Africa, the Middle East, and Europe, her novel *Black Mamba Boy* follows young Somali protagonist Jama as he moves through and across these colonial spaces. Yet the novel also speaks to our global present wherein technologies of power managing the movement of nonwhite bodies have indeed proliferated: borders, checkpoints, documents. Near the beginning of the novel, the narrator describes Jama's home, Hargeisa, Somalia, with a sense of foreboding: "A hyena-rich darkness covered the town and Jama could feel Jinns and half-men at his back stalking the alleys, making the hairs on his neck stand on end . . . Jama felt the impending bloodshed sizzle in the air and rubbed down the tiny hairs on his lower spine as they nervously stood up, as if they were frightened conscripts standing to atten-tion before a bloodied old general."[19] These sentences reflect the tension of a colonized Horn of Africa and the impending destruction on the continent by a European war. They also foreshadow Jama's own conscription by the

Italian army in Somalia as an "askari" or black soldier, so it is no accident that Mohamed uses the term metaphorically. But the brilliance of the novel is that it shows that Jama is *already* conscripted by colonial structures and systems of immigration in the high imperial era. Mohamed imagines a post-Berlin conference scene subtending the first footsteps of Jama's journey: "His land had been carved up among France, Italy, Britain, and Abyssinia . . . The British had built the road to ease their passage into and out of their possession, and now Jama trundled along it, making slow progress toward the artificial border between Somaliland and Djibouti" (77–78). Here, British roads, borders, and infrastructure, all imposed or "artificial," shape Jama's movement. *Black Mamba Boy* shows that the violence of colonialism creates the conditions for dispersal. It catalyzes displacement. In the same moment, colonial systems of immigration and its apparatuses like passports, docu-ments, or checkpoints, interdict, redirect, and reeducate that very dispersal of peoples (Jama and others in the novel) in and through colonial technologies managing movement. Jama is not simply a conscript of the Italian colonial army but more generally a conscript of migration.

Nadifa Mohamed names Claude McKay's 1929 novel *Banjo* as something of an ancestor to *Black Mamba Boy*. What they share, I argue, is a critical engagement with imperial systems of immigration as conscripting forces within the context of a globalizing racial capitalism. There is a moment, for example, in McKay's seminal 1929 text wherein Ray—the author's writerly counterpart in the novel—critiques European racism toward black French troops in Germany during World War I. In doing so he alludes to the fact that black conscripts in the war were caught up in something much bigger than an army—Western civilization itself:

> A big campaign of propaganda was on against them, backed by German-Americans, Negro-breaking Southerners, and your English liberals and socialists. The odd thing about that propaganda was that it said nothing about the exploitation of primitive and ignorant black conscripts to do the dirty work of one victorious civilization over another . . .[20]

In *Banjo*, McKay shows that black soldiers in the war as well as colonial sub-jects, black migrants, vagabonds, workers, and black intellectuals were indeed conscripts of Western civilization[21] or imperialism and its twin, racial capital-ism. Meditating on Africa, for example, Ray states, "civilization had gone out among these native, earthy people, had despoiled them of their primitive soil, had uprooted, enchained, transported, and transformed them to labor under its laws, and yet lacked the spirit to tolerate them within its walls" (McKay, 314). The terms "uprooted," "transported," and "transformed" suggest that movement in the imperial and capitalist context—being uprooted, even transported—actually transforms subjects, a variant of conscription. The larger processes of immigration (and its international systemization arising dialectically with the modern and imperial nation-state) drive global processes from colonialism to, I argue, neoliberal globalization. They solidify nation-states and economies and help divide and conquer. The state-controlled management of movement—what I am calling immigration—must necessarily have its origins in nationalist projects that define who is native and who is foreign while policing those differences in various ways. Ray's statement about "civilization"—meaning Europe—not tolerating colonial subjects "within its walls," for example, anticipates descriptions of "fortress Europe" in the twenty-first century, which Michelle M. Wright defines as "the explicit attempt to ahistoricize Europe as a 'whites-only' enclave that must protect itself against the 'invasion' of non-white hordes [similar to] increasing hegemonic aggression espoused and practiced by the United States" (271). *Conscripts of Migration* studies the ways in which Nadifa Mohamed and other contemporary African and diasporic authors take up these issues.

In a collection of essays paying tribute to anthropologist Stanley Diamond titled *Civilization in Crises*, Talal Asad begins with a quote from Diamond's 1974 monograph:

> In fact, acculturation has always been a matter of conquest. Either civilization directly shatters a primitive culture that happens to stand in its historical right of way; or a primitive social economy, in the grip of a civilized market, becomes so attenuated and weakened that it can no longer contain the traditional culture. In both cases, refugees from the foundering groups may adopt the standards of the more potent society in order to survive as individuals. But these are conscripts of civilization, not volunteers.[22]

Both Talal Asad, in his essay "Conscripts of Western Civilization," and David Scott, in his well-known *Conscripts of Modernity: The Tragedy of Colonial Enlightenment*, use Diamond's analysis of civilization as a colonizing and conscripting force to argue that modernity itself is not solely a negative, destructive power, but a productive one as well. Modernity, as constituted by transatlantic slavery, colonialism, and racial capitalism, shapes "the conditions of possible action, more specifically, shape[s] the cognitive and institutional conditions in which the New World slave," as well as colonial subjects, "acted."[23] I build upon Diamond, Asad, and Scott's important work to argue that it is precisely the management of movement, that is, the systematization of immigration by imperial Western nation-states that helps constitute modernity. If, for Donald Carter, "the nation is imagined in part through the reinforcement of boundary-maintaining mechanisms," the racialized expropriation of free movement from the individual by the state, and now the Global North, is indeed fundamental in our contemporary "age of migration" (66). Further, I argue that an analysis of transnational black migration in the twentieth and twenty-first centuries provides an incisive hinge through which to engage and challenge global processes from high imperialism to neoliberal globalization that conscript and create migrants; that they are in fact, already conscripted, much like Jama and Banjo, long before they decide to move.

It is telling, then, that Diamond uses the term "refugees" in the above epigraph to describe members of non-Western civilizations that have either seen their societies destroyed or so weakened that they must "acculturate" to Western civilization. "In both cases, refugees from the foundering groups may adopt the standards of the more potent society in order to survive as individuals. But these are conscripts of civilization, not volunteers" (204). Diamond's point suggests that in the modern era certain people across the globe are already refugees or migrants even before they move, and when they do move it is as a conscript and most certainly not as a private choice-making individual, or "volunteer," in the liberal sense. John Torpey argues that "modern states, and the international state system of which they are a part, have expropriated from individuals and private entities the legitimate 'means of movement,' particularly though by no means exclusively across international boundaries."[24] If the individual and private means of movement have been expropriated by the modern state then one cannot move freely, especially if one is from a formerly colonized space or has darker skin.

"In Europe, my brothers, you're black first, citizens incidentally, outsiders permanently, and that's certainly not written in the constitution, but some can read it on your skin" (Diome, 123–24): so reports our Senegalese protagonist in *The Belly of the Atlantic*. Salie here attempts to warn her younger brother Madické and his friends about the dangers of emigrating to France. She warns them about the dangers of being deported, about being treated as third-class "citizens," and the racist and anti-immigrant prearranged script already written for them in France. In other words, the global conditions in which African migrants and potential African migrants live will have already conscripted them into dehumanizing narratives and will materially manage their movement using borders, documents, checkpoints, ideologically tinged nationalist discourses about who is "we" and who is "them," and other technologies of power, both negative and positive. These important issues indeed warrant substantial analysis.

In chapter 2, titled "Immigration and the Phenomenology of Movement from Négritude to Shailja Patel's *Migritude*," I introduce the concept of migritude and its literary genealogies that connect back to Négritude as a way to make the claim that this particular group of diasporic African authors not only get to the heart of immigration but urge us to rethink immigration as we know it. I argue that early European management of movement was integral to the development of the nation-state, its imperial projects, and its processes of racialization in the nineteenth century and its afterlives in the twentieth and twenty-first. I also introduce the importance of the phenomenological method regarding the study of migration—that it is always ontological as such—and I read Shailja Patel's 2010 *Migritude* as a radically feminist, anti-imperialist, and phenomenological treatise on migration connecting black and South Asian diasporas.

In chapter 3, "The 'Condition d'Immigrés' in Fatou Diome's *The Belly of the Atlantic* and the Aesthetics of Migration in the Francophone African Literary Tradition," I excavate the origin of the term *migritude* from its Francophone origins and Anglophone iterations. Through an analysis of Diome's 2010 novel, I rethink Chevrier's definition of migritude, which he describes as a recent cohort of African writers in France who narrate existence between Africa and France and for whom immigration and exile are central themes. I argue more narrowly that migritude writers disclose what Diome terms the "condition d'immigres"; that is, they image the conditions and structures of immigration as a national and international network of systems expropriating the means of movement from formerly colonized peoples and that these systems have a colonial past. In addition, I unpack Diome's conversations with the Négritude tradition, noting that, at the same time she borrows from her authors, she refashions aspects of Négritude in terms of migration. I show how she reappropriates, for example, Léopold Sédar Senghor's black humanism, and mobilizes it into her global twenty-first century as a migrant humanism challenging immigration under neoliberal globalization.

Chapter 4, "'We Carry Our Home with Us': Neoliberal Globalization and the Literature of Somali-Italian Diasporas," expands new African diasporic writing beyond Francophone and Anglophone worlds, to important works of African migrant literature in Italy written in Italian. This chapter engages important historical moments including Italian colonialism, the Cold War, neoliberal economic globalization, and the ways in which these destructive histories create destabilization and thus African emigration. I use Somalia as a case study and engage with digital art and documentary film in contemporary Italy as important markers of Afro-Italian migrant cultural production. Through a close reading of Cristina Ali Farah's novel *Little Mother*, I delineate not only the pasts of Italian colonialism on the continent, but the ways in which colonial racialized modes of managing movement appear in present-day Italy, particularly since the 1980s.

In 2013 Farah's contemporary Diriye Osman wrote *Fairytales for Lost Children*, a striking collection of short stories that follow queer Somali immigrants in Kenya and Britain. It represents an important contribution to narratives and experiences of diaspora, sexuality, and modes of racialization. In chapter 5, "'A Matter of Timing': Queer Diasporas and Heteronationalism in Diriye Osman's *Fairytales for Lost Children*," I show how Osman's text teases out the intersection of migration and sexuality in his radically queer migritude text through his complex philosophy of temporality, home, and freedom. As a counterpoint, I conclude by examining instances of queer liberalism and liberal (in)tolerance of queerness in Somali writer Nurrudin Farah's *Hiding in Plain Sight* (2014). Building on Eve Kosofsky Sedgwick, Robert Reid-Pharr, and David Eng, I argue that neoliberal globalization, nationalism, and the ways in which these forces necessarily manage or police movement cannot be disentangled from heteronationalist discourses and laws circumscribing sexuality, and that queer liberalism and liberal toleration of queerness both practice and promote intolerance, given their inherent yet often disguised racialization and homophobia respectively. This is made visible through the chapter's study of systems of immigration and treatment of immigrant populations. I am also guided by queer and migrant activism on the one hand, and Osman's existentialism on the other.

Finally, I assess the imperial origins of immigration. In chapter 6 I study Nadifa Mohamed's 2010 novel *Black Mamba Boy* as a refashioning of Claude McKay's novel *Banjo*. I work through both Mohamed's novel as a migritude text itself and the ways in which it reshapes *Banjo*'s migrant pan-Africanism into a narrative that negotiates colonial structures from the perspective of Somali migration. Jama's diasporic nomadism, for example, circulates through, and is impinged upon by, both British and Italian colonial institutions and modes of managing movement. Furthermore, he is literally conscripted by the Italian army—a fate not uncommon for Somalis. Beyond the colonial setting

of *Black Mamba Boy*, Mohamed, I argue, also speaks to our twenty-first century and the ways in which immigrants from the Global South are haunted,
even conscripted, by colonial structures of immigration in the present.

African Titanics and the Immigration Crisis in the Mediterranean

According to a report by the intergovernmental organization International Organization for Migration (IOM), the Mediterranean Sea is now the
world's deadliest border, with at least 45,000 fatalities documented in the
past fifteen years.[25] The death toll for last year alone reached five thousand,
as people from various parts of Africa attempt the journey to Europe (these
are conservative estimates since lost boats and missing persons are often not
reported).[26] The process of bordering the world, along with the international
expropriation of free movement, is certainly not a new phenomenon, but it
has reached a crisis point in the twenty-first century, particularly after the
overthrow of Libya and the civil war in Syria. There are myriad news reports
detailing migrant deaths in the Mediterranean (rarely in the US mainstream
media however); there are studies like IOM, and scholarship on immigration,
yet voices or perspectives of African migrants themselves are rare.

Avid consumers of contemporary African literature will notice a burgeoning subgenre: the literature of the immigration crisis in the Mediterranean,
including authors like Cristina Ali Farah, Abu Bakr Khaal, and Nadifa Mohamed or recent collections like Warscapes' *Mediterranean*. The new African
literature of the immigration crisis in the Mediterranean, like other works
of African migrant literature, challenge the dehumanization of migrants by
1) narrating the violence of militarized borders; 2) historicizing forces that
drive and create migration itself, such as European colonialism and Euro-
American globalization; and 3) simply telling the stories of human beings
who migrate, which speaks directly against the racialized myth of invading
hordes so insidiously popular in Europe and the United States.

African Titanics, a short novel by Eritrean writer and immigrant to Den-
mark Abu Bakr Khaal, tells the story of a group of travelers making the dangerous journey across the Sahara Desert, across borders and checkpoints in
Northern Africa, to Tripoli, and, with hope, across the Mediterranean Sea to
Europe. They outrun human traffickers in the Sahara and hope to find decent
smugglers while in cramped and clandestine quarters in coastal cities. Unlike
most diasporic African literature written in the past half century, however,

African Titanics does not focus on life once in Europe or the United States, but on migration itself within Africa and the perils of the Mediterranean. In fact, Khaal's group of travelers, like most migrants, ultimately do not make it to Europe, whether as a result of death, deportation, or lack of funds. In this way, the novel reconfigures dominant narratives of immigration while suggesting conscription as a critical lens through which to assess migration.

The first few sentences of the novel, for example, describe immigration as a conscripting force. Our migrant protagonist Abdar reminisces that "migration came flooding through Africa, a turbulent swell sweeping everything along in its wake" and effecting everyone like a plague: "I was plucked from Eritrea, swept across the Sudanese border and on into Libya, in the dark of night. I was lost, and almost perished in the desert, before slipping into Tunisia. I remember feeling as though I was fated forever to continue my ceaseless roaming, and that I would never again escape the endless road."[27] Abdar metaphorizes immigration as an external force, like the sea itself and its driving waves, and an internal one, a "pandemic" leaving not a single "young soul untouched" (3). Khaal utilizes terms and phrases like "plucked," "swept," and "never-escaping" to imagine immigration anew. Abdar even describes the "dangerous lure of migration" through an image representing objects of desire: "a photo of a young friend leaning against a gleaming car in a European city" (4). Authors like Fatou Diome indeed historicize the colonial myth of Europe as paradise, a story that casts Africa as a "place of negations" in the words of the late Chinua Achebe, "at once remote and vaguely familiar in comparison with which Europe's own state of spiritual grace [would] be [made] manifest."[28] Despite the veneer of the myth itself and the photo apparently verifying it, Abdar reveals that his young friend, "in reality . . . had amounted to no more than a dog-walker," which attests, by extension, to the station and treatment of immigrants in Europe (Khaal, 4). The literature of new African diasporas repeatedly testify as much.

Consider the titular "African Titanics." Khaal's use comes from the Arabic *Titanikaat*, is discussed in his novel by hopefuls themselves, and represents the conscripting nature of immigration. In Tripoli for example, Attiah, an Egyptian fisherman exclaims to his group awaiting their smugglers,

> "Titanikaat? . . . As in al-Titanik? . . . who gave you the right to pluralise it as Titanikaat anyway?" . . . What else should we call them?"
> "Something optimistic. Noah's Ark perhaps. Or any other ship that never sank . . ." "Whatever," Attiah continues, "Just so long as you know that seventy percent of your Titanikaat sink . . . So I guess

Titanic is an appropriate name after all. Tita . . . niiiiik," he said heavily emphasizing the second syllable, transforming it into the Arabic word for "fuck." (Khaal, 60–61)

The point here is that the outcome of the voyage is predetermined: it sinks. And this has as much to do with the ways in which migration is regulated and managed by Europe, Coast Guards for their nation-states, the UN, and immigration accords as it does with overcrowded and shoddy boats (the mission of the Coast Guard is of course to guard the coast, to securitize borders, not to rescue those who are already categorized undesirable or "illegal"—an outrageous label for any human). Furthermore, well before their experiences at sea, migrants' movements are determined by checkpoints, borders, hierarchies of documentation, deportations, human traffickers, and imprisonment, all of which condition their movement, and, along with larger global processes from colonialization to globalization, set the conditions they negotiate.

Like Libya, Tunisia plays an important role for Khaal's cast of characters, who are themselves based upon contemporary African migrants and their experiences. These are important "gateway" countries in this new era of immigration and the crisis in the Mediterranean. Since the Arab Spring, beginning in late 2010 with the Tunisian revolution, soon followed by protests and revolt in Libya, Egypt, Yemen, and other countries surrounding the Mediterranean in North Africa and the Middle East, immigration to the Southern rim of Europe became, if not easier or safer, less regulated. Analyzing the aftermath of the Tunisian revolution for example, Glenda Garelli and Martina Tazzioli point out that the "newly acquired freedom [of movement] in conjunction with the president's ousting saw the disintegration of the externalized European border that Ben Ali had agreed to enforce in exchange for political and economic partnerships."[29] Prior to the Arab Spring, countries like Tunisia and Libya "sold out" to Europe and essentially became border guards for Europe in exchange for political favors. This in effect represented an externalization of Europe's border regime into Africa, and therefore an unacknowledged new wave of colonization.

The editors of *Tunisia as a Revolutionized Space of Migration* further testify that "the construction of detention centers for immigrants in Tunisia was financed by Italy as a part of the 1998 re-admission agreement with Tunisia aimed at implementing containment policies in countries of transit (Migration Policy Center 2013)" (30). These detainees were egregiously denied basic human rights in transit while the already-implemented structures of the (violent) management of movement indeed conscripted those who sought opportunities elsewhere. Bureaucracies, governmental administrative regulations, i.e., national law as well as the "international migration regime . . . [all] shape the destiny of mobile (and immobile) people across all continents" and their "economic and social conditions, be they labor migrants or asylum seekers, highly or low-skilled, educated or not, rich or poor, are inextricably anchored in national settings" (vii). Khaal's *African Titanics* not only gives voice to those travelers who negotiate these contexts from the point of view of their own experiences, as opposed to received European discourses characterizing migrants, but indeed asks readers specifically to think about borders, deportations, stereotypes, and, phenomenologically, the objects that constellate and interpellate the very being of migrants, including their precarious African Titanics.

Poetry helps make sense of impossibly violent realities. Like Fatou Diome's novel *The Belly of the Atlantic*, Khaal integrates two migrant poems in his short novel. Abdar remembers his friend Malouk's verses before he was lost on the Mediterranean Sea:

> *The Sea hurls them*
> *Like lanterns*
> *Lowered from the heavens*
> *Civilisation crucifies them*
> *Above the border's barbs*
> *Like plunder* (Khaal, 114)

The condition of migration itself "hurls them like lanterns" whether across borders, or as deportees, or upon the waves that the precariously built African Titanics navigate. "Civilization crucifies them" simply by transforming humans into immigrants, discursively, legislatively, and by gunpoint, above the "border's barbs" of the nation-state, which, protects its ill-gotten plunder, its property. Europe and the United States of course created and continue to create the migration that they then police at their borders.

After numerous failed attempts at the journey to Europe, Abdar sits peacefully in Martyr's Square in Tripoli, which was originally constructed under Italian colonial rule and was renamed after independence in 1969. No longer an immigrant, he reflects: "I'd escaped my miserable existence, cooped up waiting for the smugglers to arrive. I was no longer a migrant. I was simply a man" (82). Echoing Frantz Fanon's famous statement in *The Wretched of the Earth* that the "thing" colonized becomes human through violent anti-colonial revolution, Abdar reveals that one does not simply migrate, but is also transformed into something deemed nonhuman. Yet, to stop moving does not necessarily mark a return to humanity. Global apartheid and white supremacy often already cast black and brown folks as potential immigrants, foreigners, or outsiders. Consider Salman Rushdie's troubling yet incisive statement in *Imaginary Homelands* that even black Britons born in Britain are excluded from Britishness, and are counterintuitively designated as "from elsewhere" despite being native.[30] Global apartheid then has already conscripted its objects, just as it polices and produces their movement. It has fashioned preexisting identity formations necessarily dehumanizing, and has legislated and expropriated movement. It racializes, genders, classes, and heteronormativizes.

The novel ends with Abdar recounting the legend that emerges around Malouk. Interestingly, Khaal mixes the migrant's sober lament with what Alejo Carpentier coins as the *real maravilloso*—what would come to be known as magical realism:

> the boat's crew pulled a young African man from the waters. He was apparently walking on the crest of a wave as calmly as people walk on land . . . his rescuers embraced him one by one, as a noisy celebration broke out, pulsing with lively African music. One of the songs that was heard coming from the ship was said to be a new one by Malouk

> *To all the pounding hearts*
> *In feverish boats*
> *I will cut*
> *Through these paths*
> *With my own liberated heart*
> *And tell my soul*
> *To shout of your silenced deaths*
> *And fill*
> *Palms of dust with morning dew*
> *And song* (121–22)

Magical realism comes from Haiti, and, from within and against the context of the horrors of the transatlantic slave trade, colonialism, and the marvelous potential for liberation. And Vodoun of course traces back to Africa. Surely Abu Bakr Khaal is an odd heir to this tradition, yet Malouk's own "liberated heart" in death and his shouts against migrants' "silenced deaths" seems an appropriately radical rendering of the impossible into language. Indeed, how do we make sense of 45,000 African deaths in the Mediterranean since 2000? Is global apartheid tantamount to a slow genocide? How do we measure those "silenced deaths" at sea or above "border's barbs"? Khaal's *African Titanics*, as well as the literature of new African diasporas—and migritude cultural production—do some of the impossible yet necessary work of narrating those silences.

Chapter 2

IMMIGRATION AND THE PHENOMENOLOGY OF MOVEMENT FROM NÉGRITUDE TO SHAILJA PATEL'S *MIGRITUDE*

"Roots stretch, tighten, and snap. The plane has lifted off."[1] These lines open-ing Ivorian writer Bernard Binlin Dadié's *One Way: Bernard Dadie Observes America* (1964) evoke two important historical facts bearing upon African literary traditions and migration. The first word Dadié uses, "Roots," gestures toward the founding vocabulary of Négritude, a black literary and activist movement that would have a profound impact not just in Africa or Paris, where it originated in the 1930s, but throughout the world and in many languages. Dadié's roots are African; they are those affective and material threads that weave together his identity and sense of self, yet they "stretch, tighten, and snap" as he leaves West Africa for the United States. Négritude is arguably predicated upon the affirmation of African roots in the face of colonial racism, but as Dadié's lines suggest, also upon uprooting—through movement, migration, or diaspora—and of gaining insight precisely by leav-ing a colonized Africa for metropoles in the North.

"The plane has lifted off." Second, Dadié's concise phrase is symbolic not simply of immigration, but of a particularly modern, bourgeois mode of movement—air travel—which indicates the economic class of many Négri-tude authors in Paris. France and other colonial powers often bestowed scholarships upon the best of their African subjects precisely to showcase the success of the civilizing mission. This was the case with the Négritude authors, who represented something of an African elite in Paris. Transcon-tinental air travel indeed differs from the ways in which many migrants in the world today emigrate: those of modest or no means who would travel by foot, truck, or boat; refugees who must move quickly and without resources or the protections that citizenship and passports offer.

Contrast Dadié's inaugural sentences with the first few lines of Somali-Italian writer Cristina Ali Farah's 2007 novel *Little Mother*, another text about migration and roots, written almost fifty years after Dadié's. "*Soomaali Baan Ahay* [I am Somali], like my half is whole. I am the fine thread, so fine that it slips through and stretches, getting longer. So fine that it does not snap. And the tangled mass of threads widens and reveals the knots, clear and tight, that though far from each other, do not unravel."[2] These hauntingly beautiful opening words imagine protagonist Domenica Axad's identity as a Somali woman in Italy in the early twenty-first century. The tangled mass of fine threads figures diasporic Somali communities far from home, in which she, a single stretching thread, is interwoven. Although Farah does not mention African roots, her use of the metaphor of fine threads embedded in a "tangled mass" stretching, elongating, not snapping, simply getting finer, shares with Dadié a vision of home, elsewhere, and migrancy.

There is a key difference between the opening lines of these two texts, however. Dadié's roots snap, while Farah's threads, though elongating, do not. This distinction offers a way to begin thinking about breaks and linkages between historical and literary moments in black diasporic and African literature, past and present. The concept of African roots originates in Claude McKay's 1929 novel *Banjo*, which would subsequently inspire the Négritude authors, particularly, his use of "roots" in terms of black culture.[3] Against the historical fact of European colonialism Négritude would reinvent African roots, already snapped by imperial processes of racism that relegated Africa to prehistory and black culture to nonbeing. For Léopold Sédar Senghor it was in Paris that roots would be reconstructed after having left Africa, and for Leon Damas and Aimé Césaire it was the Caribbean—Senghor, Damas, and Césaire are the three most well-known Négritude poets. This invention, shaped by colonialism and immigration, was a reclamation of blackness, Africa, and history. Dadié's roots must snap, then, because in his colonial context it is necessarily through movement (including displacement) that reinvention becomes possible. Yet Cristina Farah's postcolonial "threads," intact yet pulled thin, are quite different from Dadié's "roots," much in the same way that conceptions of community, politics, and aesthetics differ from Négritude, to migritude's era of neoliberal global capitalism and belligerent nationalism.

Farah traces the affective and material connections of Somali women in the diaspora, those tangled masses of threads that do not unravel. She designates not a masculine politics but a mode of relation that, paraphrasing Sonali Perera, could be called a non-revolutionary ethic of the everyday.[4]

Unlike Dadié's bourgeois mode of travel, Farah's novel depicts far less elite modes of migration and community. In the following passage Farah depicts economic migrants and refugees leaving the Horn of Africa for Europe via North Africa, crossing the deadly Mediterranean by boat in the late twentieth century. She describes immigrants "arriving on those illegal boats. They land along the Sicilian coast, they are crammed into temporary reception centers. A few are allowed in for humanitarian reasons, they are released with very little money and no place to go" (26). This stark passage embodies not an air of leisure but survival. Near the beginning of her novel she describes Roma Termini station in Italy as a diasporic nodal point for the Somali migrant community: "I don't think one can write about the Somali community in Rome without starting from the Roma Termini train station, the crossroads, the scene of our longings" (25–26). These two passages are suggestive of diaspora, economic class, the production of refugees, and the historical context of the civil war in Somalia in the 1990s, itself connected to a longer history of European presence in Africa.

Tidiane Kasse argues that "the explosion of migration in recent years, despite the repressive policies in force in Europe, is explained largely by wars and civil conflicts increasing in Africa and in the Middle East. In Africa, it is the agricultural crises of the 1970s in the Sahel that generated a movement that has started to increase in the 1980s. Previously, migration responded more to a need for adventure or for political reasons, such as to escape repressive regimes (such as the Fulani of Guinea under Sékou Touré), than economic necessity."[5] This perhaps marks the difference between Dadié's adventurous tone opening *One Way* and Farah's description of the station in stark yet nostalgic language—Roma Termini becomes a metonym for both home and a symbol of abject uprooting. What Kasse fails to detail however, is the devastating neoliberal economic policies imposed upon Africa by former colonial powers. South Asian Kenyan writer Shailja Patel narrates this neocolonialism in her multimodal text *Migritude* with reference to post-independence Kenya, imposed debt, and structural adjustment programs. "The new Kenyan government was required to take loans of 12.5 million pounds from its ex-colonial master, the British government. To buy back stolen land from settlers who wished to leave."[6] Like Kenyan author Ngũgĩ Wa Thiong'o's novel *Matigari*, Patel uses the metaphor of the home to illustrate this shift from colonialism to neocolonialism: "Someone comes into your home. Evicts you at gunpoint. Occupies your property. Mortgages it three times over. To banks who know they're lending to thieves. Should you repay the debt? With penalties, late charges, 14% interest?" (37). Usurious debt, neoliberal structural adjustment policies imposed by the World Bank, and corrupt native elites, all create destabilization, conflict, and thus out-migration—the kind of migration described by Cristina Farah, Shailja Patel, and other twenty-first-century African writers.

In the broad and varying field making up twenty-first-century African literature, the texts of migritude, for Jacques Chevrier, create "a new iden-titarian space," and "designate both the thematic of immigration that is at the heart of contemporary African works, but also the expatriate status of most writers . . . [Migritude] is a third space, [a] simultaneous disengage-ment from both the culture of origin and the receiving culture."[7] Cristina Ali Farah's "tangled mass of threads" that widen and reveal the "knots, clear and tight, that though far from each other, do not unravel," are suggestive of Chevrier's third space, a space connected to yet far from Somalia. Farah's novel interweaves the narratives of economic migrants, mothers, refugees arriving by boat, and those who meet at "the crossroads" of Roma Termini station to feel closer to home elsewhere.

The problem is that Chevrier's "third space" privileges identity at the ex-pense of the material realities of immigration. *Conscripts of Migration* departs from identitarian critiques by analyzing the figuration of immigration in contemporary African literature. Developing a theory of global conscription, I show that immigration is structural, historical, and that it functions as a racializing technology of neoliberal globalization. Queer theory shows that gender and sexual normativity conscripts individuals through twin processes of inclusion and exclusion. The global expropriation of the means of free movement from individuals relies on a set of normative relations intersecting geopolitical location, race, gender, and sexuality. These relations conscript migrants from the Global South. But populations in the Global South are already faced with (or conscripted by) a set of neoliberal conditions including forced privatization and structural adjustment programs (that in effect cre-ate migration), and therefore these individuals are already, in a very general and global sense, conscripts of migration. I then return to the differences between Dadié's and Farah's beautiful opening lines, to suggest that perhaps they do not mark an irreducible difference, his set of roots snapping while her thin threads do not, but rather are suggestive of the different ways in which African actors are conscripted, not simply *as* they move, but that global conditions from colonialism to globalization already set the terms of existence and, by extension, movement. I pause on these two passages, the former of the Négritude era and the latter of the "post" postcolonial moment, as emblematic of the construction of both difference and affiliation in the phase "from Négritude to migritude," penned by Congolese novelist, chemist, and Guggenheim recipient Emmanuel Dongala.[8] Dongala's phrase represents an incisive hinge through which to analyze the contemporary phenomenon of migritude. Just as Dongala reframes the analysis of Négritude and subsequent generations of African literature in terms of exile and immigration, so migritude literature refashions the aesthetic and cultural politics of blackness, anti-colonialism, and anti-racism of the Négritude era into the era of globalization, particularly in terms of the contemporary conditions that "produce" and manage—conscript—nonwhite migrant bodies.

The term *migritude* comes to us independently from two sources: Francophone African literary studies, namely Chevrier's remarks in 2003, and from Patel's *Migritude*, published in 2010. Although there are no book-length studies of migritude fiction, Ayo Coly's *Pull of Postcolonial Nationhood: Gender and Migration in Francophone African Literature* and Mahriana Rofheart's *Shifting Perceptions of Migration in Senegalese Literature, Film, and Social Media* deftly analyze Senegalese migrant literature and film. Nigerian writer and scholar Pius Adesanmi and others contribute chapters on migritude in *Paris, Capital of the Black Atlantic: Literature, Modernity, and Diaspora*, edited by Jeremy Braddock and Jonathan P. Eburne; myself and others have published articles on the subject, while still more work is now being done on Shailja Patel as well.[9] Additionally, there are new and exciting discussions that include reference to migritude authors, their predecessors, or the themes subtending migritude embedded in studies of "Black France," "Black Paris," or "Paris Noir," by authors like Michel Fabre, Bennetta Jules-Rosette, Dominic Thomas, Tyler Stovall, Alec Hargreaves, Tricia Danielle Keaton, T. Denean Sharpley-Whiting, Pius Adesanmi, Brent Hayes Edwards, Gary Wilder, and others.[10]

Migritude describes the work of a disparate yet distinct group of younger African authors born after independence in the 1960s. Most often they have lived both in and outside Africa and narrate the being-in-the-world[11] of the migrant within the context of globalization, yet they emphasize that the "past" of immigration and conceptions of the immigrant are irreducibly entangled with the history of colonialism. They confront issues of migrancy (forced or not), diaspora (forced or not), errantry, departure, return, racism against immigrants, identity, gender, sexuality, and postcoloniality. Going beyond narrativizing the individual lives of people who cross borders, these writers, I suggest, consider the modes, structures, conditions, and subject-positions of being migrant. They inaugurate a phenomenology of borders, both material and imagined—and what it means to move across them by the majority of the world's population; they offer a phenomenology of checkpoints, passports, residence permits, all of which necessarily disclose larger apparatuses such as nation-states and the international system they are embedded in.

I want to pause here briefly on the importance of the phenomenological method. Edmund Husserl's phenomenology bridges the gap between empiricism and rationalism by arguing that consciousness is always directed at something out in the world like objects or others, but instead of isolating the object itself, or consciousness itself, he analyzes the active mental processes and content created in the relationship between the two—how the world shapes us in time and how we shape the world.[12] Consciousness is directed toward objects, but those objects also make impressions upon us and orient us, thereby shaping and changing us.[13] This radically dislocates the (colonial) Western subject (which dislocated others). Husserl's is not simply a metaphysical claim but an ontological one, regarding what Heidegger would later call being-in-the-world (*Ideas*, 40). Neither an individualist narrative, therefore, nor a sociology of, migration, would get us to a more capacious phenomenology of movement. A substantial study of phenomenology, migration, and globalization would need to take into account not only the classic philosophers following Husserl, like Heidegger, Merleau-Ponty, and Sartre, but the groundbreaking feminist phenomenology of Simone de Beauvoir's *The Second Sex* (1949); Frantz Fanon's, Lewis Gordon's, and Michelle M. Wright's phenomenology of blackness in *Black Skins White Masks* (1952), *Bad Faith and Antiblack Racism* (1995), and *Physics of Blackness: Beyond the Middle Passage Epistemology* (2015); Sara Ahmed's important queer migrant phenomenology of gender and the enforcement of heterosexist object choices in *Queer Phenomenology: Orientations, Objects, Others*, and others.

Migritude writers indeed offer a phenomenology of migration, often challenging what Balibar calls the "gigantic inequality" of globalization and mobility. Balibar calls for a phenomenology of mobile inequalities structured by neo-imperialism and racial capitalism. "What we need is a complete description of this inequality as a transnational social relationship. Its phenomenology includes *dissymmetries* (think of the access to passports and visas, the fact that certain strategic borderlines can easily be crossed one way but not the other way) and includes differential *repression* (from this point of view, the so-called undocumented migrant emerges as an economic institution of globalization in its own right, an essential element of global employment and wage labor)."[14] *Conscripts of Migration* represents in one sense this kind of orientation as it looks not only to the conditions and structures that shape and impinge upon the very being of the African migrant but also appraises Balibar's "differential repression" and the world of immigrant objects: passports, visas, borders, and even bodies that circulate as materialized labor under racial capitalism. This affords a critique not just of recent machinations of global capital and the abject inequity of people in the world but a rethinking of colonialism and the ways in which its management of movement, predicated upon the construction of race and tribe, remains constitutive of modernity.[15]

Migritude cultural production is also historical, often drawing upon early and mid-twentieth-century anti-colonialist thought and literature such as pan-Africanism, Négritude, the literature of the black diaspora, and African literature and history. These writers refashion political and literary moments within these larger paradigms for their own context of late twentieth- and early twenty-first-century global capitalism and "new" economic and cultural configurations ushered in by our age of asymmetrical flows of capital and people—globalization. The phrase "from Negritude to migritude" is sugges- tive of the acknowledgment of, and debt to, earlier international black radical writers by their migritude "children of the postcolony."[16] Yet migritude writers also challenge the texts of their forbears. For example, West African writ- ers Fatou Diome and Alain Mabanckou, both of whom now live in France, acknowledge the promise of Négritude in their novels at the same time that they problematize its failures. Négritude emerges refashioned, in a sense, as twenty-first-century writers take on the racialization of immigration in addition to its gender normativity.

I locate migritude in four general geographical locales or spaces: 1) the Global South (hereon specific to Africa, I analyze Senegal, Kenya, and Soma- lia); 2) the Global North (more specifically the Global South *in* the Global North or, for example, immigrant neighborhoods within Northern nation- states such as France, Britain, Italy [recall the Roma Termini train station in Farah's *Little Mother* discussed above], and the United States, like "banlieues"[17] or "ghettos"; 3) the transnational in-between spaces such as Lampedusa, the Libyan coast, immigration centers, or refugee camps, airports, checkpoints, and immigration control, each mediated by nation states or the international system of nation states, and that operate beneath or outside of them; and 4) colonialism as a historical space that continues to impinge upon the present, since so much of what catalyzes and shapes immigration in the twenty-first century has roots in the practices of empire. This is made poetically explicit in Shailja Patel's *Migritude.*

Orienting Immigration: Diaspora Phenomenology and Shailja Patel's "Migrants with Attitude"

Lisa Lowe's monograph *The Intimacies of Four Continents* addresses the global-historical processes that shaped both African and Asian diasporas from the transatlantic slave trade and racial capitalism to indentured labor in the era of high imperialism.[18] In *Migritude*, Patel traces South Asian diasporas in East Africa and her own migrations from Africa to England and the United States to, in a way, stage these fraught and historied intimacies of Africa, Asia, Europe, and the Americas. Patel's East African Asian contemporaries like M. G. Vassanji, Parita Mukta, Yasmin Alibhai-Brown, and others, are similarly global and diasporic in scope. Yet, Patel's project *Migritude* refashions Négritude-era identity politics and engages the material histories of migration and empire to challenge systemic violence against immigrants under neoliberal globalization. Indeed, Patel connects immigration itself directly to past imperial processes and illustrates the ways in which, in the present, immigration involves an ever-broadening network of borders, passport controls, checkpoints, and modes of "othering." Patel then calls for a "migrant attitude," the loud and proud diasporic voices that would speak out against systemic national and international expropriation of movement from nonwhite peoples. Indeed, she states in an interview: "I was looking for a word that captured migrant attitudes or the idea of migrants with attitude, a generation of migrants who don't feel the need to be silent to protect themselves."[19]

Shailja Patel's *Migritude* therefore is timely, as it speaks to our moment when "fortress Europe" refuses to address the growing immigration crises in the Mediterranean and elsewhere, and the United States' immigration policies in the Trump era remain belligerent and xenophobic. For Patel, delineating colonial pasts is necessary for any understanding of immigration in our post-postcolonial moment. Vijay Prashad evidences this point in his introduction to *Migritude*:

> "Immigration," as a concept, is born in the era of imperialism. "Immigrants," in this context, are not just those who cross boundaries, but those who pointedly enter the advanced industrial states from lands of dusky skin. Immigration is always already about mobile capital and immobile race. Colonial rulers went where they willed, and they even moved people from one colony to another; but the colonized were not to be fully welcomed in the heartlands of Empire,

in Europe, in the United States. If they came, they were allowed in for their labor, not for their lives.[20]

Building upon Prashad's framing of immigration and empire, I approach immigration phenomenologically and as a conscripting system, as interrelated techniques of power that manage and discipline the movement of migrant bodies, both interdicting and catalyzing movement. These material structures succeed their *concept*, that is, the idea that there are insiders and outsiders and that both, in different ways, must be relieved of their capacity to move freely, without surveillance, without monitoring. The synthesis of the concept, institution, and practice of immigration creates what I call, paraphrasing Senegalese-French novelist Fatou Diome, the condition of immigration as it shapes not just the ways people move or do not, but their very being (Diome, 172). Shailja Patel's relationship to Négritude opened up the possibility and the terms that would challenge white supremacy and would allow her to connect racism and imperialism to immigration.

For Patel, the Négritude poets Aimé Césaire and Léopold Sédar Senghor were "not direct influences or primary sources for *Migritude*. But the political and cultural space they opened up through Négritude, and the discourse that continues from that, were the soil in which *Migritude* could germinate" (144). In an interview with Khainga O'Okwemba, Patel reflects upon the legacy of Négritude and the ways in which aspects of it might be mobilized and refashioned for the figure of the migrant within globalization:

> When I coined the term I was looking for a word that would draw from the legacy and tradition of Négritude that reclaimed and celebrated African cultures, black cultures around the world as powerful and central in their own right, and not as something that always needed to be measured against, and compared to European culture. . . . I wanted to claim that same power for migrant cultures, for all migrant populations, that there is a culture, a space, a place where we inhabit, that world that does not need to be assessed against where we came from, or where we are, how well we have assimilated, that migrants have an unapologetic voice, and world view that enriches the world and that we need to claim and celebrate.[21]

What both Négritude and migritude share here, in Patel's description, is a critique of imperial and neo-imperial modes of "measure," those networks of laws, technologies, practices, and discourse, that create the fantasy of a "citizen" over and against an "other." In other words, white superiority under colonialism refracts into the twenty-first century as European and American anti-immigrant rhetoric and law, the former, producing anti-black practice and discourse justifying conquest, and the latter, symptomatic of differentiated citizenship or non-citizenship in the late-twentieth and twenty-first centuries.

Jiwon Chung argues that the term migritude as Patel has crafted it "shares the richness of connotation and inspiration of Négritude, as applied to immigrants: a celebration and revalorization of immigrant/diasporic culture and identity, its greatness 'measured by the compass of suffering' (Aimé Césaire), with overtones of spiritual and political liberation" (*Migritude*, 143). If *Migritude* is a revalorization of "immigrant/diasporic culture," it also traces the global imbrication of African-Asian diasporas within imperial and neo-imperial histories—it is both identitarian and materialist. *Migritude* is a reparative celebration of migrants and, as Patel proclaims, "unabashedly political—feminist and anti-imperialist" (137). In this sense, *Migritude* corrects for a blind spot often operating in in the first few generations of Négritude writing and its scholarly interpreters: the lack of focus on women of color and gender.[22]

Migritude the text is based on Patel's one-woman performance-theater show, which debuted nationally and internationally in 2006. It included poetry, dance, and utilized set pieces like Patel's trousseau and saris. As a spoken-word performance piece, it follows Patel as she unpacks her trousseau of saris given to her by her mother while narrating her own diasporic movements. These movements, as a South Asian African woman in Kenya, Britain, and the United States, allow her to engage with and challenge global processes like neocoloniality, repression of migrants (particularly migrant women), and imperial histories while sharpening focus on South Asian East Africa. That her project began as an activist performance suggests that embodiment is important to Patel, both in terms of the ways that bodies express meanings and are subject to, for example, gendering or imperial mapping. "Theatre is relationship," Patel argues. "A body in front of other bodies. Unfiltered, unedited, unmanipulated. In real time. If I screw up onstage, everyone participates in that moment."[23] Against the flattening of subjects in migration as data or rhetorically invested stereotypes, Patel's performance embodies immigrants by inflecting movement with history, culture, and traditions; her own trousseau of saris passed down to her by her mother incisively images the fullness of being as she unpacks the history and culture in her saris—onstage and in text—tries them on, and thus crafts possible identities.

Migritude the text and the performance piece dramatize these processes in different ways and yet are explicit in terms of arguing that imperial pasts shape the present.

In the prelude to the text-based version, for example, entitled "How Ambi became Paisley," Patel begins by illustrating how imperial world-level processes shaped and commodified—or better, conscripted—Ambi's historical and migratory movements. This "stylized rendition of the date-palm shoot, tree of life, fertility symbol" would move from Babylon to the Middle East and India when, in the colonial era, its movements would be drastically redirected (4). Adopting an anti-colonial Marxist perspective along with echoes of J. M. Coetzee's critique of imperialism in *Waiting for the Barbarians*, Patel muses, "Enter the Barbarian. Imperialism. Armed with a switchblade, designed to slice out the heart of craft. To separate makers from the fruits of their labors" (5). British capitalism would export the production of Ambi to another colony, Scotland, to a town called Paisley, propping up British manufacture at the expense of the original Indian textile industry. Weavers of Paisley, Patel remarks, "learned how to churn out imitation Ambi, on imitation Kashmiri shawls, and [unlike South Asian workers under British rule], they got to keep their index fingers and thumbs" (5–7). Referencing the brutal practice of torture for resisting slavery under colonialism, Patel's tracing of the colonial commodification of a pattern and fabric provides an illuminating instance, and unsettling depiction of, racial capitalism and movement in the colonial era.

"Bengal was known for its fine cotton, now extinct, and for the excellence of its textiles, now imported," Noam Chomsky notes.[24] The British East India Company had undermined their "rivals in the colonies by recourse to state power and violence" (13). A British enquiry commission concluded in 1832 that "The misery hardly finds a parallel in the history of commerce. The bones of cotton-weavers are bleaching the plains of India" (17). Karl Marx lamented in one of his dispatches for the *New York Tribune* in 1853: "It was the British intruder who broke up the Indian hand-loom and destroyed the spinning-wheel. England began with driving the Indian cottons from the European market; it then introduced twist into Hindostan, and in the end inundated the very mother country of cotton with cotton."[25] Later in 1857 Marx would remark: "To characterize that rule, it suffices to say that torture formed an organic institution of [England's] financial policy" (234). The British Empire's colonial violence, including "free-trade" economic policies, destabilized what would become known as the Global South for the benefit of northern industry. *Migritude* records the intimacy of free trade and force:

The British weighed [mosuleen] down with an 80% duty. But that wasn't enough. They needed to force India to buy British cloth. So down the alleyways of Dhaka stamped the legionaries—British this time, not Roman. Hunted down the terrified weavers, chopped off their index fingers and thumbs. (5)

"How Ambi became Paisley" marks the violence of imperial racial capitalism not solely by reiterating history like Marx and Chomsky's important work, but by producing a poetic phenomenology of the movement of colonial objects like Ambi and the global processes disciplining workers and markets. Patel ends the section with postcolonial irony, connecting imperialism to the economics of twenty-first-century appropriation under globalization: "Until Kashmiri became cashmere. Mosuleen became muslin. Ambi became paisley / And a hundred and fifty years later, chai became a beverage invented in California" (7). Patel shows how objects and people were conscripted under colonial globality and how echoes of that very commodification and circulation hew into the fabric of contemporary corporate capitalism.

For Patel, these are the histories she did not learn in school and that do not now appear in the media or national discussions. Patel reports, for example: "This is the history we didn't learn. From 1952 to 1960, the people of Kenya mounted a fierce guerrilla struggle, the Mau Mau uprising, to reclaim their land and freedom from the British. The British incarcerated, tortured, and murdered approximately 25,000 Kenyans. Men, women, and children. More than a million Kenyans were detained for over eight years in concentration camps—barbed wire villages where forced labour, starvation, and death were routine" (17). Kenyan author Ngũgĩ Wa Thiong'o's important novel *Grain of Wheat* also narrativizes the Emergency and is therefore perhaps one of the literary antecedents Patel utilizes precisely to connect imperial pasts to the present. The colonial structures that Patel's *Migritude* grapples with, for example, would have significant effects in the postcolonial period, particularly on South Asian diasporas in Africa. Patel shows that histories of South Asian migrants in Africa are catalyzed and disciplined by imperial structures. I here relate what she titles a "migritude timeline," appended to her text.

1895–1902 32,000 indentured Indian labourers imported by British to build African railway. About 2,300 die during their contracts.

. . .

1905–1917 Maji Maji uprising in Tanzania against German occupation.

. . .

1920 British East African Protectorate becomes Crown Colony, renamed Kenya. Indian indentured labour ends in Kenya. About 6,700
Indians choose to stay in Kenya to work as shopkeepers, artisans,
clerks, and administrators. (130)

The South Asian postcolonial present is shaped by the colonial constitution
and management of a diasporic population in the imperial era. Later, in
1972, Patel reminds us, "Idi Amin, military dictator of Uganda, expelled the
country's entire Asian population. I was born and raised in Kenya, Third-generation East African Asian" (10). She continues: "Secret documents, declas-
sified in 2001, show that Britain, Israel, and the United States instigated and
backed Idi Amin's military coup, which overthrew Uganda's democratically
elected government. What followed were eight years of terror that devastated
Uganda, left hundreds of thousands dead. British Foreign Office documents
describe Idi Amin as *a man we can trust*" (10–11). Important here is the way
in which Patel exposes the Global North's violent neocolonial posturing as
she reclaims her diasporic or migrant identity—her proud "third-generation
East African Asian." This seems to me not only an important identitarian
gesture, sharing in the irreverent spirit of Négritude, but an abiding critique
of material imperial and post-imperial histories that shape migration. In
other words, the processes that shaped South Asian migration from Uganda
to Kenya were not limited to Amin and the baleful state policies of Uganda
but global, given the state structure of Uganda's colonial past and the neocolonial machinations of the United States and Britain.

In her poem "Shilling Love Part I," Patel describes a post-independence
Kenya and the neoliberal economic policies of the North, while at the same
time weaving together memories of her parents, love, childhood, and immigration:

> My parents never say / they love us . . . Those words were not / in any
> language / spoken by my parents . . . save and count / count and save
> . . . 1975 fifteen shillings to the British pound . . . Thirty shillings to the
> pound / forty shillings to the pound / my parents fight over money
> . . . As yet another western country / drops a portcullis of immigra-
> tion spikes / my mother straps my shoulders back with a belt / to
> teach me / stand up straight . . . Seventy shillings to the pound / they
> hug us at airports / tearless / stoic / as we board the planes for icy /
> alien England / cram instructions into our pockets like talismans.
> (25, 27, 28)

Patel's formal innovation here, in which she interweaves a horizontal personal narrative into the crashing vertical movement of the value of the Kenyan shilling in relation to the British pound, poignantly illustrates the ways in which neoliberal market colonialism, or for Patel, "neocolonialism," impinge upon domestic spheres, creating hardship and tension, even catalyzing migration. Michel Chossudovsky notes: "Currency devaluation is often demanded (as a pre-condition) prior to the negotiation of a structural adjustment loan: the destabilization of the national currency is a key objective of the IMF-World Bank's 'hidden agenda.' . . . The social impact of the IMF-sponsored devaluation is brutal and immediate: the domestic prices of food staples, essential drugs, fuel and public services increase overnight."[26] In Kenya, Joseph Kipkemboi Rono describes the general decline of the economy in the past few decades "which has impacted negatively in nearly all areas of development. This is mainly attributable to the introduction of [Structural Adjustment Programs] in the 1980s and the 1990s."[27] This decline did not affect everyone evenly. Folasade Iyun notes that since "a feature of SAPs is the reduction of government expenditure, particularly on social welfare programs . . . mothers and children in particular become marginalized."[28] Patel's poem illustrates the gendered effects of neoliberal policies as mother counts and saves rather than says "I love" while preparing terrified daughters for "alien England." The phrase "portcullis of immigration spikes" suggestively refers to what has been called "fortress Europe"[29]—the increasingly harsh policies of containment and exclusion Europe has developed against Africa and elsewhere in the past few decades. Yet the European portcullis of immigration, as the poem demonstrates, is inextricable from the West's global policies—"forty shillings to the pound . . . As yet another western country / drops a portcullis of immigration spikes" (28).

Migritude ties the conditions of immigration to gender and imperialism. For Patel, her project is "a tapestry of poetry, history, politics, packed into a suitcase, embedded in my body, rolled out into a theatre. An accounting of Empire enacted on the bodies of women" (96). The poem "The Making (Migrant Song)" acts as the *raison d'être* for Patel's *Migritude* project, the "why?" behind the performance piece and text. "The Making" is bookended with italicized personal reflections beginning with her sari and family. "*Make it out of the sari that wraps you . . .* make it out of every scar and callous / on your father's hand" (32, emphasis in original). She segues into a narrative about everyday features of migrant life: "We overdress, we migrants. We care too much how we look to you. We get it wrong. We ought to look like we don't give a fuck" (33). But Patel argues that the quotidian is connected to larger

structures symptomatic of immigration as a system: "We absorb information without asking questions. Questions cost us jobs, visas, lives" (33). This
statement, indeed Patel's project, is ontological. Therefore I read *Migritude*
as a phenomenology of movement that records the immigrant condition
and the ways in which immigration *conditions*—in often violent, gendered,
and racialized ways—the very being of those who move. In "Shilling Love
Part II," for example, Patel narrates her parents' first journey to see her in the
United States as they travel from Kenya.

> Four hours / after their plane landed / they have not emerged / and
> we know / with the hopeless rage of third world citizens / of African
> passport holders / that the sum of their lives and labour / dreams
> and sacrifice / is being measured / sifted / weighed / found wanting
> / by Immigration . . . / [She continues in her mother's voice speak-
> ing to American immigration officials who ignore her] listen to me
> / I'm the one / who filled in the visa forms . . . these Americans / so
> advanced so / modern but still / in the year 2000 / they think it must
> be the husband in charge / they won't let the wife speak (57, emphasis
> in original)

Patel illustrates above not only the trials of traveling from Africa to the
United States as a person of color and on an African passport (and this is
pre-9/11), but that women are differentially targeted, "measured," *in* movement, *between* home and hostland, and *within and across* (often militarized)
spaces like checkpoints, Immigration Control, the island of Lampedusa (ad-
dressed in Cristina Ali Farah's *Little Mother*; see chapter 4), and other liminal
and disciplinary spatial structures. In the passage above, Patel's mother is
silenced and rendered invisible as she is marked as other via her gender—her
husband's masculinity conversely renders him more legible. While there is
a growing and important literature on women's experiences living in diasporas as well as in the Global South,[30] what is unique about Patel's text
and other works of migritude literature such as Diriye Osman's *Fairytales
for Lost Children* or Diome's *The Belly of the Atlantic* (see chapters 6 and 3
respectively), is that they illuminate the gendering, racializing, and often
heteronormativizing techniques and practices of power *in transit* that are
fundamental to nation-states and the international system in which they are
embedded. Patel's mother is both gendered in migration and racially profiled.
Her father "refuses to travel any more to the U.S. Post 9/11, he gets racially
profiled. Every time" (91). At Heathrow she watches security force a "Sikh

man [to] strip, right down to his underwear. Remove his turban to reveal his knot of hair" (91). Regarding her live performance of these poems, these vignettes, she reveals that in the "finale of the show, the audience has finally earned the right to see the saris in all their splendor. Because they've engaged with the violence and violation beneath . . . Listened to the voices of women from within the bootprint of Empire" (95). As a performance, as a staging, both live and textual, *Migritude* therefore is a feminist and diasporic South Asian–African invocation of the globalized crimes of empire that continue in, and subtend, the present. And for Patel, immigration control and policy in the twenty-first century does not exist outside of the bootprint of empire.

Immigration is a system. Here I do not indicate the movement of individuals from one place to another, but rather that the network of national and international institutions that regulate and manage the movement of peoples. Immigration in this sense is an integral and originary component of the modern nation-state as it developed in the West. Eithne Luibhéid argues for example that "immigration control is not just a powerful symbol of nationhood and people but also a means to *literally* construct the nation and the people in particular ways" (*Entry Denied*, xviii). It is necessary to historicize immigration itself, in terms of both the movements of people and the larger structures and conditions that shape or impinge upon movement like European and US nation-states, racism, and imperialism. John Torpey's immeasurably useful *The Invention of the Passport: Surveillance, Citizenship, and the State* argues that in the past century or so, modern nation-states and the international system of which they are a part, have "expropriated" the means of movement from individuals: "the emergence of passport and related controls on movement is an essential aspect of the 'state-ness' of states . . . documentary controls on movement were decisively bound up with the rights and duties that would eventually come to be associated with membership—citizenship—in the nation-state."[31] In other words, just as Karl Marx argued that the central experience of the modern involved "the expropriation of the 'means of production' from workers by capitalists," and for Max Weber, "the successful expropriation by the state of the 'means of violence' from individuals," Torpey's project demonstrates that "modern states, and the international state system of which they are a part, have expropriated from individuals and private entities the legitimate '*means of movement*,' particularly though by no means exclusively across international boundaries" (4). Immigration control, passports, borders, deportations, identification cards, residence permits, legal categories such as "illegal alien," "undocumented," or *sans-papiers* and so on have all become naturalized over the past century, just as their proliferation in the late twentieth and twenty-first centuries goes relatively unchallenged. Free movement has become alienated from individuals and communities as the institutions policing movement are increasingly perceived as natural or essential, even as Torpey and others in the social sciences and African diasporic writers at the level of literary production show their pernicious, historical, and systemic national and international situatedness.

Paul Gilroy makes a parallel argument about the naturalization of race and racism in *There Ain't No Black in the Union Jack*: "The oscillation between black as a problem and black as a victim has become, today, the principal mechanism through which 'race' is pushed outside of history and into the realm of natural, inevitable events. This capacity to evacuate any historical dimension to black life remains a fundamental achievement of racist ideologies in this country."[32] Just as mechanisms of racism and nationalism present themselves as natural and ahistorical, so immigration as a system, bound up with racism, nationalism, colonialism, and capitalism, is construed as inevitable. Salman Rushdie analyzes the British context as well, noting that, although "the facts are that for many years now there has been a sizeable amount of white immigration as well as black, that the annual number of emigrants leaving these shores is now larger than the number of immigrants coming in; and that, of the black communities, over forty per cent are not immigrants, but black Britons, born and bred, speaking in many voices and accents of Britain, and with no homeland but this one. *And still the word 'immigrant' means 'black immigrant'*; the myth of 'swamping' lingers on; and even British-born blacks and Asians are thought of as people whose real 'home' is elsewhere" (132). This attests to the fact that "immigrant" is a discursively weighted word not least in terms of race. "Immigrant" is coded black or brown by virtue of its colonial ideological index.

Salman Rushdie in the above quotation refers to an interview in 1978 wherein Margaret Thatcher claims that, "people are really rather afraid that this country might be swamped by people of a different culture. The British character has done so much for democracy."[33] This conforms to the imperialist racial hierarchy in which Europe defines itself as superior, civilized, and modern, while at the same moment constructing Africa as its opposite: primitive, unenlightened, and so on.[34] Rahul K. Gairola argues in his article "A Critique of Thatcherism and the Queering of Home in *Sammy and Rosie Get Laid*," that in the 1978 *Granta* interview, "Thatcher foregrounds her nativist racism, colonial nostalgia, and 'family values' under the patriotic sign of the Union Jack, which affords 'home' to white Britons while leaving out immigrants, queers, and those who did not neatly fit into her heralding of neoliberal economics" (124). Building upon the work of Torpey, Balibar, Gilroy, Hobsbawm, Rushdie, Gairola, and Cedric Robinson, I therefore analyze immigration regimes and their twin processes of exclusion and inclusion, as fundamental to the modern nation-state, not adjunct to it, ultimately introducing migritude literature and thought as an antidote to border-thinking.

For Cedric Robinson in *Black Marxism: The Making of the Black Radical Tradition*, "the historical development of world capitalism was influenced in a most fundamental way by the particularistic forces of racism and nationalism"—that both racism and nationalism "anticipated capitalism in time."[35] He argues that, "the bourgeoisie that led to the development of capitalism were drawn from particular ethnic and cultural groups; the European proletariats and the mercenaries of the leading states from others; its peasants from still other cultures; and its slaves from entirely different worlds" (26). Eric Williams, following C. L. R. James, then seems to get it wrong when he states that modern "slavery was not born of racism: rather, racism was the consequence of slavery . . . the reason [of slavery] was economic, not racial."[36] If, for Eric J. Hobsbawm, the *concept* of the nation, or nationalism, "comes before nations, [that] nations do not make states and nationalism but the other way around," then there must, for Robinson, be a racial dimension to both the nation and its predecessors, nationalism and capitalism.[37] In other words, racial capitalism, its various nationalisms, as well as the contemporaneous management of movement, precedes chattel slavery. Spain's nationalism, for example, would then have to precede its imperial ventures in the fifteenth and sixteenth centuries and thus its status as an empire. How then does immigration substantially enter into these histories?

Torpey's study of the history of passport controls and more generally the regulation of movement by burgeoning nation-states illuminates the ways in which the movement of people and racialization were bound up in the origins of the modern nation and its imperial projects. For Torpey, "the institutionalization of the idea of the 'nation-state' as a prospectively homogenous ethnocultural unit [was] a project that necessarily entailed efforts to regulate people's movements" (1). And later, "documents such as passports and identification cards that help determine 'who is in' and 'who is out' of the nation here took center stage, and thus became an enduring and omnipresent part of our world. These documents were an essential element of that burgeoning 'infrastructural' power to 'grasp' individuals that distinguish modern states from their predecessors" (121). The infrastructural "grasping" that Torpey refers to is a part of a larger process of conscription both domestically and abroad. Nation-states, for example, did not distinguish between insiders and outsiders only as a form of isolationism, but as burgeoning colonial powers attempting to mobilize public support for conquest. It follows that colonialism, in addition to immigration as a system and racialization within a capitalist economic system, was integral to the rise of the nation-state as well. Hobsbawm finds in his study of the nation and nationalism, for example that, "In practice there were only three criteria which allowed a people to be firmly classed as a nation," 1) "its historic association with a state"; 2) having a "long-established cultural elite, possessing a written national literary and administrative vernacular"; and, 3) "a proven capacity for conquest" (*Nations and Nationalism*, 37). Immigration, the nation, racism, and nationalism, then cannot be thought apart from the historical processes of colonialism.

The word *nation* was not used in its modern sense until European colonialism was almost at its zenith. The year 1884 marks this transition, and was, not coincidentally, the year of the Berlin conference, wherein Europe carved up Africa like a cake. Hobsbawm notes: "The Dictionary of the Royal Spanish Academy, whose various editions have been scrutinized for this purpose does not use the terminology of state, nation and language in the modern manner before its edition of 1884 . . . 'a State or political body which recognizes a supreme center of common government' and also 'the territory constituted by that state and its individual inhabitants, considered as a whole'" (15). The British *New English Dictionary* followed suit shortly thereafter.[38] For Hobsbawm, nationalism, the management of movement, and racialization helped mobilize public support for imperial ventures: "The period from 1880 to 1914 was also that of the greatest mass migrations yet known, within and between states, of imperialism and of growing international rivalries ending in world war. All these underlined the differences between 'us' and 'them.' And there is no more effective way of bounding together the disparate sections of restless people than to unite them against outsiders" (91). In *Migritude*, Vijay Prashad's argument that immigration has its origins in imperialism, then, makes sense.

The point must be made that if immigration and the nation (in the European context), are contemporaneous and historical, the nation itself (as well as immigration) cannot be understood nationally. The nation and its nationalists have a vested interest not in truth, but in the reproduction of the nation. Hobsbawm paraphrases this point in Ernest Renan's "What Is a Nation?" quite poignantly: "Nationalism requires too much belief in what is patently *not so*. As Renan said:[39] 'Getting its history wrong is part of being a nation'" (12, my emphasis). Étienne Balibar would later describe a "fictive ethnicity," a national mythology developed in the production of the citizen. In *Race, Nation, Class*, Balibar considers the way in which "the people" are "produced" as such. For Balibar, "A social formation only reproduces itself as a nation to the extent that, through a network of apparatuses and daily practices, the individual is instituted as *homo nationalis* from cradle to grave, at the same time as he or she is instituted as *homo economicus, politicus, religious* . . . I apply the term 'fictive ethnicity' to the community instituted by the nation-state."[40] Produced ethnicity is fictive in that it imposes homogeneity upon a heterogeneous group loosely bound by geography and a state. This process has material effects, since one is compelled to act according to certain laws and norms, is protected and given access to resources, etc.; in the same way, one who arrives is immediately clothed in a sort of fictive otherness and produced as an "immigrant"—as migritude writers like Patel show—and is also compelled to act in other ways, is disafforded protection and access while being branded or reduced.

The management of movement in the heart of empire was mirrored by the construction of immigration in the colonies. If, for Donald Carter in "Navigating Diaspora: The Precarious Depths of the Italian Immigration Crisis," "The nation is imagined in part through the reinforcement of boundary-maintaining mechanisms," then empire in the colonial era maintains itself through policing movement on a global scale (66). Furthermore, colonialism itself created much of the very migration it attempted to control. Both settler colonialism and the imposition of infrastructure under non-settler-administered colonization created mass (and gendered) displacement. Abdoulaye Kane and Todd H. Leedy note that historically "colonial capital created sites of raw material production for European industries that attracted rural labor migrants. During the colonial period, both rural-rural and rural-urban migrations in Africa were predominantly male" (*African Migrations*, 2). Note that in the late twentieth and twenty-first century labor migration will be substantially more female; women will also represent the majority of factory workers in the Global South, and care workers in the Global North.

Although, for Prashad, "colonial rulers went where they willed, and they even moved people from one colony to another . . . the colonized were not to be fully welcomed in the heartlands of Empire, in Europe, in the United States. If they came, they were allowed in for their labor, not their lives" (*Migritude*, ii). This intolerance of colonial subjects reveals that imperial racial hierarchies (and gender and sexual hierarchies) and immigration are intertwined. Paul Gilroy describes a "new racism," taking Britain in the 1980s as his case study: "It will be argued that its novelty lies in the capacity to link discourses of patriotism, nationalism, xenophobia, Englishness, Britishness, militarism and gender difference into a complex system which gives 'race' its contemporary meaning" (*There Ain't No Black in the Union Jack*, 43). Gilroy analyzes the British Immigration Acts of 1968–81 to suggest that immigration control and its attendant national ideologies are inextricable from the racism-nationalism dyad: "The 1971 Immigration Act brought an end to primary immigration and instituted a new pattern of internal control and surveillance of black settlers. It was paralleled by a new vocabulary of 'race' and crime which grew in the aftermath of the first panic over 'mugging'" (62). Although anti-immigrant racist rhetoric varies and shifts over time, the 1980s marked a severe turn by Britain, the United States, France, and later Italy in the era of Reagan and Thatcher and the return to colonial-era racism.

Migritude literature discloses the violence of systems of immigration and provides a challenging retort that, necessarily, cannot come from Western nations themselves. Gilroy analyzes the reuse of earlier moments in black radicalism by actors in black urban struggle in Britain:

> Such conflicts are possible because black Britain's repertoire of symbols is relatively unfixed and still evolving. It includes the language of Ethiopianism and Pan-Africanism and the heritage of anti-colonial resistances as well as the inputs from contemporary urban conflicts. These diverse elements combine syncretically in struggles to reconstruct a collective historical presence from the discontinuous, fractured histories of the African and Asian diasporas. (236)

Migritude is, in part, born of these urban struggles in Northern metropoles. And its refashioning of the black radical tradition, from pan-Africanism and Négritude to postcolonial African literature, provides both a sophisticated understanding of immigration in the era of global neoliberal capitalism, and resistance to it with reference to Africa and Africas *in* the Global North.

In the present, immigration control, passports, borders, deportations, identification cards, residence permits, and legal categories such as "illegal alien," "undocumented," and "*sans-papiers*" have all become naturalized over the past century as their proliferation in the late twentieth and twenty-first centuries continues unchallenged.[41] "*I excavate the words that hid in my churning stomach through visa controls*," writes Patel in *Migritude*, "*words I swallowed down until over the border*" (35, emphasis in original). The description here of a kind of tortured passing, of forced silence and alienation, seems at odds with liberal and neoliberal discourses conceptualizing immigration in terms of personal choice and free movement. Both in fact erase the realities of white privilege, the nearly unrestricted mobility of capital, and asymmetrically valued European and American passports. When Shailja Patel narrates her parents' experiences at American immigration control above or her own experiences as a South Asian Kenyan in the mechanized and biopolitical border spaces of what she calls "the global North," she creates a literary, phenomenological, and activist iteration of the "migrant attitude" so necessary at our contemporary juncture (37).

Immigration is never solely an individual action in which one moves from one place to another. It is always already mediated by systems or sets of conditions that shape or interdict one's movements, one's world. For Saskia Sassen, "migrations do not simply happen. They are produced. And migrations do not involve just any possible combination of countries. They are patterned."[42] Labor migrations, for example, "are embedded in larger social, economic, and political structures, and . . . they are consequently bounded in their geography, duration, and size. There is a geopolitics of migration and there is the fact that migrations are part of systems: both set parameters for migrations. . . . [We should] accept the fact that migration is not simply an aggregation of individual decisions, but a process patterned and shaped by existing politico-economic systems" (155–56). Migritude authors negotiate and challenge extant politico-economic systems wherein the movement of capital, information, and the elite are intensified, yet conversely, the movement of poor and working-class migrant bodies and refugees are more intensely managed. Under globalization, for Étienne Balibar, "what becomes intensified is not only the circulation of commodities, capital, and money but above all the circulation of *information*. . . . On the other side, what becomes increasingly controlled, differentiated, and, for some categories, restricted, is the circulation of *persons*" ("Toward a Diasporic Citizen?" 216). Far from the liberal/neoliberal lauding of globalization as creating a free and open world, it creates "a gigantic inequality with regard to the right of circulation and the mobility of persons" (217).

These contexts shape migritude fiction itself. Senegalese-Italian writer Pap Khouma, for example, in his 1990 *I Was an Elephant Salesman*, states: "Africa is poorly governed. There are too many people making a profit at her expense . . . *and so the people must leave.*"[43] Khouma goes on to reference colonial histories in Africa and migration as he narrates his experience as an African elephant salesman in Italy. A migrant phenomenology must pay close attention to material changes under globalization. Take labor itself as movement. For Leila Simona Talani, under globalization

the labour structure . . . changes, with substantial reallocation of la-
bour-intensive production [to] Third World countries . . . where it is
possible to exploit the advantages of lower production costs and/or
in the form of lower costs of primary resources . . . the populations of
those marginalized zones of the globe, whose economic conditions
are deemed to worsen as a consequence of the process of globalization, experience an increased incentive to leave their home countries
and move to more developed regions of the world in search of better
life standards. This produces the two interrelated phenomena of the
"brain drain," when highly skilled or highly educated labour flees the
country of origin, and "mass migration," when migratory flows interest unskilled labour.[44]

Neoliberal economic policies such as structural adjustment programs, imposed on African nations by the International Monetary Fund, also create
gigantic inequalities and subsequent "interrelated phenomena." In "The Neo-
Liberal Agenda and the IMF/World Bank Structural Adjustment Programs
with Reference to Africa," Gloria Emeagwali analyzes the Nigerian situation:
"In the case of Nigeria, the defining moment was the Babangida countercoup
of 1985, sometimes dubbed 'the IMF coup.' Fluctuating interest rates, corruption and poor economic planning were at the root of the debt crisis in
Nigeria, by the early 1980s. . . . Despite numerous student protests and riots
against the adoption of IMF programs, the new regime rapidly adopted such
policies. Under the weight of IMF *conditionalities* the Nigerian economy was
soon sapped. The removal of subsidies and on health and education took
its toll on wide segments of the population."[45] Italian digital artist Marco di
Prisco (discussed in chapter 4) poignantly shows the experience of Nigerian
farm workers in Italy who, after having left a destabilized Nigeria, migrate
to Italy to find work. These men, allowed in for their labor, were met with
abject hatred for their blackness and were physically attacked. Diaspora
and immigration studies therefore must take into account not simply the
journey and the destination, but the material conditions of reality in the
home country, and further, the complex relationships between the three.

In *Critical Perspectives on Neoliberal Globalization*, Sidonia Jessia Alenuma-Nimoh notes that subsidies in the Global North undermine farmers and
businesses in the Global South. For example, "cotton is a key crop in central
and western Africa, yet the global price of cotton is 20% lower than it could
be without US cotton subsidies."[46] Governments in the Global North are
allowed to subsidize their industries while institutions like the World Trade

Organization, the International Monetary Fund, and the World Bank forbid countries in the Global South from implementing subsidies or tariffs that would help their industries. This leads Aviva Chomsky to note that "Free-market policies may be associated with democracy in the United States and elsewhere in the industrialized world, but in the Third World, they more commonly come with the disappearance of democratic rights."[47] Mass unemployment and cuts in social services can exacerbate intra-ethnic tensions in an already unstable environment due to colonial legacies and corruption and thus lead to conflicts, famine, war, and flight.

Women are perhaps most significantly affected by these processes. In "Gendered Globalization: A Re-examination of the Changing Roles of Women in Africa," Alenuma-Nimoh continues:

> In accordance with the philosophy of neoliberal globalization, state intervention in the economic life of the people, under all circumstances, is undesirable because it is considered unproductive. Globalization subsequently entails trade liberalization, the devaluation of national currencies against "major" currencies (especially the U.S. dollar), and deregulation of the public sector, or simply, privatization of public utilities. These policies have resulted in retrenchment of workers and consequently, massive unemployment, reduction in government spending on social infrastructure, cuts in government subsidies for social services wherever they are available, and increased cost of these services. Women, especially those in Africa bear the brunt of these changes because of their already marginalized status. (*Critical Perspectives*, 88)

There is a necessary burgeoning literature both in academia and in fiction on women's experiences in the diaspora, detailing, for example, increasing demand for domestic or care labor.[48] But it is important also to pay careful attention to conditions in the Global South as well. This important fact is not lost upon Sonali Perera, who in *No Country* presciently argues: "in the contemporary historical moment, the 'new proletariat' is best represented by the figure of the woman worker in the periphery. Separate from organized labor in industrialized countries of the North, the occluded agent of production in this 'postindustrial' age is the super-exploited worker in postcolonial, 'developing' countries with extraverted, rather than autocentric, economies" (79). Furthermore, migrant women from "developing" countries such as those in Africa mentioned above are targeted differentially within migration, that

is, via locations in between homeland and host land like immigration control, checkpoints, airports, refugee halfway points like the Italian-run island
of Lampedusa—a kind of migrant purgatory—and various other spaces
within movement. In chapter 3 I discuss protagonist Salie's bio-political
and gendered examination at immigration control in France, having come
from Senegal, in Fatou Diome's novel *The Belly of the Atlantic*. Shailja Patel's
mother, as we saw above, is treated differently than her father by American
immigration control officers as they (almost) arrive from Kenya to America
in *Migritude*. These instances and others reveal not only the racialization
of nonwhite bodies in migration but the gendered and heteronormative
techniques of power mobilized by international system(s) of immigration
within globalization. Patel traces South Asian diasporas in East Africa and
her own migrations from Africa to England and the United States. This
tracing stages the fraught and historied intimacies of Africa, Asia, Europe,
and the Americas.

I began this section of the chapter by praising the critical globality of
texts like Lisa Lowe's *The Intimacies of Four Continents*. Patel's *Migritude* can
be read as taking up similar work yet in different form. In a poem nearing
the end of her text she writes: "At 6pm she heats the oil. / I've made the puri
dough . . . *Don't worry / about the size and shape, / just do your best. /* Mine are
shaped like countries. / Kenya. England. India. America . . . *No one in America
knows / how to make good puris*" (106). Patel's project traces the intimacies
of four countries, and the violence that subtends and creates those intimacies: imperialism, racial capitalism, and neoliberal globalization. Yet she
phenomenologically weaves small or everyday objects (both domestic and
national) like Ambi and puri dough, or visas and passports, into the macro-
societal-global. Patel's poetic entanglement here at once represents both a
phenomenological "attitude" in the sense of perception, objects, and being in
the world on the one hand, and *having* an attitude, i.e., the politicizing "voice
of a generation of migrants who speak unapologetically, fiercely, lyrically, for
themselves" on the other (137). Just as, for Léopold Sédar Senghor, Négritude is not solely an affirmation of one's blackness, but a "rooting oneself in
oneself, and self-confirmation: confirmation of one's *being*," so *Migritude* is
similarly ontological, affirming, and political.[49] Shailja Patel and other migritude writers, whether novelistically or poetically, trace the being of those who
move from the Global South to the North and those already there; they take
up the conscripting structures and conditions that manage the movement
and being of their subjects as well as the histories of those structures and
conditions themselves—marking a novel and twenty-first-century mode

of analysis, politics, and creativity. Building upon Patel's essential work, I argue that it is necessary to rethink immigration in terms of the material systems and histories that create, shape, and manage it—moving away from privileged liberal and neoliberal understandings of immigration that can reproduce anti-immigrant racisms and the contemporary global conditions of inequality. And if, for Shailja Patel, "art is a migrant," the artistic figure of the migrant in literature, and the "migrant attitude" itself, novelly take up and engage these conditions (137).

THE *"CONDITION D'IMMIGRÉS"* IN FATOU DIOME'S *THE BELLY OF THE ATLANTIC* AND THE AESTHETICS OF MIGRATION IN THE FRANCOPHONE AFRICAN LITERARY TRADITION

"The country says Black or French / The Country says that one can only be black or French / The thinking of the country in binary . . . the best / Is to go beyond the limits of the Nation / To see more largely."¹ In *Ecrits pour la parole*, contemporary Cameroonian-French writer Leonora Miano poetically suggests that racism, nationalism, and immigration are fundamental to the European nation-state. "The Country" here represents the French state while the word "French" in "black or French"—meaning "white"—repeats a kind of racial nationalism or the idea that to be French is to be white, which is in turn, incommensurable with blackness. For Miano, the nation-state is therefore premised upon state-sponsored racism and nationalism; it thinks in binary, it includes and excludes. People from elsewhere are other-than, and black people native to France are considered, counterintuitively, from another place. Miano speaks to contemporary and historical French contexts in which black people are not included or partially included under the aegis of "Frenchness," which is perhaps why she makes the powerful argument that, "the best is to go beyond the limits of the Nation / To see more largely."

Her irreverent unfaithfulness to formal grammatical structure parallels her challenge to the tacit racism and anti-immigrant nationalism of the French nation-state. Grammar and the language it organizes are not only historically situated and carriers of culture or value, as Frantz Fanon, Ngũgĩ Wa Thiong'o, and Lisa Lowe have argued, but also conscripting (colonial) forces. For example, Miano's contemporary, Senegalese-French novelist Fatou Diome, uses the term *nègre*, much like the négritude authors before her, as both a challenge to and reappropriation of its white supremacist usage, showing how it constructs black identity and conscripts black bodies (I discuss this in more detail later in the chapter). Achille Mbembe reminds us that although the term *Nègre* originates in Iberia, it entered into common usage in France in the eighteenth century, not coincidentally at the precise moment the transatlantic slave trade would reach its zenith.[2] Phenomenologically, he argues, "the term first designates not a significant reality but a field—or better yet, a coating—of nonsense and fantasies that the West (and other parts of the world) have woven, and which it clothed people of African origin long before they were caught in the snares of [racial] capitalism" (38). Terms like *nègre* constellated as a field, catching people of African origin with prefabricated identities, roles, and values.

Of course, language as a conscripting force indeed has a colonial history. In *Culture and Imperialism*, Edward Said reminds us that "the division between 'francophone' and 'anglophone' African states today exactly mirrors the distribution of the French and British colonial empires" (76). The French discourse of assimilation (an ideologically weighty term itself) that began "under the Revolution[,] collapsed, as theories of racial types . . . guided French imperial strategies. . . . At best, France's relationship with Algeria, Senegal, Mauritania, Indochina, was one of *association* through 'hierarchic partnership'" (170, emphasis in original). Miano deconstructs both the specious language of "partnership" with its colonies and colonial subjects in France, and its linguistic hierarchy itself, precisely by breaking (with) its formal structure or grammar. Rosemary Haskell notes that Miano's contemporary Fatou Diome recently denounced "contemporary French right-wing politicians' support for 'assimilationism,' which Diome ties to then-presidential hopeful François Fillon's declaration that 'la France n'est pas une nation multiculturelle!' (France is *not* multicultural!). This assimilationist ethic's denial of otherness—'une négation de l'altérité' (a negation of otherness)—is exploded by Diome as a cover for an exclusionary Frenchness that particularly targets Africa and Islam."[3] Like Miano's poetics, this politics is reflected in the language Diome uses.

I must note here that due to the limits of my own learning, I have, for the most part, read the following "Francophone" texts in their English translations—which admittedly, is not the best way to go about things. That my understanding of these texts is therefore mediated through *two* colonial languages suggests a kind of double bind, which I hope the reader will carefully consider. However, in the spirit of transnationalism and the multilinguistic literatures of diaspora, it is still important to cross (in both senses of the word) the colonial linguistic boundaries that demarcate "Francophone," or "Italophone," or "Anglophone," even at the disadvantage of reading in translation. Like Diome and Miano, many African authors break with the formal structure of the colonial language they utilize. Authors have integrated words or idioms in their native language (think of Achebe and Ngugi's use of Igbo or Kikuyu, or their great debate about the use of African versus colonial languages). Migritude authors including Abu Bakr Khaal and Shailja Patel often integrate poetic form as well as history into the language of their novels, crossing the formal structure of the novel itself. I begin with one such example from Diome's novel *The Belly of the Atlantic*, a novel that follows protagonist Salie, a young Senegalese migrant living in France, and her younger brother Madické, who lives on their native island Niodior, just off the west coast of Senegal. I mine her integrated poem for what it might tell us about conscription and, in the following sections of the chapter, trace what I call the aesthetics of migration in Francophone African literary traditions while close-reading Diome's novel through the lens of conscription.

The Belly of the Atlantic itself represents not so much a linear narrative but rather a tapestry of the experiences of Senegalese migrants in France. Near the end of the novel Salie reflects upon her migration to France from Africa and her experience with immigration control in the form of a poem. Salie pens the following lines: "Passports, permits, visas, / endless red tape, / The new chains of slavery / Bank branch, account number, / Address, ethnic origin, / The fabric of modern apartheid" (154). For Salie, the endless red tape constricting those migrants from outside the geopolitical West, the connection of "account numbers" and "bank branch[es]" to "ethnic origin," are already woven into the fabric of "modern apartheid," and thus represent, ideologically and materially, the "new chains of slavery." Salie's migrant poem indicates a kind of global conscription. It is not simply that Salie fits a profile and therefore sets off the alarms of "fortress Europe" or that France's immigration regime (like other nation-states') is, despite exceptions like these, legitimate. These regimes are, rather, symptomatic of an illegitimate rule, a global and historical force that has already conscripted nonwhite actors from the Global South or within the North, and has already scripted their narratives. I have argued that the United States' and Europe's global economic and political policies, from regime change to forced privatization and structural adjustment programs, create the destabilization and therefore out-migration that they then attempt to police at their own borders. Diome's "new form of slavery" then represents precisely conscription into these contemporary conditions, which look more like a "modern apartheid" than a "global village."

Diome's *The Belly of the Atlantic* narrates diasporic life for African migrant populations in France. Although the novel focuses on Salie and Madické's experiences and relationship across the distance between France and Senegal, as well as their backstories, the novel is structured as a palimpsest of the narratives of various islanders who become migrants. Numerous characters like Moussa and the man from Barbès emigrate to France and ultimately fail (or are failed by their various environments). Consider the scene, for example, in which Afro-Parisians from Senegal celebrate wildly in the streets of Paris. Set against the historical event of the Senegalese football team's victory over France in the 2002 World Cup, Diome's narrator describes an unprecedented postcolonial moment:[4] "So, naturally, with Senegal's World Cup triumph, the black population of France was singing and dancing; for once they were invited to play with the big boys who, what's more, were saying good things about them" (172). This postcolonial victory, however, allows Diome to reflect upon the failure of the postcolonial condition and the ways in which immigrants are conscripted. As the weight of global capitalism in Africa creates migration via destabilization, continued racism in France makes life in the segregated and impoverished *banlieues* difficult, even perilous, for immigrant and second-generation populations.

For the majority of African migrants in France, Senegal's triumph would be bittersweet. "Even those who were afraid to go home [to Africa] with their suitcases stuffed with failure, humiliation and disappointment came out of their cramped tower blocks to shout about their pride regained in France. They managed to forget that no one ever spoke of gratitude toward them or even simply citizenship, but only of tolerance and integration into the mould of a sieve-society in which they are the lumps" (172). If France's black diasporic subjects manage to forget—if but for a moment—white France's hostile attitude toward them, their structural segregation, cramped tower blocks, and the indignity of being "tolerated" without rights or citizenship, their amnesia represents a commensurate feat, rivaling Senegal's World Cup victory. "As the Parisian Senegalese rejoiced, parading down the Champs-Elysées, they were overtaken by their *condition of immigrants* and its corollary, contempt. The Arc de Triomphe isn't for negroes!" (172, my emphasis). Diome's novel indeed narrates the "condition d'immigrés"[5] in France for Senegalese migrants. Her cast of characters in *The Belly of the Atlantic* are faced with detention centers, racial profiling, deportations, passport control, and immigrant under- or unemployment. The above passage evokes immigrant affect produced by both cultural and economic humiliation, impoverishment, and the fear of returning home (or the inability to), experienced by many

Africans in France. It is for these reasons that we must necessarily think about the conditions of migration in terms of conscription rather than the conventionally accepted idea of free movement.

Furthermore, Diome's incisive description of the condition of immigrants more generally reconfigures the ways in which we conceptualize immigration, engaging not solely with immigrants themselves but with the structures, apparatuses, and institutions that catalyze, reshape, or interdict their movement. Fatou Diome's novel stands among a number of twenty-first-century works of African literature ushering in new genres—including migritude—whose authors figure immigration anew. Fatou Diome goes beyond writing what is already a wonderfully global novel replete with literary-genealogical references to a bevy of Négritude writers of generations past while narrating her own ambiguous adventure as an African woman in Paris. She responds to a conscripting global apartheid through both her *rehearsal* and *re-fashioning* of Léopold Sédar Senghor's "black humanism" by 1) meditating upon the condition of what Miano terms the "Afropean"[6]—the mixing of African and European identity and culture, also a preoccupation of Senghor's; and 2) inaugurating what I call a migrant humanism. Since racial discrimination is outwardly frowned upon in some places and in some spaces illegal, anti-immigrant rhetoric and practice transforms itself so that it can continue to racialize subjects in different ways, thereby reaffirming racist practice and discourse. Migrant humanism is not solely a challenge to this contemporary and highly adaptable anti-immigrant rhetoric and law, essentially new codes for an old racism (racism itself is not monolithic but highly protean). The migrant humanism of Diome or of Shailja Patel's *Migritude* narrates the experience of migrants, particularly women, while borrowing from the black philosophy of Négritude and other moments in black and brown radical traditions. It therefore creates an (ontological) phenomenology of the being-in-the-world of those who—to paraphrase Simone de Beauvoir in a different context—"become" migrants, an important field in its own right indispensable for any understanding of our global present (see chapter 2 for more on the importance of the phenomenological method and migration).

~

Migration itself is perhaps one of the few shared commonalities in Francophone African literature. Before Bernard Dadié's famous 1959 migratory travel narrative and philosophical tract *Un Nègre à Paris*, Négritude authors of the 1930s and 1940s like Léopold Sédar Senghor and Aimé Césaire commented on black migration to France and diasporic pan-African experience, an experience necessarily inextricable from the historical context of colonial racism. for example, one of the recently acknowledged godmothers of Négritude, Paulette Nardal, wrote a short story titled "In Exile" in 1929 detailing the stark economic conditions facing black migrant Caribbean women in Paris. Isaie Dougnon reminds us that in addition to "prestige migration," wherein colonial empires invited their best and brightest subjects like the Négritude authors in the 1920s to France to illustrate the "progress" of empire, "colonial empires [also] attempted to control the migration of their subjects [in the colonies], especially to keep subjects from working in another colonial empire."[7] Gary Wilder's *The French Imperial Nation State* documents European management of African mobility beginning in the colonial era. In French West Africa in 1928, for example, through a "decree establishing an Office of Emigration and Immigration in each colony, [Jules] Carde created a formal apparatus for policing native mobility. It prohibited Africans from traveling outside their colony of origin without first obtaining a permit, an official identity card (including the bearer's photograph, fingerprints, race, and kinship lineage), and for those traveling to Europe, proof that they could support themselves once there."[8] If policing migration both materially and discursively is a fundamental preoccupation of the Western colonial nation-state (see chapter 2), it would certainly appear to shape the lives and narratives of those it touches.

From the first Négritude prose-novel—Cheikh Hamidou Kane's 1961 *Ambiguous Adventure* and Ousmane Sembene's groundbreaking 1966 film *La Noire de* (*Black Girl*), visualizing a black woman's migration and alienation, to contemporary Congolese migritude author Alain Mabanckou's 2009 *Black Bazaar* and many other recent works, in literature African migration to France has been both significant and inextricable from the historical fact of European colonization (out of which the concept of immigration itself arises), racism, and global capitalism. Although migration and diaspora are significant themes taken up by a substantial number of authors within what we might call late twentieth- and twenty-first-century global literature, I choose Fatou Diome's text here because it joins a rather small number of contemporary African diasporic texts that detail the very materiality of immigration through what is really a complex phenomenology of movement, including challenges to global apartheid as well as forging a migrant humanism—the recapturing of the category of "immigrant" as positive and human against the abject dehumanization of migrants throughout the world, from the African migrant crisis in the Mediterranean and the Syrian refugee crisis to the recent humanitarian crisis at the US–Mexico border substantially exacerbated by the Trump administration.

Exile and its condition of possibility, migration, are major themes in African literature.[9] Perhaps it is most pronounced in the French context. For Dominic Thomas, exile and immigration subtend black literature in French. In *Black France: Colonialism, Immigration, and Transnationalism*, Thomas argues that "exile itself constitutes the entry into writing . . . the Congolese novelist Emmanuel Dongala has underlined how both negritude and the more recent concept of 'migritude' emerged from these circumstances" (5). In his lecture "From Négritude to Migritude: The African Writer in Exile," Dongala traces the development of the "Francophone African novel through the lens of exile,"[10] suggesting that what these two generations of black writers share across a half-century or more is the experience of exile—a theme that is, not coincidentally, significant in Diome's *The Belly of the Atlantic*; Salie, for example, describes herself as "a permanent exile, I spend my nights soldering the rails that lead to identity. Writing is the hot wax I pour between the furrows dug by those who erect partitions" (182). It is through exile that the entry into writing is marked. Diome negotiates the specific experience of immigration, illustrated here in her reference to partitions, which signals borders, checkpoints, passport control—the stuff of migritude experience. Just as she is shaped by them, she writes to protest anti-immigrant milieus in her twenty-first-century context.

If Négritude centers upon the being of the black man in the colonial era, his experiences, and finally, the construction of an oppositional identity that would counter racism while forging a pan-African community, then migritude literature constructs a migrant-focused literature, identity, and solidarity. For Thomas, "whereas protagonists of colonial-era texts navigated their way through France primarily for the purpose of education and travel, those in contemporary novels experience detention centers, are faced with legal procedural issues, are often categorized as illegal, clandestine, or undocumented" (4). Alain Mabanckou's migritude novel, ironically titled *Bleu-Blanc-Rouge* (*Blue White Red*—the colors of the French flag), opens, for example, in a detention center in France and closes with the deportation of his protagonist, an undocumented migrant or *sans-papiers*. This allows Mabanckou's narrator to illustrate both the plight of those who are "undocumented—sandwiched between complex and draconian laws," and the politics of French xenophobia "used as a political football to win a vote or two from intolerant French people. The abandoned and undocumented horde was considered a pressure on French society."[11] Mabanckou's commentary is suggestive of the legislative, political, and cultural structures and conditions that shape migrants' lives. These preexisting structures produce immigrants in the sense that there are already discourses such as anti-immigrant rhetoric or racial nationalism that interpellate or conscript diasporic subjects in France, while material structures (legislative and disciplinary) contain or manage them.

Migritude writers ask us to think not simply about those who move across borders or oceans, but about the techniques of power utilized by states, governments, transnational corporations, and "natives" to manage, contain, and surveil immigrant populations biopolitically: they illustrate how "condition" works both as a noun and verb, and show how these apparatuses operate within, along, beneath, and as, state structures. Michel Foucault, whose key terms I borrow here, analyzed migration as early as *The History of Sexuality Vol. 1.* For Foucault in 1976,

> The old power of death that symbolized sovereign power was now carefully supplanted by the administration of bodies and the calculated management of life. During the classical period, there was a rapid development of various disciplines—universities, secondary schools, barracks, workshops; there was also the emergence, in the field of political practices and economic observation, of the problems of birthrate, longevity, public health, housing, and migration. Hence there was an explosion of numerous diverse techniques for achieving the subjugation of bodies and the control of populations, marking the beginning of an era of "biopower."[12]

Foucault tracks the proliferation of these "techniques," including the observation and disciplining of migration, beginning in the eighteenth century, that are necessarily bound up with the development of capitalism in Western countries (141). Foucault's vocabulary allows for a more precise parsing of the proliferation of apparatuses and techniques of power that in the context of migritude describe border control, detention centers, checkpoints, deportations, the distribution of passports, and population management, whose function is to manage the movement of nonwhite people in the postcolonial era of global capital. He defines biopower as "the set of mechanisms through which the basic biological features of the human species became the object of a political strategy, of a general strategy of power, or, in other words, how, starting from the eighteenth century, modern western societies took on board the fundamental biological fact that human beings are a species."[13] In this sense, just as for Foucault the "homosexual" was invented as a "species" beginning in 1889, so the immigrant was produced as such in the same era of high imperialism. Migritude literature shows how terms like *sans papier* or "undocumented" in Mabanckou's France, "immigrant" or "illegal alien" in the US context, all become categorical terms, "species," that are both legislated and discursively weighted.

Biopolitical colonial techniques indeed adumbrate the management of movement under globalization. In *The Belly of the Atlantic*, for example, Diome's narrator illustrates how twenty-first-century passport control is shaped by an imperial past:

> On my arrival in France, before being issued with my residency per-
> mit, I'd been called into the International Immigration Office for a
> full X-ray. Free of scabies and pustules and not harboring any shame-
> ful diseases, I'd been sent, along with a bill for 320 francs, a medical
> certificate, which stated: fulfils the requisite health conditions for au-
> thorization to reside in France. So illness is considered an unaccept-
> able defect that bars access to French territory. Mind you, in the days
> when Negroes, ebony and spices were sold any which way, no one
> bought a sick slave. And in the colonies, for a long time the natives
> believed that the master never fell ill, so cleverly did everything con-
> spire to maintain the myth of his superiority . . . Did the immigration
> office think it was teaching me to toe the line? One thing's for sure:
> they wanted to know everything about me. They'd seen me wearing
> Senghor's Negritude on my face and were unsure which role I would
> play in Les Misérables. (153)

The above passage begins by showing how the French nation-state has ex-propriated the free means of movement from Salie at the same moment that it biopolitically enfolds her: it examines her physically, keeps records, and through the language and attitude of its employees, racializes and silences her, all while externalizing the costs—she receives a bill for "320 francs." Representative of the practice of French neocolonial biopower, Salie's body itself, as well as her movement, is integrated into a dynamic system of control; this passage also alludes to the fact that bodily controls have proliferated rather than decreased, as proponents of globalization claim, from the colonial period in to the late twentieth and twenty-first centuries. Salie however, is quick to make the parallel between twenty-first-century France and the techniques—material and otherwise—it uses to condition Salie, and the colonial policing of migration, slavery, and interestingly, *Les Misérables.*

Like other colonial powers, France engaged in cultural colonization as well, which meant among other things, the imposition of French education on its colonized populations. So instead of reading Serer or Wolof poetry and history, for example, students were taught Victor Hugo and French history; they were conscripted into a discourse that would value French culture at the same moment it devalued their own. However, Salie strategically refers to Senghor—"They'd seen me wearing Senghor's Negritude on my face"—as an anticolonial response to French cultural racism that she remobilizes in her own context as she negotiates passport control and the immigration officers. Salie's conscious awareness of, and subtle resistance to, conscription as I've outlined it, pushes against the biopolitical creation of the immigrant subject, and exposes it as a colonial practice in the present.

Abdourahman A. Waberi's Djiboutian Francophone novel *Transit* provides another illuminating instantiation of colonial processes in the present. In this novel, Ali Aref—president of the French colony of Djibouti in the Horn of Africa—takes a cue from European models of population control: "Ali Aref and his supporters had done all they could to sort people out, and anathema and exclusion were the rule. Your membership in a tribe, or more precisely a clan, contrary to the common appellation, was stamped on your identity card, and as if that weren't enough, they invented a new population category, decreed non-native on the pretext that they were supposed to be from Somalia."[14] Waberi's narrator details the categorization of peoples and apparatuses like identity cards and checkpoints developed to manage movement. "Anathema" and "exclusion" also direct our attention to the rhetorical regulation of immigration through the construction of a discourse or ideology around questions of who or what constitutes "outsiders" and conversely who or what counts as a national or ethnic "we."

Mabanckou ironically uses the term "horde" in *Blue White Red*, which immediately calls to mind anti-immigrant rhetoric reminiscent of colonial-era racist attitudes. The perception of black immigrants as an "abandoned and undocumented horde [who create] a pressure on French society," as they are sarcastically described by Mabanckou's narrator, is instructive here. From "the black threat on the Rhine" propaganda against black French soldiers in Germany in 1920, to Jacques Chirac's "notoriously expressed distaste for the 'noise and smell' of France's immigrant population"[15] in France in the early 1990s, nonwhite populations in France, elsewhere in Europe, and in the United States were and are subject not only to discriminatory laws and policies but to ideological defamation as well. I here pause briefly to discuss the important *literal* conscription of West African subjects into the French

army in World War I, to which the "black threat on the Rhine" refers. Myron Echenberg notes that although many European powers used colonial
African conscripts in both world wars, "France was the only colonial power
to bring Africans by the thousands to the trenches of Northeastern Europe
in the First World War."[16] There were racist reactions throughout Europe
(including the panicked German "terror on the Rhine" which Claude McKay
eloquently critiques—see chapter 6), and racist responses to black troops in
Hitler's *Mein Kampf* and H. G. Wells's speculative fiction *The Sleeper Awakes*
(Echenberg, 2, 34). Many Africans derided these soldiers as cronies of colonialism, yet Echenberg points out that although these African soldiers were
indeed "part of the coercive state apparatus of rule [they were] themselves
coerced into service" and indeed many resisted conscription (3, 100). The
mutiny at Thiaroye, Senegal, for example, has been lauded in both Ousmane
Sembene's documentary *Camp de Thiaroye* and a poem by Leopold Sedar
Senghor, "Poéme liminaire." Echenberg also points out that although these
African soldiers fought and died to save "France and humanity from Nazi
totalitarianism . . . [they were met] with the crude racism of white officers and
civilian society"—a discursive and legal practice at odds with France's myth
of universal brotherhood and equality, precisely what the French-African
authors discussed in this chapter chastise (164, 165).

These contexts illustrate why for Diome, in the epigraph framing this
chapter, the corollary of the immigrant condition is contempt. In theorizing
the immigrant condition, the terms delineated above shore up analyses of
migritude literature by allowing the thinking of seemingly disparate phenomena such as deportation laws, discriminatory hiring practices, racist
colonial propaganda, or the manufacture of anti-immigrant panic and its
attendant epistemic violence, as actually interrelated techniques of power
(biopolitics) leveraged to maintain control. Elisa Camiscioli, for example,
shows that "racial hierarchy was a constitutive feature of immigration discourse in Republican France" in the early twentieth century.[17] Although white
foreigners in the French imperial era would be assimilated, "immigration
discourse explicitly and repeatedly referred to people of color as impossible
to assimilate because they were not members of the white race" (157). Immigration, she correctly argues, "was therefore one component of a larger
state project of constituting citizens and subjects, political identities which, I
have argued, cannot be extracted from their gendered and racialized embodi-
ments" (157). This larger state project reveals the entanglement of empire with
the management and categorization of the movement of people, things, and
ideas. Building upon Camiscioli, I frame immigration as more than simply

"one component" of state and imperial projects but indeed fundamental to it, and that postcolonial experiences of immigration in the present illustrate its tenacity. Colonial racial hierarchies indeed refract into the present as anti-immigrant discourse—which amounts to newly flexible coding for anti–black and brown.

So why not just return to Africa? Although narratives of return certainly abound in colonial and postcolonial African literature, for a variety of historical, economic, cultural, and other reasons, there is rarely a salutary "return" to Africa in the literature of migration. "It is precisely the inability of the new immigrants to envisage or entertain a permanent return to a postcolonial space bereft of agential possibilities that Paris," for Pius Adesanmi, "ironically, regains a problematic status as a site of redemption in migritude narratives."[18] So Mabanckou's migritude narrator in *Blue White Red* ponders this "new immigrant" double bind: "Foreigners in France, they would be equally foreign in their own countries. After all, one can't just go back, impulsively, after an absence" (107). For Fatou Diome's protagonist Salie in *The Belly of the Atlantic*, there is no return to Africa from France since she feels as alienated upon her return trips home as in France. For Salie,

> the urge to return to the source is irresistible, for it's reassuring to think that life is easier to grasp in the place where it puts down its roots. And yet, for me, returning is the same as leaving. I go home as a tourist in my own country, for I have become the other for the people I continue to call my family, (116, emphasis in original)

Upon arrival home, and because she speaks "France French" and has accrued French mannerisms, Salie is treated as somewhat foreign in Niodior. She is also expected to provide gifts and capital to the village, the logic being, that since she lives in France she must be rich—a leftover colonial myth.

Dominic Thomas helps excavate the origins of migritude literature in this French context: "this neologism [migritude] designates both the thematic of immigration that is at the heart of contemporary African works, but also the expatriate status of most writers . . . their inspiration comes from their hybridity and decentered lives, elements that now characterize a kind of French-style 'world literature' [Chevrier] . . . In this way 'migritude' symbolizes a kind of 'third space' that comes from a 'questioning of certain prevalent discursive configurations' and 'simultaneous disengagement from both the culture of origin and the receiving culture . . . within a new identitarian space'" (*Black France*, 5). Chevrier's definition here utilizes key terms in postcolonial theory in the 1990s focusing on identity such as hybridity, decenteredness, and liminality. Though important, these terms foreground identity while often eliding the material institutions and economic processes that shape subject positions. The concept of "hybridity," for example, has come under fire for solely representing elite postcolonial subjects with the resources to travel and live across borders. A contemporary example of this can be found in the debate around Afropolitanism and narratives like Taiye Selassie's *Ghana Must Go* and others, which have been criticized for focusing on affluent diasporas and branding. Most famously, for example, see Binyavanga Wainaina's keynote address at 2012's African Studies Association UK titled "I am a Pan-Africanist not an Afropolitan." Yet the allure of Afropolitanism lingers on given the multiple panels addressing it at literature conferences (see 2018's African Literature Association conference).[19] Issues of immigration are highly intertwined with class. Therefore, I resist conflating hybrid elite cosmopolitan writers—often not subject to the same kinds of institutional apparatuses managing immigration that refugees or economic migrants are—with the majority of immigrants or migrant writers. Fatou Diome's novel indeed revises Senghor's black humanism within the context of non-elite diasporic and migrant subjecthood as a challenge to, and negotiation of, the neoliberal conditions that produce and shape diaspora and movement—contributing to a migrant humanism.

Like all literary movements however, these writers are shaped by historical literary contexts. For Abdourahman Waberi, these "children of the postcolony . . . are also a *'generational* phenomenon.' [They represent a] 'fourth generation,' the first three being the pioneer writers of 1920–1930, the negritude movement from 1930–1960, and finally decolonization and postcolonial disillusionment from the 1970s onward" (quoted in *Black France*, 20). The fourth generation would be publishing from around 1990 and on into the twenty-first century. These temporal categorizations are purely heuristic and nowhere near absolute, but are useful in some ways as road markers upon complex genealogical, historical, cultural, and geographical literary fields. Although for Thomas the second-generation Négritude writers were always already "immigrant writers," he cites Mamadou Diouf, who presciently suggests: "One must also speak of a new, extraordinary literature, that of novelists who are no longer the novelists of the in-between, of Africa and France, but rather novelists of Africa *in* France . . . They present a history and forms of modernity that are quite different from colonial and postcolonial modernities" (*Black France*, 23, my emphasis). Migritude modernities include both first- and second-generation immigrant communities and thus Africa can be both central and secondary. The paradox of some children of the postcolony (or writers of this new, "extraordinary" literature of Africa in France), is that while they are "French" (or "English," or "American"), given their skin color, they are considered outsiders and are treated inhospitably.

Writer Faïza Guène, for example, narrates a scene between her young Arab protagonist and an old white (racist) neighbor, who yells at Doria for mispronouncing the biblical Job's name in a kind of rote repetition of Chiracian, racialized anti-immigrant rhetoric. "She shouted at me because when I read, instead of pronouncing it like Job-rhymes-with-globe, I said 'Jahb.' Like what they call your work in America or the name of that fat guy in *Star Wars*. And that crazy old bag Mme Jacques accused me of 'sullying our beautiful language' and other stuff just as stupid. Nothing I can do, I didn't even know this Job guy existed. 'It's the faaaaulttt of people like yooouu that our Frrrench herrrritttage is in a coma!'"[20] "Sullying" here evokes Thatcher's "swamping" and chastises former president of France Jacques Chirac's racist anti-immigrant discourse as well. In many contexts, paradoxically, immigrant comes to mean simply black or brown, regardless of where one is born. This contradictory social construct, coding nonwhites as foreign is readily apparent in "*beur*" literature (of the 1980s) and "*banlieue*" literature (1990s and beyond) in which the protagonists are born in France to North African immigrant parents. Azouz Begag's autobiographical *Shantytown Kid* (1986) is often considered the first *beur* novel along with Mehdi Charef's *Tea in the Harem* (1983), which is also considered an early example of later *banlieue* literature, which includes Faïza Guène's *Kiffe demain* (2004), Alain Mabanckou's oeuvre, and others. This literature arises within and in response to impoverished urban spaces in Paris at once targeted and neglected by the French government (see the 2005 Clichy-sous-bois riots in Paris), populated largely by North African Muslims as well as sub-Saharan and Caribbean black populations. For Alec Hargreaves these groups and the urban spaces "were targeted in Le Pen's attack on the alleged evils of 'immigration' and 'Islam' . . . In popular discourse, North Africans have often been labelled as 'Arabs,' a term that frequently carries pejorative connotations inherited from colonial times. Tired of this stigmatization, during the 1970s second generation North Africans in the Paris conurbation began calling themselves *Beurs*, a self-valorising piece of *verlan* (backslang) formed by inverting and partially truncating the syllables of the word *Arabe*" ("Banlieue Blues," 215–16). The urban spaces in the novels are called *banlieues*, roughly meaning "suburbs" but with very different connotations from the English term. The terms "project" or "ghetto" might better serve as loose US equivalents.

Buer and *banlieue* writing represents a close affiliate to migritude literature since it documents and philosophizes upon the immigrant condition in French urban spaces. For Hargreaves, "these spaces are characterized on the one hand by acute material deprivation and on the other hand by extraordinarily rich and dynamic cultural diversity" (212). In *Tea in the Harem*, Charef narrates this acute material deprivation endemic of urban immigrant spaces as Majid, his friend, and a young woman, Solange, who also happens to be a prostitute from their tenement building, walk toward another *banlieue*:

> They walked through the long wild grass by the side of the disused railway line, to the hostel where the immigrant workers live. Solange complains endlessly. "How much further is it?" she asked. "I've got stones in my shoes." As she walks, she treads on the hem of her long, crumpled, Indian skirt . . . The barracks consist of rows of prefabs on a starch of stony, dusty wasteland, which turns into a mud patch in winter. These barracks are run by local employers, and they house workers from North Africa and the Mediterranean. They live here like animals, excluded from the normal life of the city, stuck between the roadworks on the motorway, the railway line and the harbor, in a work-camp surrounded by a wire fence.[21]

An important question these novels ask is: Is this dehumanization—"they live here like animals"—an aberration in Paris (or in any other northern metropole such as New York or London), or is the exclusion of various groups "from the normal life of the city" *constitutive* of the City of Lights? Migritude discloses a reality that reflects the latter.

Tea in the Harem invokes a common theme, often rehearsed in immigrant literature: "At the time, Majid and his parents were living in Nanterre bidonville—the rue de la Folie—the largest and cruelest of any in the Paris suburbs. Shantytowns that could equal anything in Brazil, but without the sun and music. When Majid's dad had sent for his wife and son to come from Algeria, he'd not told them about the cold, smoky barracks. When she first saw the place, Malika burst into tears, and Majid wondered if it was some kind of practical joke, because back home there was never enough to eat, but at least you had your little stone-built house; at least you had a home" (96). In Faïza Guène's novel *Kiffe Kiffe Tomorrow*, published twenty years later, Doria describes living in those same *banlieues*: "My mom always dreamed that France was like in those black-and-white films from the sixties. The ones where the handsome actor's always telling his woman so many pretty lies, a cigarette dangling from his lips . . . So when she and my dad arrived [from Morocco] in Livry-Gargan, just north of Paris, in February 1984, she must have thought they'd taken the wrong boat to the wrong country. She told me that when she walked into this tiny two-room apartment the first thing she did was throw up" (11). Migritude literature is predicated upon the vomiting up of colonial myths like the "Mirage of Paris" fed and swallowed by colonists and colonizer alike since the dawn of imperialism—a consistent theme in Diome's *The Belly of the Atlantic*.

The *"Condition d'Immigrés"* in Fatou Diome's *The Belly of the Atlantic*

Fatou Diome's *The Belly of the Atlantic* was written in French in 2003 and translated into English in 2006. It is a timely novel of African migration in general, and of the perils of emigration under and alongside global capitalism in the twenty-first century in particular. *The Belly of the Atlantic*, like other great works of African literature—both old and new—engages the history of imperial rule and the ways in which colonialism, and its vestiges in the present, have controlled and continue to mediate the movements of people, things, and ideas. Yet *The Belly of the Atlantic* speaks to a global world, not solely a Francophone one, in which Coca-Cola, American songs, and the global phenomenon of football deeply touch the small island of Niodior, Senegal, from whence its protagonists journey and tell their stories.

Ayo A. Coly points out that, around the time Diome begins to write *Belly* in the late 1990s, "African capitals became stages for mass demonstrations against structural adjustment programs, and an expanding group of African thinkers set themselves to exposing the neocolonial processes of globalization."[22] For Coly, Diome's embeddedness in the context of anti-globalization movements "feeds an anticolonial and nationalist narrative of home and migration" (99). Diome's novel, which I will argue is not nationalist, does necessarily speak to the destabilization of Africa by neoliberal economic policies wielded by the Global North, such as devaluation.

Manthia Diawara analyzes the 1994 currency devaluation imposed on Francophone Africa by European and American financial institutions.[23] For Diawara, many in West Africa conceptualized this move as "the recolonization of Africa by international financial institutions such as the World Bank and the International Monetary fund" (104). Diawara shows how the CFA devaluation affects all walks of life in West Africa: farmers, students, factory workers, and women and children. "Imagine the farmer being told that his harvest is only worth half of its real value, or the head of a household of sixteen now having to spend for the equivalent of thirty-two"; or imagine students, who "because of the recent structural adjustment programs and the devaluation . . . are being treated to reduced scholarships, higher admission standards, school closures, and the lack of jobs after graduation" (105). Diawara details how workers are negatively affected, while Folasade Iyun, in her study of Structural Adjustment Programs (SAP) in Nigeria, notes: "A feature of SAPs is the reduction of government expenditure, particularly on social welfare programs . . . [as a result] mothers and children in particular become marginalized."[24] How then do these neoliberal relations (a term which in this book is also taken to mean neocolonial) between France and Africa, often catalyzing emigration, get taken up by migritude writers?

Dominic Thomas reminds us that "migration to the French metropole has been a constant feature of francophone sub-Saharan African literature from colonial times to the contemporary moment of postcoloniality" (*Black France*, 185). However, a particular set of neoliberal economic policies has produced massive African destabilization that, by extension, produced mass migration in the 1980s and 1990s. For Thomas, "Whereas writers during the colonial era such as Ousmane Socé, Cheikh Hamidou Kane, and Bernard Dadié (all of whom Diome alludes to in her novel) were concerned with the 'ambiguous' nature of the cultural encounters with France . . . Diome extends and updates the implications and parameters of her work in order to situate her observations and critique within the contextual framework of a reflection on globalization and its impact on Africa" (*Black France*, 186–87). Twenty-first-century Francophone African writers respond to and challenge these very shifts in cultural and economic configurations. "Even in these regions," Diome's narrator reflects, where "drinking water's still a luxury, Coca-Cola brazenly comes to swell its sales figures. Have no fear, Coca-Cola will make the Sahel wheat grow!" (*The Belly of the Atlantic*, 6).

Building upon Coly and Thomas's important work, I argue that a close reading of Fatou Diome's novel allows for a substantive unpacking of Dongala's pithy phrase "from Négritude to migritude," and begins to answer the question of the theoretical and genealogical import represented in the shifting of the prefixes "*Nègre-*" in Négritude to "*migra-*" in migritude. Perhaps this linguistic permutation, for example, mirrors changes in radical lineages or traditions, from the racial identity politics of blackness in the colonial period to the critique of the codification of nonwhite bodies as "migrant" in our global present. Writers like Fatou Diome also reflect upon what stays the same, given that, though African nations have what Julius Nyerere calls "flag independence," for many little has changed in terms of cultural, economic, and other freedoms.

Like Diome herself, the protagonists Salie, a young writer and maid in Paris, and her younger brother Madické, an obsessed football fan ("soccer" in the United States), hail from the tiny Senegalese island Niodior off of the west coast of Africa. Salie leaves the island, "a scrap of land stuck to the gum of the Atlantic," to pursue her education in Dakar and then Paris, where she marries a Frenchman (2). She continues her grueling work as a maid after her husband divorces her due to the pressures of his family, who wanted "only Snow White" (26). She regularly spends a fortune calling her brother back in Niodior since Madické insists she update him on all the football matches he misses (there is only one television in the village and it often stubbornly refuses to cooperate). The narrative begins with Madické excitedly watching a football match in Niodior while Salie, in France, reflects upon leaving the island: "It's nearly ten years since I left the shade of the coconut palms. Pounding the asphalt, my imprisoned feet recall their former liberty, the caress of the warm sand, being nipped by crabs and the little thorn pricks that remind you there's life even in the body's forgotten extremities. I tread on European ground, my feet sculpted by African earth" (2–3). This passage beginning the novel is subtended by movement—the practice of walking—but it also suggests that the place within which one moves (and the in-between of those spaces) sculpts not only movement but the *way* we move, just as for Fanon the language we speak not only determines the words we say but how we think.

Like the spaces of Africa and later Europe, which mold Salie's identity, the materiality of the sand and concrete mediate her "body's forgotten extremities." Salie's positional in-betweenness, what Ayo Coly calls her "nomadic homelessness," shapes Diome's migrant narrative (Coly, 122). Salie is statedly "always in exile, with roots everywhere, I'm at home where Africa and Europe put aside their pride and are content to join together: in my writing, which is rich with the fusion they've bequeathed me" (*The Belly of the Atlantic*, 127). This fusion is best illustrated through her "hybrid" literary upbringing under Ndétare, the exiled Marxist schoolteacher in Niodior, who takes pity on Salie and becomes her mentor as she is orphaned and subsequently raised by her grandmother. "I owe him Descartes, I owe him Montesequieu, I owe him Victor Hugo, I owe him Molière, I owe him Balzac, I owe him Marx, I owe him Dostoevsky, I owe him Hemingway, I owe him Léopold Sédar Senghor, I owe him Aimé Césaire, I owe him Simone de Beauvoir, Marguerite

Yourcenar, Miriama Bâ and the rest . . . I owe him in short my *ambiguous adventure*" (41). *Ambiguous Adventure* references Senegalese author Cheikh Hamidou Kane's novel of the same name about the very alienating fusion of African and French culture. Further, in the above passage two-thirds of the Négritude poets are named, in addition to one of the godmothers of feminist African literature in Miriama Bâ, who also hails from Senegal. The French and African philosophical and literary traditions join German, American, and Russian greats in uneasy yet promising company. Diome's hybridity revises earlier uses of the term that are perhaps too narrowly identitarian by the foregrounding material conditions that shape both movement and diasporic identity.

Diome also situates her writing within the black radical tradition, drawing from it just as she refashions it. Salie's intellectual genealogy, for example, echoes Senghor's black humanism, which is predicated not upon racial exclusion or isolation but on African and European interconnectedness. In 1956 Senghor argued that "we are all cultural half-castes"[25] and suggested: "we are now living the final stage of world unification through interdependence. Thus, though our humanism must have West African man as its major objective, it cannot without peril, end with West Africa, not even with all of Africa. An effective humanism must be *open* . . . I dare say, pan-humanism—a humanism that includes all men on the dual basis of their contribution and their comprehension."[26] For Souleymane Bachir Diagne, "Negritude is not the ideology of separated identities that, despite his protestations, many critics of Senghor have taken it to be. Hybridity is always at work deconstructing his essentialist assertions and the Senghorian obsession with mixture is a Penelope ceaselessly making sure to undo fixed differences: 'the humanism of hybridity' could very well have been one of the poet's slogans."[27] And like Blyden before him and Mbembe after, Senghor thinks world interdependence: "Once again it is a matter of decolonizing and developing beyond the value of *négritude* our civilization and our African personality. *For the very being of being is to persevere in one's being* . . . It must be the contribution from us, the peoples of sub-Saharan Africa, to the growth of *Africanity*, and beyond that, to the building of the *Civilization of the Universal*" (*Prose and Poetry*, 97). Though Senghor castigates colonialism and the West elsewhere, his rhetoric here is more utopian and futural then say, Kane after him (note, however, that Senghor references the nineteenth-century godfather of pan-Africanism E. W. Blyden's concept of "African personality"). Salie similarly utters a sort of utopian humanism in *The Belly of the Atlantic*: "I'm at home where Africa and Europe put aside their pride and are content to join together" (127). Diome's black/migrant futurity exists in uncomfortable tension alongside the novel's portrayal of the violence of dispersal and the perils of emigration within which Diome embeds her critique of the neocolonial and neoliberal globalization of the West, and its not-so-distant colonial past.

In addition to the central stories of the two main protagonists in the novel (Salie and Madické), there are several parallel stories (set in the late twentieth and early twenty-first centuries), each telling the story of an African who migrates in one way or another, usually ending badly. Furthermore, Diome deconstructs the conventional reasons to migrate, downplaying representations of Africans as impoverished and starving, looking to fulfill their dreams in the various paradises of the North. It is rather *les mirages* of Paris and their function as discursive apparatuses—dialectically underwriting material exploitation of the South by the Global North—that Diome and her protagonist Salie take to task. The young football fan Madické, for example, his peers, and others in the village fall prey to the myth of France, or what Ndétare calls the chimera of red, white, and blue.

France is tantamount to paradise for Madické (meaning at the very least that his sister must watch all the football matches he misses): "In paradise, you don't struggle, you don't fall ill, you don't ask questions: it's enough to be alive, you can afford everything you desire, including the luxury of time, and that automatically means you're available [for football on TV]" (26). As Salie struggles to pay rent, work a decidedly unglamorous job, write (which is her true passion), study, and keep up with football matches for her brother, her reality has a much different hue from his imagined France: "It was no use telling Madické that as a cleaning woman my survival depended on the number of floor cloths I got through, [because] the Third World can't see Europe's wounds . . . For Madické, living in a developed country was in itself a huge advantage I had over him, he with the family and the tropical sun. How could I have made him understand the loneliness of exile, my fight for survival and the permanent effort my studies demanded?" (26). Here Salie refers not only to a colonial "illusion" or mirage "third worlders" subscribe to about France but also to her job as a maid to a French couple, picturing a reality in which demeaning jobs are reserved for black (women) immigrants (see Nardal).

Interestingly, Senegalese filmmaker and author Ousmane Sembene's 1966 film *La Noire de . . .* (*Black Girl*) is an incisive critique of just such a condition, as young protagonist Diouana labors away for her liberal white French employers, themselves clinging to colonial-era racial hierarchies in the just post-independence era of the 1960s. Her interior monologue would echo in

Diome's novel as Diouana in the film muses, "back in Dakar they must be saying Diouana must be happy in France. She has a good life . . . But France for me is the kitchen, bathroom, living room, and my bedroom. Did the mistress bring me here to shut me in?"[28] And then later, before she ends up committing suicide, Diouana laments, "I am a prisoner here. I know no one here. That is why I am their slave" (*La Noire de*). Diouana's voiceover, along with Sembene's wonderful shots and mise-en-scène, give us a clue as to the perspective of those "back in Dakar" who hold fast to a colonial mythology of metropolitan France, as well as the jolting view of the actual reality of the black immigrant condition—a technique that Diome both borrows from Sembene and refashions within her twenty-first-century narrative.

For example, as the narrative progresses in *The Belly of the Atlantic*, Salie warns Madické that papers, passports, residency cards, checkpoints, and border control all shape the migrant and her movement in one way or another. Further, "illegal" immigration can be fatal as we see in Moussa's story. Salie argues with Madické here: "'I'm not trying to stop you but to warn you. If you turn up without papers, you're going to run into serious problems and have a miserable existence in France'" (123). Madické stubbornly responds, however, that "'Hey we're hard workers, we are! Aren't we guys?' . . . needlessly urging on his allies, who were already on a war footing. 'We're capable of finding jobs and holding onto them like real men. You managed it, and you're only a girl'" (123). Salie's following response to Madické's gendered dismissal of her admonition is something of a migritude manifesto in miniature, a statement not only addressing the perils of immigration but a challenge to those, like Madické and his starry-eyed friends, driven by survival, who firmly hold onto the myth of the "first" world:

> You're wrong. In the past, just after the Second World War, the French welcomed lots of people with open arms because they needed workers to rebuild the country. They hired immigrants from all over the place who agreed to go and risk their lives down the coal mines to escape poverty . . . Successive waves of African immigrants have all ended up in slums. They dream nostalgically of an unlikely return to their homeland, a land which, to be honest, worries them more than it attracts them because it's changed while they've been away, and when they do go back for rare holidays they feel like foreigners. Their children, who've grown up with the refrain "Liberty, Equality, Fraternity," no longer have any illusions once they realize, after a long battle, that their hard-won naturalization doesn't improve their op-

portunities . . . In Europe, my brothers, you're black first, citizens incidentally, outsiders permanently, and that's certainly not written in the
constitution, but some can read it on your skin (123–24).

Salie first references the second post–World War II diaspora in which people
from former colonies in Africa, the Caribbean, India, and elsewhere migrated
to the "mother country." Some who fought in the war alongside their white
brethren believed (mistakenly) that, for their service, decent treatment in
Northern metropoles would follow.[29] As we saw above, many West Africans
were indeed conscripted into French military service. Some came to help
rebuild Europe as jobs were opening up. Black migrants from Senegal in
France, as Salie notes above, often ended up in "slums" or *banlieues* and
were subject to racism—"my brothers, you're black first." And as the passage describes above, a return home is just as "unlikely" and fraught with
contradictions as European hospitality.

"*Liberté, Egalité, Fraternité*," France's national slogan, an "illusion" for
Salie, is shown to encompass its opposite both historically—slavery—and
contemporarily in the exclusion of blacks, immigrants, and others at the
same moment France targets them with, as Mabanckou puts it, "complex
and draconian laws."[30] Furthermore, Ndétare in *Belly* deconstructs another
liberal yet contemporary neoliberal catchphrase in France: "*Blacks, Blancs,
Beurs*—Blacks, Whites and Arabs—is nothing more than a slogan stuck on
their international showcase, like a bad Benetton ad . . . if French society
were truly integrated, they wouldn't need to invent a slogan" (Diome, 125).
Ndétare remarks here upon France's World Cup win in 1998, its team including football stars of Algerian immigrant parents (Zinedine Zidane) and an
immigrant from the Caribbean (Lilian Thuram). This multiracial team was
then used to laud supposed French multicultural equality, liberty, and brotherhood. Haby Assevero lucidly describes this context: "When France won the
World Cup in 1998 on their home soil it wasn't just a sporting achievement,
it was a social phenomenon . . . This team, they told us, was the ultimate
proof that integration had been a success. There was nothing, they said, that
prevented the children of immigrants succeeding in French society. 'Black,
Blanc, Beur' was the slogan."[31] However, for Assevero, and Ndétare in the
novel as well, "integration in France, if it ever truly happened, was most defi-
nitely not the resounding success people would have you believe. Those same
young people that look up to Zidane and other French soccer players, are
the ones burning cars in suburbs of France's major cities as we speak. Their
dream is to be like Zidane but their every-day reality is much harsher. They

live in slums, they are undereducated and/or unemployed and the future looks bleak" ("Black, Blanc, Beur"). Thus "Black, Blanc, Beur" joins "*Liberté, Egalité, Fraternité*" on a long list of rhetorically seductive European slogans dating back to the colonial era that, in this case, create Nardal's mirage of Paris, used to justify Northern control while contributing a bait-and-switch model of migration—hiding the peril with the lacquer of paradise.

Moussa's tale is another important narrative of African migration in *The Belly of the Atlantic* that uses the subject of football to make an argument about Franco-African relations and immigration. That our narrator begins Moussa's tale with "All that remained of Moussa was a yellowed photo, sent from France" suggests that this story, like the man from Barbès and Salie's, does not conform to the narrative of France as paradise, a colonial myth (63). Moussa is described as a promising football prospect, a village boy made good by his athleticism, ready to make the big journey to Paris, possibly to become a star athlete. He is targeted by a French scout (who turns out to be unscrupulous) and, rather than a rags-to-riches tale, Moussa sees the realities of the system from inside, and his tale, like Samba's ambiguous adventure, ends in death. His perspective from within Paris shatters the image of Paris he had consumed, like Coca-Cola, in Niodior. Further, Moussa's narrative deconstructs the workings of the global football racket:

> Moussa was incensed at the buying and selling of players, and he'd end up ranting at the phenomenal transfer sums: Real Madrid bought that kid for how many million French francs? Much as he enjoyed this calculation, imagining himself as the object of such a transaction, he didn't like the process, which smacked of slavery. But he had no choice; he was a part of this sporting cattle market now. Moussa knew that if he wasn't taken on by the club backing him, he'd have to reimburse Sauveur himself for the expenses he'd incurred: the plane ticket, bribes, accommodation costs, training, etc. (65)

This often meant working execrable under-the-table jobs in which his meager salary would be taken by his agent, Sauveur. Moussa's narrative also challenges the notion of "Black, Blanc, Beur" that Ndétare critiques above, detailing the experience of racism in Paris. His fellow "teammates" shout "'Hey! Darkie! Pass! Come on! Pass the ball, it's not a coconut!'" (66). Both Moussa, the man from Barbès, and Salie negotiate the various ways in which racism is mobilized against immigrants in France, as encapsulated in Salie's warning "you're black first" and citizens only "incidentally."

On April 27, 2014, Al Jazeera America posts on an incident symptomatic of Europe's continued structural racism in the realm of football. Eliot Ross and Sean Jacobs report that "when a spectator threw a banana [during a match] at the Brazilian footballer as a racist insult, he quickly picked it up, peeled it and ate it" and that, "of course we should all applaud Barcelona's flying fullback, Dani Alves, for his inspiring protest action during a Spanish league match Sunday."[32] However, this ugly gesture does not represent an isolated incident limited to one individual but rather an abiding condition in Europe. For Ross and Jacobs, it reflects "the deep-rooted racism that persists across European societies, on the institutions and authorities whose years of lip service have so dismally failed to protect black players and on all those in the game, as in society, who stand silent and thus complicit" ("The Banana that Revealed Europe's Persistent Racism"). So it is with Mario Balotelli in Italy (see chapter 4). Moussa's tale in *The Belly of the Atlantic* parallels the treatment of Alves, showing the "persistent racism" subtending European society—yet Moussa isn't a football star and thus certainly doesn't make the news, like so many other African hopefuls; he therefore falls through the cracks and ends up dead in the Atlantic. And so Salie grapples with her brother Madické's dream to become a football star like his hero, Maldini, knowing the reality beneath the veneer for African immigrants.

The man from Barbès, of an older generation of Senegalese migrants, both subscribes to and reproduces the mirage of Paris. He had "seen some of his friends return to the village in crates packed with ice—killed by tetanus, an ammonia leak or crushed beneath tons of rice—but he'd kept going" (*The Belly of the Atlantic*, 16). In other words, he sees clearly an African migration in which "death scythes widely," to use Césaire's phrase, but he represses these facts so that, through the reproduction of the Parisian colonial and neocolonial myth, his own legacy and social capital might be reproduced as he accumulates relative wealth by Niodior standards—"that television was there in his huge house as a sign of his success" (15). Upon his return from his seventh trip abroad, "the man from Barbès built a well-stocked shop at the entrance of his house and moved to the village for good. As the symbol of successful emigration, his advice was now sought after on every matter . . ." (18). However, "his flood of tales" about Paris-as-paradise that he recites for the young football fans of the island, held rapt by his tales and habitus, "never hinted at the wretched existence he'd led in France. How could he, scepter in hand, have admitted that in the beginning he'd hung out in metro entrances, picked pockets to relieve his hunger, begged, only survived the winter thanks to Salvation Army before finding a squat with his companions in misery? . . . As a perpetually illegal immigrant, he later travelled the length and breadth of France at the beck and call of less than scrupulous employers, equipped with a false residency permit, a photocopy of a friend and accomplice's residency card" (59). The man from Barbès, as he is called (Barbès being a primarily African and North African Parisian neighborhood populated by migrant communities) heavily edits his own narrative, refusing to acknowledge the "wretchedness" of the black immigrant experience. Interestingly, in Mabanckou's novel *Blue White Red*, this editing is used to exploit recent migrants in Paris to benefit more seasoned migrants, who become inured to the immigrant condition, essentially enacting a transference of violence beginning with France's treatment of immigrants and passing it along to newer immigrants in an ugly cycle of manipulation and survival. The complicity of many immigrants in the oppression of other, newer migrants, as a capitalist mode of survival, continues the work of conscription but, rather than from above, it marks a lateral conscription, illuminating the not quite all-encompassing fabric of global apartheid.

After regaling the boys with his tales, the man from Barbès retires to his bedroom. The following passage suggests that, in a sort of *Picture of Dorian Gray*–esque way, the longer he represses the brutality of Paris and hides from consciousness his actual fraught personal history (and thus "consolidating his status"), the more pained and alienated becomes his soul: "Biting the inside of his cheek, the man from Barbès threw himself into bed, relieved that once again he'd succeeded in preserving, even consolidating, his status. He'd been a *nigger in Paris*, and as soon as he'd returned he'd set about sustaining the illusions that gave him an aura of success" (58–59, emphasis in original). It is important to note here that the original French in Diome's passage is "Il avait été *un nègre à Paris* et s'était mis, dés son retour, à entretenir *les mirages* . . .";[33] and though *mirage* was translated as "illusions," in the English edition it is clearly a reference to Soce's *Mirages de Paris* or perhaps even Paulette Nardal's 1929 short story "In Exile" before that, which also uses the phrase. And while *un* nègre à Paris refers to Bernard Dadie's *Un Nègre à Paris*, translated in English *An African in Paris*, mitigating the valences of *nègre*, Ros Schwartz and Lulu Norman translate *nègre* as "nigger" in the English version of *The Belly of the Atlantic*, keeping the term's politicized and violent history. In fact, Diome brilliantly shows how he had already been caught up in, or conscripted by, the term itself and its entanglement within and mobilization by white supremacist discourse.

At night the man from Barbès fails to keep his memories of Parisian realities at bay with as much success as he has with an audience during the day. He remembers that as a night watchman in a big supermarket, he'd wander the aisles, salivating at the sight of goods that were beyond his reach. To avenge his frustration, he'd sniff out the thief among those fellow travelers he considered so arrogant as to do their shopping like whites, or too poor to be honest. Sometimes, North African or African prey would be gripped in his hawk-like talons, ensuring his boss's approval. His victims eventually came to understand that the foreigner's worst enemy isn't the native racist, that kinship doesn't guarantee solidarity. As his peace of mind grew, a gang from his estate decided to make him pay for his devotion to the rich: he left two teeth on the pavement (60).

The man from Barbès in the above passage represents the "successfully" assimilated immigrant who identifies with colonial whites against his fellow black travelers, a crime for which he is relieved of two pearly whites. In the end, the man from Barbès does "successfully" emigrate and return to Niodior from Paris since he accumulates a house, a television, and attendant prestige. However Diome problematizes this neoliberal notion of success, itself striated with the contradictions of the failures of African migration within a global capitalism helmed by the states and transnational corporations of the North. Yet the novel also shows that, in this era of globalization, the techniques of control used to manage and codify nonwhite bodies are as varied as they are manifest. In Moussa's experience, for example, "one morning a policeman arrived, smiling broadly, and threw an official paper at him with a flourish: 'there you go, your invitation!' It was an IFQ, an invitation to quit France. Twelve hours later an aeroplane spat him out on the tarmac at Dakar airport" (73). Salie is also met with repressive techniques managing the movement of nonwhite bodies, as we saw earlier.

As migritude writers generally show, there is no salutary return to Africa. Salie is othered at home at the same time that she is held accountable for something like remittances upon return. "Despite the whispering, [villagers would] lower themselves to extract money or a T-shirt from me in the name of a custom—one that prevents many poorer migrants coming home for the holidays—which has it that the returning migrant must bring presents, presents whose values is calculated by how far you've come and your relation to the recipient" (38). For Moussa this custom seals the tragedy of immigration. His fate is far worse than Salie's or the man from Barbès. Upon returning, Moussa is shunned by his family, and by extension his village, as he is branded a failure—he does not enrich the village either economically or symbolically; those who have adopted the France-as-paradise myth expect the returned to uplift their families as well as the community. The ostracization he is met with ultimately leads him to commit suicide by drowning himself in the belly of the Atlantic: "The fisherman had caught Moussa's inert body in their nets. Even the Atlantic can't digest all that the earth throws up" (77). "Nor could Ndétare's memory absorb Moussa's adventure. It stuck in his throat every time his protégés, pleading their passion for football, let themselves be blinded by the red, white and blue chimera . . . 'Be careful, my boys' he'd conclude. 'Go and watch that upstart's TV, but please don't listen to the nonsense he spouts. France is not paradise. Don't get caught in the net of emigration. Remember, Moussa was your brother, and you know as well as I do what happened to him" (77). Ndétare presents a much different and less self-interested story of migration to the young boys than does the man from Barbès. Diome provides a sophisticated literary critique of the "net of emigration" as "net," here, more than a poetic continuation of the titular metaphor, indicates the interwoven techniques of power managing, reeducating, and interdicting black movement in ultimately fatal ways.

For Diome these stories are not necessarily exclusive to the Senegal-France relationship, but are global. The United States is invoked, for example, when an extended family member, after having been deported back to Senegal, literally sings the United States' praises: "*Everything you want, you've got it!*" A cousin who'd been deported from the USA never stopped listening to that song and translated it for everyone who wanted to hear: where there's a will there's a way, he would say" (12). Interestingly, Diome keeps the English in her use of Roy Orbison's American original, itself misremembered by the nameless cousin (the original is "*Anything* you want—you got it"). Orbison's song, of course, is not about the American Dream or a panegyric about the riches of Americans or those who immigrate there, but a fairly clichéd love song about a man who would give his paramour anything to win her love. This moment of meaning lost in translation is suggestive of the ways in which ideology interpellates its subjects, coloring, even changing original meaning. In this case Orbison's love song becomes a metonym not for the country of its origin but the *idea* of American supremacy and excess. Though much less salient in the novel than the myth of France, the novel here indeed critiques the myth of the United States as a "paradise" for immigrants as well. It thus speaks to a nationally grounded yet global system, or what presciently

Salie calls "the kingdom of capitalism which stretches into the shade of the coconut trees" (140).

There are moments throughout the novel, woven in between migrants' narratives, in which Salie-as-narrator takes on this global system: "All those legions of third-world areas colored red on the map, soon decimated by AIDS, dysentery, malaria and the economic bazookas aimed at us from the west. Devaluation. Demolition of our currency, of our future—of our lives, pure and simple! On the scales of globalization, the head of a third-world child weighs less than a hamburger" (140). Salie, specifically referencing the CFA devaluation discussed earlier as one of many "economic bazookas," also discloses the global guns of the IMF, World Bank, and Structural Adjustment policies that were being protested, and continue to be critiqued, since Diome began writing the novel. She also reproduces, whether as a critique or not, the CNN/Western media preoccupation with Africa as "AIDS, dysentery, malaria,"–ridden and war-torn. The difference is Diome engages with histories and economic contexts and does not solely rely on Afro-pessimistic narratives prepackaged for white liberal consumption or conservative repulsion.

Salie, for example, takes on the problems with aid. "Listening to the news, I realize that religious hypocrites are invading the country, opening institutes under cover of humanitarian aid and building Arab schools in remote parts of the country-side so they can spread their doctrine . . . Naturally, the state sees no harm in it and uses the excuse of progress to avoid resolving the problem. As with colonization, by the time we wake up, it'll be too late, the damage will already be done" (132). Again, she critiques the problems connected to globalization that cannot be disentangled from their colonial past. Finally, she introduces the problem of Western tourism as an apparatus of global capitalism, which, far from creating jobs and benefiting "natives," at best bequeaths only "a bone for the poor." At a resort town in Senegal Salie muses, "third-world hotels are only for the tourist's benefit . . . [They] stand there, hideous on their gilt pedestals. As the state is so keen for revenue from tourism, it lets foreign investors take over the most beautiful stretches of coast and pay their staff peanuts. Steak for the powerful, the bone for the poor! So be it in the kingdom of capitalism which stretches into the shade of the coconut trees" (140). The owners of the means of production (white and European or American) exploit a native workforce held at the bottom rung of the global economic ladder and "pay their staff peanuts," thus reproducing that "kingdom of capitalism"—perhaps a more apt term than globalization, since upward economic mobility for "third world" countries and their populations is feudal and thus futile.

It is important for Diome to extend a line of Senegalese feminist writers like Miriama Bâ and Ken Bugul. In the following passage, Salie relates her discomfort at what she considers the patriarchal nature of tradition in Niodior: "Men don't like details, and [Madické], even as a kid, had it drummed into him that he must behave like a man. He's been taught to say 'Ow!,' to grit his teeth, not to cry when he's hurt or afraid. As a reward for the courage he had to show in all circumstances, a throne had been built for him high above the female sex . . . I'm only a moderate feminist, but really, that's going too far" (24). I can't help but think back to the ways in which Chinua Achebe both represents and critiques patriarchal gender roles in *Things Fall Apart*. In a particularly insightful passage, Achebe exposes the violence associated with masculinity while providing an alternative to that violence in the character of Nwoye, a male with an uneasy relationship to received masculinity: "Nwoye knew that it was right to be masculine and to be violent, but somehow he still preferred the stories that his mother used to tell."[34] Nwoye, then, understands his societal role as a male but hesitates to "perform" gender in that he prefers the opposite, represented in his mother's tales. For Salie, only a "moderate" feminist—perhaps a mode of distancing herself from white middle-class feminism—such roles "go too far."

Sankèle's story, for instance—also a story of migration—is one catalyzed by the violence of patriarchy. She is a young woman who, on the verge of being forced by her father into an unwanted arranged marriage that would economically and socially benefit him, has an affair with her true love, a younger Ndétare, with whom she has a child. Ndétare, who would go on to become Salie's mentor, is unacceptable to the community as he is a "foreigner" (he comes from mainland Senegal), and feels exiled in the village: "As an unmarried mother, [Sankèle] was denigrated, then banished from the community, and finally exiled herself with her son to the city. Some say she worked as a maid; others imagined a less respectable activity" (*The Belly of the Atlantic*, 35). For Ayo Coly, "The story of Sankèle who rebels her arranged marriage and is forced into exile by her father offers a symbolic frame for Salie's emigration" (112). We will remember that for Salie, returning home is the "same as leaving," as she feels exiled at home. Her language, demeanor, education, and privilege already mark her as more French than the villagers, and since she was already an orphan as a child, home in this sense was never home to begin with. Coly argues that Diome uses gender to revise her "narrative of home dictated by [her] antiglobalization agenda" (111). Take Sankèle's narrative of resistance for example: "Since diplomacy is fine-tuned between a woman's thighs, declarations of war may also issue from there. Sankèle knew this. To become an unmarried mother was the most *radical* way to reduce her father's matrimonial strategy to dust" (*The Belly of the Atlantic*, 88, my emphasis). Diome adds a radical (and tragic) level of resistance to traditional patriarchy but within a global configuration, and echoes Gayle Rubin's theory of the patriarchal traffic in women in her "Notes on the 'Political Economy' of Sex." In other words, Sankèle refuses to relinquish her own freedom simply because, by accident of birth, she was not born with a "throne" waiting for her as would a male child. Sankèle's rebellion is radical because *everything* is on the line, including home itself.

Near the end of the novel, Salie takes a break from "home" and travels to the Petite Côte of M'bour just south of Dakar (which is where she meditates upon tourism and globalization, as above). As she hears the rhythms of a Senegalese band she muses, "No daughter of Africa can remain indifferent to the sound of the tom-tom, even after long years of absence" (137). Earlier she mentions that immigration officers in France had "seen me wearing Senghor's Negritude on my face" (153). These two references to Négritude in the novel by a "daughter of Africa," first implied and then named, answer in some ways, the above question. Diome's gendered revision of home is also a revision of Négritude's "black humanism" as inaugurated by Senghor within what is a different context in time and space among a different cohort of writers (largely women) who narrate immigration precisely *because* the management of immigration is the mechanism of control that in our twenty-first century allows us to figure and figure out modernity, a modernity that, for Ndétare has "left us high and dry" (126). It's not so much a temporal leaving that would allow for a more precise picture of modernity and home (though it does seem apt to pair this "leaving" with Salie's description of the economic "bazookas" "aimed" directly at the Global South from the "ahead" of the West), but also something like a "hopping over," to paraphrase the words of James Ferguson, that incisively depicts the economic and cultural configurations that Diome challenges with her migrant narrative of movement.

In his article "Seeing Like an Oil Company: Space, Security, and Global Capital in Neoliberal Africa," Ferguson explains the contradiction that Africa, so rich in resources (oil, for one), is yet so poor in actual wealth. Ferguson points out that this significant discrepancy is explained by looking at the way global capital moves (we will remember Salie's opening refrain about walking in Africa and Europe and that place shapes movement itself): "It is worth noting that the movement of capital that is entailed in such enterprises [large multinational corporations and their African partners] is 'global' in the sense that it crosses the globe, but it does not encompass or cover contiguous geographic space. The movements of capital cross na-tional borders, but they jump point to point, and huge areas are simple bypassed."[35] Capital then is by no means evenly disseminated; just as Salie's feet don't land everywhere she walks, capital only lands in certain places, usually where and when it benefits elites. Ferguson notes, for example, that "the Angolan government receives something on order of $5 billion in oil revenue each year [yet] very little of the oil wealth even enters the wider society" (378). Thus Ndétare's deceivingly simple yet profound "modernity's left us high and dry" can be rephrased: it simply hops over us, at most paying "peanuts" to non-elite populations. But of course Ndétare is correct in his implication that the African economy was shaped by colonialism. Stephen Ocheni and Basil C. Nwankwo show that "Africa was compelled or forced to accept the international division of labour which assigned her the compulsory role of production of agricultural raw materials required by the industries of Europe. This explains why up till today, the role of [the] African economy and states in the world market or international trade is the production of primary goods and agricultural products."[36] In no uncertain terms, then, Africans are already conscripted into a particular global condi-tion, the terms of which were set by empire.

But Salie is not just a "daughter of Africa"—or of Senghor even—but is also in some ways a daughter of Europe. By that simple fact, home and move-ment are revised as such by: 1) the highly asymmetrical movements of people and movements of capital, 2) by its imbrication in the production of not simply gender but the construction and reproduction of the nonwhite body moving across space itself. If we remember Salie's biological examination at the state level as well as her white ex-husband's family desiring only "Snow White," thereby reproducing conventional (white) notions of French belong-ing, we are led by Diome's sophisticated narrative to formulate the following argument: it is through the black *immigrant* woman's body specifically that technologies of power managing movement culminate in sustaining both notions of national belonging and global hierarchical figurations. Perhaps this is why Salie chooses to foreground her own cultural hybridity, as she identifies as an African-European fusion, and chooses furthermore (regard-less of its unhappy ending) an interracial spouse. In this way she refashions a Senghorian black humanism of the Négritude era into the literary-historical context of migritude in the era of globalization.

In closing this chapter on *The Belly of the Atlantic*, I return to Salie's migri-tude poem and Leonora Miano's prose-poem in *Ecrits pour la parole* opening the chapter. Diome pictures what in the next chapter I call moving globality:

> Shut in, cooped up,
> Captives of a land once blessed,
> Hunger our only comfort,
>
> *Passports, Permits, Visas*
> *And endless red tape,*
> *The new chains of Slavery.*
>
> *Bank branch, account number,*
> *Address, ethnic origin,*
> *The fabric of modern apartheid,*
>
> *Perennial mother Africa suckles us*
>
> *The west fuels our desires*
> *And is deaf to our hungry cries.*
>
> *African globalization, generation*
> *Enticed, then sifted, dumped, ejected, wounded.*
> *We the unwitting travelers.* (154)

The speaker of this poem represents a voice in the diaspora much like Diome's narrated cast of Senegalese migrants in France such as Salie, Moussa, and the man from Barbès, each "shut in" and "cooped up," eternally hungry while struggling to get ahead. Yet these lines also reference earlier characters in the Franco-African migrant tradition, like Elisa in Nardal's short story "In Exile" (which I have written about elsewhere), Samba in *Ambiguous Adventure*, or Diouana in Sembene's film *Black Girl*, and as such, they delineate black movement from Négritude to migritude.[37] But just as earlier generations of black writers speak to their own colonial and postcolonial context, Salie here speaks to new and proliferating technologies controlling movement as she phenomenologically and literarily examines "passports," "visas," "permits," and the "endless red tape" reeducating African migration, demonstrating that they are conscripted in various ways. It is not inaccurate for Salie to name this new era under global capitalism a "modern Apartheid." Achille Mbembe argues that "Europe has developed over the last 25 years or so an attitude of containment in the sense that the biggest preoccupation has been to make sure that Africans stay where they are," and that—as Salie also appears to suggest—"the fixation with the question of immigration has jeopardized to a large extent the development of more dynamic relations between Africa and Europe."[38] In this newer global era of surveillance and management of black bodies, the tracking of "account numbers," and "bank branch[es]" are connected to "ethnic origin," as the placement of words in the third stanza suggest. In the phrase near the end of the poem "African globalization, generation," the word "generation" is suggestive both of genealogy (successive generations of family or literary movements), and of a biological reproduction shackled to "new chains of Slavery" and new modes of conscription.

The novel ends with Madické opening a small shop on the island. He is able to purchase the shop because Salie finally saved up and sent him enough money to bring him to France, his initial dream. He chooses, however, not to migrate to France. Ayo Coly therefore deems the narrative a "nationalist narrative of home," as Madické finally opts to stay in and contribute to the island community. However, given Ndétare's narrative (a Senegalese man not from Niodior who is not accepted in Niodior), as well as Salie's stated "hybrid" or migrant humanism "fusing" Africa and Europe, I do not call the narrative "nationalist" as such. *The Belly of the Atlantic* is both African and highly local, insofar as it embodies both "Africa's" relationship to France and the world, and the "tiny island" of Niodior, which is not a nation, and its relationship with the rest of Senegal, West Africa, France, and the United States. The novel is rather, a sustained engagement with conscription. Given that it is predicated so fundamentally upon the condition and structures of movement and migration, it is, about the *"condition d'immigrés."* Finally, I close with migritude writer Leonora Miano's poetic reflection upon what she calls the "Afropéan."

> The country says Black or French The Country says that one can only be black or French The thinking of the country in binary . . . the best Is to go beyond the limits of the Nation To see more largely. The best is merger: French Black The best thing is the addition: French and black which opens up a third term more than a third . . . Afropéans.
> (Miano, *Ecrits pour la parole*)

Chevrier's "third space" in which he locates migritude, Salie's migrant humanism, or Miano's "addition," what she calls the Afropéan, is the "best thing"; they problematize the global imperial history of the nation-state and the international system of immigration of which it is a part.

Chapter 4

"WE CARRY OUR HOME WITH US"
On the Literature of Somali-Italian Diasporas

We carry our home with us, our home can travel. It's not fixed
walls that make a home out of the place where we live.

—Barni, in *Little Mother*, **Cristina Ali Farah (226)**

African immigration to European countries like France or Britain began *en
masse* during the post–World War II and independence era. In Italy however,
perhaps due to its relatively short-lived colonial project (save in Somalia),
influxes of African immigrants would arrive only later, in the 1980s.[1] The
global recession in the 1970s, the global turn by Western powers to neoliberal
economic policies such as deregulation and liberalization of African markets,
Western conditionalities imposed on African states by the World Bank and
the International Monetary Fund, as well as corruption and the detritus of
structural colonial legacies all led to massive destabilization across Africa,
which in turn led to conflict, war, and mass unemployment.[2] Migration
almost always follows. It was therefore beginning in the 1980s that Europe,
and Italy in particular, saw a substantial increase in the number of African
immigrants arriving on its southern shores and in its cities. Subsequently,
there have been significant new waves of African migrant literature published
in Italy, some works cycling into world literature markets that would be
translated into English and other languages.[3] *I Was an Elephant Salesman*
(1990) by Senegalese-Italian author Pap Khouma, for example, is considered
one of the first great Afro-Italian migrant narratives. More recently, Somali-
Italian author Cristina Ali Farah's 2007 novel *Little Mother* (translated into
English in 2010), parses questions of home and African immigration in both
intensely personal and socio-structural ways.

Fig. 1. "Hugging Hope." Illustration by Marco Di Prisco © 2014.

Immigrants contribute both economically and culturally to their new homeland, even catalyzing new conversations in art. For example, the recently designed digital image "Hugging Hope" (see Fig. 1), by little-known contemporary Italian artist Marco di Prisco, provides a poignant and almost uncanny parallel to the characterization of home and immigration in Cristina Farah's above epigraph—"We carry our home with us, our home can travel."[4] "Hugging Hope" depicts a collage of African figures migrating across a gray sea on a wooden dhou. Referencing the thousands of African migrants and refugees arriving by boat, many of whom perish along the way, this work of digital art takes its place among the aesthetic and cultural production of Africa in Italy. In the foreground of "Hugging Hope" a large man, also on the small craft, clutches his miniature house while shedding a red tear. He carries his home with him; as in Farah's epigraph, his home travels. In contrast to elite cosmopolitan representations of travel, the African figure carrying his home in di Prisco's piece grimaces along his perilous journey with few earthly belongings.

Pap Khouma begins *I Was an Elephant Salesman* by asking "how does it feel to be an illegal immigrant?" answering starkly: "Terrible."[5] Francophone writer Fatou Diome's narrator equates "the condition of immigrants" to "contempt" or hardship while philosophizing upon the structures of immigration (see chapter 3). Taageere in *Little Mother*, after having just arrived in America as a Somali immigrant, relates to the (contemporary) sadness produced by the experience of being "immigrant":

> At that time I was overwhelmed by sadness, by a deep and shabby sadness, a crazy sadness that sprang from the cold and the disillusionment . . . And it was during this time that I saw how much sadness there is in the West, that there are many more homeless people in the streets than we imagine, in fact we can't even imagine how many homeless people there are here when we're back home and hear of these countries that are doing so well. (Farah, 57–58)

Taageere's monologue suggests both that immigrant experiences are not isolated to a particular nation but are global, and that the "immigrant experience" is not simply a matter of individuals but is a "condition," as Diome's narrator describes it. What these writers, artists, workers, farmers, mothers, and daughters show is that immigration is never solely about moving from one place to another but is ontological; it is about the production of immigrants as such. The "sadness" of those who move has as much to do with national and international institutions put in place to manage movements and populations—particularly in terms of their disciplinary, punitive, and racialized nature—as they do individual feelings of homelessness in diaspora.

Second-generation and immigrant populations, whether citizens or not, are excluded from basic rights, a reality in deep conflict with the multicultural and democratic rhetoric of many European nations and the United States.[6] Migritude authors like Farah negotiate these issues—how institutionalized techniques of power managing movement such as checkpoints, borders, immigration control, residence permits, and others, impinge upon and shape existence. To negotiate, reflect upon, and challenge these material processes by way of cultural production, to indeed *live in* immigration, is to engage with being itself. Farah, di Prisco, and others produce what I have called the phenomenology of movement wherein migrant cultural production shows how objects of immigration, from as large as a border

Fig. 2. "Postcard from Rosarno, Italia." Illustration by Marco Di Prisco © 2014.

to as small as an identification card, constellate how they shape the world. These migrants are conscripts, in both an immediate or bodily sense and a general, even philosophical one.

Marco di Prisco's "Postcard from Rosarno, Italia" (see Fig. 2) subtly indicates the African immigrant experiences of exploited workers in orange orchards in Rosarno, Italy, the objects constellating their world and, therefore, migrant being. Ghanaian and Nigerian immigrants in Rosarno have been subject to intense racism and physical violence, and in 2010 were ultimately expelled from the area for no crime other than being born elsewhere.[7] This precipitated the creation of "Postcard,"[8] which pictures a black shirtless figure sitting down with his[9] head on his knees and mostly submerged in an orange-hued sea. Only a small part of his back and the back of his head rise above the water. His face rests immersed underwater. An orange slice sun peeks over the horizon as a few tiny tents and a tree rest upon the figure's back just above the water line, making up a small encampment.

The submerged portion of the figure's body spans the width of the piece. This brings to mind the final words of Caribbean poet and philosopher Kamau Brathwaite's short 1974 book *Contradictory Omens*: "The unity is submarine."[10] Brathwaite suggestively images the connection between Africa and the Caribbean both in terms of slaves' bodies drowned along the middle passage and the cultural and linguistic connections crossing the Atlantic submerged by colonial processes and history making. Di Prisco's "Postcard from Rosarno, Italia," provides an incisive parallel to Brathwaite's phrase, as the Mediterranean Sea connects Africa to Italy in this more recent of African diasporas. And just as the middle passage was strewn with submerged black bodies, so the Mediterranean Sea, between Africa and Italy, has more recently seen tens of thousands of drowned African migrants. "I think there are more Somalis at the bottom of the sea or lost in the desert than there are left in our land," ominously notes Jibreel in *Black Mamba Boy* (see chapter 6).

Cristina Ali Farah's *Little Mother* narrates this continuing humanitarian crisis. Barni speaks to a woman working on a project about the Somali diaspora, musing, "Boats have been coming and unloading illegal immigrants across Italian coastlines for a long time now. The tides go in and out and the beaches keep filling up with garbage: tomato cans, shards of green glass, small tubes of medicine, clumps of tar, and plastic bags, more and yet more plastic bags. And, carried by the sea, lifeless bodies, wearing tattered clothes, their purplish skin blotched with white salt" (14). What would it mean to envision these new paths from Africa to Europe as middle passage–like, as a product of global domination by the Northern and its various apparatuses? Or to suggest that the relatively recent creation of "fortress Europe" bears the vestiges of a highly asymmetrical colonial system, perhaps producing the kind of material and affective migrant "sadness" of which Taageere speaks?

In addition to challenging contemporary global systems with structural ties to colonialism, di Prisco and Farah's work picture migrant ties and community. More abstractly, for example, "Postcard" points us toward black diasporic connection as the African migrant's submerged body symbolically spans the length of the ocean. There is something profound in di Prisco's piece, particularly in the submerged figure's bridge or island-like quality, especially in conversation with Brathwaite's phrase "The unity is submarine." If we think "Postcard" diasporically, the encampment upon the figure's back would be populated by Africans coming from various places in Africa, suggesting that the wealth of the Global North was indeed built upon the backs of blacks—just as the figure bears the weight of the encampment and the orchard, represented by a single orange tree on his back. Alternatively, the black figure literally supports the migrant encampment, perhaps evoking black unity-in-diaspora.

Farah depicts unity, or the multiple connections in the black diaspora in Italy (in this case the Somali diaspora), as a "tangled mass of threads." One

Fig. 3. "Men on Wire." Illustration by Marco Di Prisco © 2014.

of the main protagonists, Dominica Axad, opens *Little Mother* by addressing these threads in relation to identity in migration. "*Soomaali Baan Ahay* [I am Somali], like my half is whole. I am the fine thread, so fine that it slips through and stretches, getting longer. So fine that it does not snap. And the tangled mass of threads widens and reveals the knots, clear and tight, that though far from each other, do not unravel" (1). Farah's tangled mass of fine threads describes a diasporic Somali community far from a Mogadishu originally called home, in which she, a single stretching thread, is interwoven among many other refugees and immigrants. In another digital piece, di Prisco images African figures (one of which carries an outline or cutout of Africa) walking on a single red thread that connects two cliffs (see Fig. 3). These migrants not only cross via paths as precarious as thin threads but indeed sustain cultural connections in diasporas. For Farah, in her novel, these fine threads, like ties to home or community, might stretch but do not snap.

The three works of art I have briefly analyzed included in di Prisco's digital quadriptych of African immigration to Italy and Cristina Farah's novel *Little Mother*—a story of the Somali diaspora in Italy—provide an illustrative if complicated window into issues of immigration in the geocultural and historical space of Italy, while showing the ways in which literature and art negotiate immigrant experiences, questions of home and movement, identity and gender as well as structures, systems, and patterns of immigration. Importantly, *Little Mother* pays specific attention to women in diaspora. This chapter parses the history and politics of Somali immigration to Italy and its causes with respect to gender and Italian imperial and global neoliberal formations in Africa, which ultimately connects to historical and contemporary immigration. The chapter converses with other African-Italian migritude texts such as Pap Khouma's *I Was an Elephant Salesman* and Igiaba Scego's works such as her short story "Sausages" and novel *Adua*. As diasporic refugee Domenica Axad in *Little Mother* "wanders around and between Europe" attempting to find those missing threads that would strengthen her sense of herself, she dreams of making a documentary about the Somali diaspora in Italy, which is precisely the conceit of Farah's novel itself—documenting the diaspora. Although the film does not get made in this novel, there is something akin to it in contemporary Afro-Italian filmmaker Fred Kuwornu's 2011 documentary *18 Ius Soli*. His film documents the children of immigrants from Africa, Asia, and the Middle East born in Italy as well as young adults who, though immigrants, have grown up in Italy; it illustrates the daily challenges they face in a primarily anti-immigrant and racist society. I close the chapter by briefly drawing upon Kuwornu's film about the experience of immigrant and second-generation young adults in Italy and debates around national citizenship. It is my claim that these particular angles or viewpoints into immigration ultimately show various levels and scales of conscription. And since migration is fundamentally human, they reveal something substantial about our world itself.

Migration Italy: Somalia as a Case Study

In "Black Italia: Contemporary Migrant Writers from Africa," Alessandra di Maio addresses African immigration to Italy beginning in the 1980s and proposes a rethinking of diaspora studies: "The recent arrival of a plethora of migrants from the four corners of the world, many from African countries . . . has inscribed Italy as a site of the African diaspora, offering new perspectives and directions to the field of Black diaspora studies."[11] Indeed, relative to global Anglophone and Black Atlantic studies, Italy as a site of the African diaspora and the Afro-Italian writing that those diasporas produce, has been, with some exceptions,[12] under-theorized. Theorizations of diaspora (Black Atlantic studies or studies of black France or Paris, for example) often fall short by privileging the destination of immigrants and their experiences in Euro-American metropoles. These studies are important, but they must not come at the expense of attention to the material conditions of reality in homelands and the reasons behind the "why" of migration, the catalysts that shape movement. When left to the (Western) press, the answers to these questions often reproduce racist and uncritical depictions of Africa as the site of "failed" states, dictators, famine, tribal conflicts, and so on—essentially aggregating into a twenty-first-century iteration of the "Heart of Darkness."[13]

African diasporic literary studies must focus not solely on destination countries but on the widely varying places on the continent from which people emigrate, as well as immigration patterns; focusing on these issues, recentering or de-provincializing Africa, can tell us as much about the construction of immigration in Euro-American centers as it can about Africa and the global/local processes that create immigration. It would also tell the stories of those metropolitan centers themselves but not *by* themselves, highlighting their imbrication in global processes from colonialism to globalization. Contrary to both contemporary and historical depictions of Africa as a homogenous center of chaos, corruption, or famine, which irresponsibly and speciously answers the question of why Africans leave, the real reasons behind emigration are much more complex from location to location, and often have as much to do with neoliberal economic policies imposed from the Global North, colonial structures still in place, and foreign aid and intervention than with an essentialist view of Africa itself as failure or victim. Cristina Farah's novel is indeed about her own life as a Somali-Italian in both Somalia and Italy—two places historically intertwined and deeply connected.

Somalia was an Italian colony from 1888 to 1941, at which point Britain took control. Many of the characters in Farah's book speak Italian, one reason being that Italian colonial structures like education were still in place during her childhood (though she was born in Verona to an Italian mother, Farah would spend significant amounts of time during her childhood and adult life in Somalia).[14] Middle-class and elite Somalis often spoke Italian. Somali novelist and thinker Nuruddin Farah notes that Mogadiscio ("Mogadishu" is the English spelling) is the *Italian* name for the capital most familiar to

Westerners. In fact, "Xamar" is the Somali designation for the once cosmopolitan pearl of the Indian Ocean.[15] Nuruddin Farah begins a story that reveals Italy as responsible, in part, for today's state of Somalia and *a fortiori* for its peoples' emigration:

> In drawing arbitrary imperial borders, builders of empires [like Italy] create a network of political and economic tensions, with a legacy both explosive and implosive. I do not have to remind anyone of how in the Horn of Africa the implosive nature of the crisis helped engender tensions among the different nationalities in the region; how the explosive tendency of the conditions would every now and then prevail, bursting outward in a full-scale war between countries. The 1977 war between Somalia and Ethiopia claimed at least two and a half million lives . . . (52)

Noted Ethiopian writer Nega Mezlekia also notes that "many of the present-day Somali problems have their root in the European scramble for African territories, not to mention Ethiopia's own imperial ambitions. The recent bloody breakup of the country into five different pieces, for instance, stems from attempts to force a fiercely individualistic, clan-minded people, through colonial influence, into the mold of a nation."[16] The story of massive destabilization in Somalia culminating in the 1991 civil war therefore begins in Europe, at the dawn of colonization. Colonial destabilization would continue into the postcolonial period, much to the chagrin of newly independent nations hopeful for a new future. In addition to tensions that arbitrary imperial borders create, the 1977 Somalia-Ethiopia war was significantly exacerbated due to Cold War–era posturing by the U.S.S.R. and the United States, both of whom would not only pick sides, fund, and provide massive amounts of weapons for their own political gain in the great battle between communism and capitalism, but would in fact switch sides!

Having firsthand perspective, Mezlekia remembers this period well. First the Soviet Union backed Somalia, making the Somali dictator Said Barre's army "the fourth largest fighting force in Black Africa," while the Americans had traditionally supported Ethiopia (201). However, after the communist military junta in Ethiopia in 1974, "the Americans refused to send arms to Ethiopia . . . and offered its hand to Somalia," which was then abandoned by the United States' rival the Soviet Union, making Barre furious with the Soviets for sending arms to his opponent, Ethiopia (203). Somalia was then badly defeated. This brief foray into history simply suggests that the civil war was not due to its own failure or retrograde "tribal" nature, as racialized Western accounts would have us believe, but in this case Somalia would become something like a casualty of two playground bullies making the world their stage—and with a staggering body count.

Alessandra di Maio stresses the importance of more nuanced and historicized perspectives like Mezlekia's and Farah's: "Nuruddin Farah explains in an important work of nonfiction, *Yesterday, Tomorrow: Voices from the Somali Diaspora*, that, unlike what the mass media seems to suggest, the [Somali] civil war cannot be explained merely on the basis of tribal violence and warlordism, nor exclusively by referencing clannism. Rather, it is the ultimate result of a historical process which began with Europe's prolonged colonization, continued with brief independence, and was followed by Siad Barre's oppressive regime (which received backing from powerful players in the international arena) until its eventual downfall" ("Pearls in Motion," xvi–xvii). It is important to engage with colonial and postcolonial historical moments wherein Western powers directly and indirectly interfere and or control African nations, in this particular case, Somalia. This goes a long way toward not only the deconstruction of popular discourses around Africa, immigration, and Somalia but also understanding immigration to the Global North and the multiple diasporas therein.

Yet, what N. Farah and di Maio do not mention is that, in addition to colonial and neocolonial Western domination, Somalia and other African nations faced economic and social destruction by the neoliberal economic policies of the World Bank and International Monetary Fund beginning in the 1970s. In "The Neo-Liberal Agenda and the IMF/World Bank Structural Adjustment Programs with Reference to Africa," Gloria Emeagwali points out that some of the destabilization that led to Somalia's 1991 civil war was indeed due to foreign economic and social control:

> when in 1981 the IMF forced the government of Somalia to liberalize the economy, privatize public services, devalue the currency and cut back in public sector spending, it actually laid the foundation for ruin and disaster. Somalia's currency was devalued by 460% between 1987 and 1989. The cost of food and transportation skyrocketed. In keeping with IMF prescriptions, numerous workers were laid off, thus swelling the ranks of the unemployed. . . . The IMF program exacerbated intra-clan conflict. Remarkably, Somalia, in that moment of economic crisis [on the eve of the Civil War], transferred 47.4% of its export earnings to its debtors . . . (9)

The "ruin and disaster" wrought by neoliberal economic policies of the Global North—what Senegalese migritude writer Fatou Diome calls "economic bazookas," or what Ann Stoler calls "imperial debris," the very real detritus of the colonial system—as well as postcolonial Cold War policies, mismanagement, and corruption by African leaders (dictators such as Siad Barre) indeed set the stage for humanitarian crises that catalyze movement, immigration, and the massive influx of refugees to both other countries in Africa, Europe, and, to a lesser extent, the United States (which currently bans all people from Somalia and six other countries).[17] Attention to these "imperial formations," for Stoler, "rather than empire per se [registers] the ongoing quality of processes of decimation, displacement, and reclamation"; and "unlike empires," imperial formations are "processes of becoming, not fixed things," that then change and shift yet remain embedded in contemporary neoliberal and global structures (8). These fluid formations then continuously conscript those who move, creating the conditions that, even if one stays home, conscript them into a particular kind of globality, or what Jennifer Lloyd calls global apartheid. For N. Farah, therefore, it is important to view the Somali civil war diachronically, that is, to consider the historical detritus of imperial formations and the ways in which they impinge upon, surface in, and shape the present, conscripting people in/into the present.

Given the history of Somalia and Italian colonialism, N. Farah notes that it is ironic that Somalis have not always been granted asylum in Italy. Writing at the turn of the twenty-first century, Farah writes, "the majority of Somalis do not qualify for refugee status, according to the Italian authorities' close reading of the 1951 Refugee Convention and Protocol, because they have no tangible evidence that, as individuals, they are fleeing persecution in their land"; he also notes that "Where, in their homeland, the Somalis were seen as subhuman by the [Italian and later British] colonists, it appears that they are not doing much better in Italy, not after the collapse of Somalia. They are not classified as refugees" (*Yesterday, Tomorrow*, 62). Although these practices change over time (more Somalis are being granted asylum), the colonial relationship between Italy and Somalia does not necessarily translate to recognition of actual circumstances and histories.[18] As Fred Kuwornu's documentary *18 Ius Soli* shows, because of Italy's *jus sanguinis* (bloodline) citizenship law, even Afro-Italians born in Italy are denied citizenship and thus equal rights.[19] Somalia is only one of many examples of African countries, each with varying histories, who share the experience of colonial, neocolonial, and global-neoliberal economic conquest. These are places across Africa and the Global South that are originally called home by those who leave.

Aviva Chomsky, in her important and highly accessible work on immigration, relates the fact that there is always a "push/pull" dialectic in terms of patterns of migration. She notes that although immigrants come for individual reasons, "patterns of immigration have structural and historical causes. . . . Poverty, lack of opportunity, and danger 'push' people to leave; opportunity, availability of jobs, education, and safety 'pull' people elsewhere" (121–22). In other words, for an individual there is a push to leave a geographical homeland ranging from a number of structural and historical factors at the same time there exists the "pull," imagined or not, of the destination nation—the desire for a living wage or for a safe environment. These two forces are mutually constitutive. Above, I have outlined in the case of Somalia some of the structural forces or catalysts "pushing" Somalis to leave their home. There are, in addition, reasons Italy and other places are considered desirable destination by migrants. Graziella Parati, in her introduction to Pap Khouma's important Italophone migritude novel, states that,

> While social discourse immediately identified immigration as a "problem," it was a response to Italy's own economic demands: migrants are still widely employed in the care of young children or the elderly, the very individuals that the welfare system in Italy should provide for but cannot. Immigration was also motivated by the demand for unskilled labor in agriculture both in tomato fields of the south and in the fruit orchards of the north. However, stereotypes of migrants as criminals, as intruders, as invading hordes, and as interlopers into superior culture multiplied in the press and in public discourse. [Subsequently] racist attacks against immigrants started to increase in the late 1980s. (xii)

As Marco di Prisco's recent works of art analyzed above reveal, particularly "Postcard from Rosarno," there is a double bind of immigration: cheap immigrant labor is needed and often exploited, as in the orange orchards in Rosarno, at the same moment that Italy—its government, media, and public—rail against immigrants, attempt to deport them, promote ideological warfare, and even perpetrate and encourage racist attacks against immigrants. Of course, those decrying immigration are often ignorant of Italy's own implication in Africa's destabilization as outlined above, which created the very immigration lamented in the first place (this applies to the United States as well, given its imperial status dating back at least to 1898).

In "Black Italia," di Maio continues: "as an emigrating nation, Italy had neither laws nor social policies nor yet a language to address its new immigrant reality . . . multiculturalism was countered by racism . . . acceptance and solidarity [by] a relapse into nationalism. . . . Newcomers were more often than not forced to the margins by the 'welcoming' Italian society" (124). Pap Khouma's African-Italophone novel reflects this complexity as he highlights the passing of Italy's 1987 law granting some immigrants permission to stay. "In 1987 the new year brings us a special gift: the famous law. . . . In the end they really gave us the *permessi di soggiorno* [residence permits]. Here they are, shiny and beautiful. Even our association is inspired with new courage"; but, he asks, "have our troubles really ended?" (123). Khouma answers in the negative: "I hate to say it, but after we get the *permessi di soggiorno* the heavens are still not quite within our reach. Our days as illegal aliens are behind us, but to live we have to keep selling and no one is happy about this. We still work outside the law. . . . In fact, thanks to the rights we have obtained, our problems grow. Both local and state police are now very suspicious" (123). In the context of racist nationalism and neoliberal economic policy, then, rights can usher in their very opposite. It seems that, more than three decades after the law has passed, things still have not gotten better for either immigrants or second-generation children born in Italy to immigrant parents, perhaps given that "rights" means something different for each group: for Westerners (white natives born of white natives) rights are unquestioned givens, while for immigrants or second-generation children, rights are privileges doled out sparingly by the state.

Italian immigration scholar Alessandro Dal Lago echoes Khouma's narrative in his 1999 *Non-Persons*: "After 15 years of migration flows that show a certain degree of consistency, immigrants still do not have the civil rights (not to mention the social and political rights) enjoyed by Italians and other foreigners, European or Western, present in Italy."[20] Like Aviva Chomsky's work on the United States confronting popular and often racist myths, Dal Lago deconstructs the primarily spurious ideas and policies on immigration in Italy: "Nearly all of the dominant affirmations regarding the threat that migration constitutes are debatable, if not simply false. It is not true that Italy, since the mid-1980s has been invaded by foreigners, that its extensive borders enables the entry of illegal immigrants more than in other Mediterranean countries, that migrants demonstrate a higher propensity to commit crimes, or that they tend to take jobs away from our youth" (17). Although numerous scholars, public intellectuals, and activists have disproven these fallacies, they remain entrenched in the societies of the Global North.

I suggest that one (if only partially) successful mode of resistance to these myths and their attached iterations in law is the production of a migrant literature (collections of stories in whatever form) that reaffirms the human-ity of immigrants while disclosing and challenging repressive and racist laws and xenophobic public discourse surrounding immigration. Di Maio notes: "Among these African migrants [in Italy] are a number of emerging writers whose increasingly flourishing literary production has been reshaping Italy's contemporary letters, but whose voices, more often than not, have been ex-cluded by the dominant literary discourse in ways that seem to reproduce the social marginalization to which the African Italian community has generally been subjected" ("Black Italia," 120). There have been a number of popular African-Italian migrant texts (Pap Khouma, Igiaba Scego, and Cristina Ali Farah). Khouma, Farah, and more recently Scego have been picked up by the world literature market as all have been translated into English (and while this is promising, it still begs the question of excluded voices in terms of who and why). In what follows, I focus on Cristina Ali Farah's novel *Little Mother*, which, as a migritude novel, philosophizes and challenges the issues of im-migration in Italy and emigration from Somalia outlined above while giving voice to women and mothers in the Somali diaspora. *Little Mother* therefore contributes to the important work of "reshaping of Italy's contemporary letters" and of reshaping Italy itself.

Little Mother and Migritude

As di Maio notes in her introduction to *Little Mother*, Farah was born in Verona, Italy, in 1973 to an Italian mother and a Somali father (xv). Farah grew up in Mogadishu, Somalia, until age eighteen, when she and her newborn joined a large number of compatriots fleeing the civil war in 1991 (xvii). She wandered Europe until settling in 1997 in Rome, where she began attending university. She published a book of poetry on migration in 2006, *Ai confini del verso: Poesia della migrazione in italiano*, and her first novel *Madre Piccola* in 2007, which would be translated into English in 2011 as *Little Mother*. One of the main characters in *Little Mother*, Domenica Axad (who is also half Italian and half Somali), is involved in a film project documenting the lives of Somalis in the diaspora both in Italy and elsewhere. This parallels the novel itself, which, though following two main female protagonists and one male, each accorded one of three sections of the novel within an overarching narrative, represents a rich patchwork of the tales and experiences of many other migrants in the diaspora interwoven into the novel set in and between Italy, Somalia, North America, and the Netherlands. In fact, di Maio argues that the "the implicit protagonist" of Farah's novel is the Somali diaspora itself (xv). Farah's character Domenica Axad uses the poignant metaphor of threading as a way to describe herself and others in the Somali diaspora in Italy. The novel parses these tangled diasporic threads, immigration, and questions of identity.

As a migritude text, *Little Mother* goes beyond narrating the stories of individuals and families who migrate, who cross borders; it also philosophically engages with the structures and conditions underwriting, creating, and shaping immigration from Africa to Italy and the production of the "immigrant" subject-position. It analyzes and challenges the ways in which Italy has created those structures, through the use of both discourses shaping public opinion (the construction and repetition of the idea that Africans are "other," criminal, represent an undue societal burden, and are usurpers of jobs), and material law (the actual policing and legislating of immigrants). These structures—both ideological and concrete—mark the conditions that immigrants face and that shape their experience and their identity as well as their dignity and well-being. *Little Mother* is also a political project, reaffirming Somali-Italian humanity[21] by relating the everyday lives of individuals, families, and communities, and is thus valuable as both global novel of migration and contribution to the cultural production of black Italy.

As others have noted, the novel also narrates the embodiment of a dual or split identity in that both Farah herself and protagonist Domenica Axad are half Somali and half Italian, creating various complexities—racially, linguistically, and culturally. Indeed, scholars have approached Farah's novel in terms of hybridity or plural identities.[22] Farah himself, however, approaches this complexity as a structural-existential one—as much a product of the condition of immigration as it is a psychological one. In the novel, Axad uses the term "existential," which comes out of Heidegger's work and later Jean-Paul Sartre's philosophical program that would also be taken up by Négritude. Axad expresses her existential condition as mother and migrant, Somali and Italian. I begin then, with Domenica Axad's use of the term "existential" in the novel, demonstrating how *Little Mother* is both an intensely personal feminist migrant narrative, and a larger and structural-phenomenological engagement with immigration and patriarchy.

Little Mother follows two friends, Domenica Axad and Barni, who, as cousins, grow up together in Mogadishu; they lose touch, and finally reconnect in Italy as adults. The novel also tracks Taageere, Domenica's estranged husband, also from Somalia, who migrates to the United States. Barni is a midwife, or a "little mother," and narrates her experience in the Somali diaspora while attempting to solve the mystery of a mute Somali refugee who winds up in her hospital. This formal device allows Barni to sort through the "tangled mass" of Somali immigrants in Rome. Taageere's chapters detail his experience in the United States while Domenica Axad's narrate both a working through of her experience as a migrant via her friend's film on the diaspora, and the melancholy she feels due to her perceived personal fragmentation (which is inextricable from the actual structural fragmentation caused by immigration) she feels as the child of an Italian mother and Somali father. She finally ends up reclaiming her Somali roots by choosing her Somali middle name "Axad" over her Italian first name "Domenica" and by reconnecting with the Somali language.

After fairly substantial mental health issues, Domenica Axad traces her genealogy at the behest of a therapist, allowing her to "rebuild the complex existential path" that she has since lost. She writes:

Dear doctor:

... let me tell you that I deeply appreciated your willingness to work with me. I am sure this decision will help me rebuild the complex existential path that will enable me to assume with integrity the responsibility of motherhood that lies ahead. It is much easier to narrate the events in writing since my relationship with words is still an emotional and fragmented one. It's not unusual to digress or to follow the thread of a thought that ends up folding back on itself. As you have helped me understand, this is not unusual in people who come from a history of migration. Even if I'm not—technically—an immigrant, I fully understand your remarks about Domenica having lived through estrangements and readjustments that are typical of immigrants. The family tree you suggested I draw took days to prepare, surprising even me with its complexity. I don't deny that such a wide-reaching tree is essentially a feeble attempt to reclaim family ties that I feared were too tenuous . . . I hope that writing down my story will help me become . . . whole. (193–94)

Axad's letter details fragmented identity, motherhood, migratory paths, and roots. Axad, who refers here to her other self, Domenica, in the third person, continues this section of the novel by describing her childhood in

Mogadishu, her subsequent migrations, and the alienation she feels. The above passage highlights the ways in which the movement of people is shaped by the structures of immigration—the reasons those "who come from a history of migration," those who face "estrangements and readjustments that are typical of immigrants" develop existential complexes contributing to their subject-positions; some like Domenica Axad, develop almost dual personalities, fragmentation, and identities that are not "whole." Her relationship with language even, the precariousness of spoken words along with the comfort in writing, is perhaps symbolic of the alienation embedded in her unconscious as a symptom of the material separations produced in part by immigration as a system within which the pain of a dual identity is exacerbated. Writing, and language itself, also represents those fine threads that connect individuals and communities in diaspora, but that can also be pulled apart or cut.

It is not movement itself, suggests *Little Mother*, but the ways in which movement is managed—immigration—that reeducates the movement, identity, language, and even desires of migrants themselves in variously repressive ways (both physically and mentally), hence Domenica Axad's fragmented self. Interestingly, since she has dual citizenship, she is "not technically an immigrant"; but as we well remember, in the words of Salman Rushdie even native-born blacks "are thought of as people whose real 'home' is elsewhere" (132). Thus Domenica Axad is still subject to being-immigrant and so she writes her story and her genealogy in order to name and thus come to terms with the being-in-the-world of the migrant, that "complex existential path."

Immigration dehumanizes, mentally, physically, culturally, and so on. Even with dual citizenship, for Axad the price of the ticket to Italy would be costly given the requirements expected of immigrants. For her, "the move to Italy [had] implied the complete erasure of my short past" (210). To survive, to fit in, she abandons "Axad" (the Somali part of her) for "Domenica" (the Italian part), and forgets the Somali language as well as the cultural signifiers she was brought up with as a child. Conversely, as many immigrants do, she adopts the Italian language and culture. "My dear Barni," she writes, "there's nothing left of the person I was when you knew me. . . . I quickly erased the Somali language. That's what our mind does: it removes things, it locks things up in closets" (86–87). Euro-American policies of assimilation were and continue to be dehumanizing since "assimilation" not only calls for an abandoning of one's self (the erasure of "Axad") but also categorizes the migrant within a valued hierarchy wherein the top tier is reserved for white males.

Farah refashions a Fanonian critique in the context of twenty-first-century globality in terms of women in diaspora, and therefore takes her place within the black radical tradition(s) that Frantz Fanon contributed to over a half century earlier. The novel suggests that, for example, with immigration automatically comes what Fanon names, in *Black Skin White Masks*, a "psychoexistential complex" (14). His important work analyzing colonialism and race is inextricable from questions of immigration and diaspora, given that some of the complexes he sees alienating black men stem from the colonial assimilation policies that the colonized are confronted with in metropoles of the North. His goal is "the disalienation of the black man" with reference paid to both economic and psychological realities (13). When Domenica Axad reflects that "being an emigrant in both directions is quite exhausting, especially for those who, like us, lived in economic circumstances that necessitated daily sacrifices," she reveals both the psychological effects of transmigration as well as economic ones (C. Farah 204). The daily economic sacrifices are by and large representative of immigration and represent one side of the mutually constitutive dialectic of material realities and ideological "superstructures" or "epistemes."

Looking back upon her migratory "peregrinations" and alienation (the condition of immigration), Axad muses: "Exist, one could exist anywhere. For me, for all of us, it didn't matter where. You simply had to get used to a different set of store signs, different prices, and draw up a new map: a map of your links to the others, and of the junctions of places where we could meet. . . . By alienating ourselves we continued to live" (100). To "exist anywhere" in migration necessitates the separation of the self from itself, alienation, and thus, to "draw up a new map" is to become inured to a repressive situation through the very erasure of selfhood. The beauty of *Little Mother* is that it confronts myriad structures of immigration in terms of both personal issues shaping immigrant subject positions, and the material, economic, and legal institutions of immigration that also shape migrant subjects as well as the "maps" migrants must make and remake.

For example, the Italian government does not recognize Taageere and Shukri's official Islamic divorce, leading Axad to think about the consequences of immigration in a systemic way, as conventions not only do not travel but are erased by an ironically inhospitable "welcoming" society: "What happens to laws and conventions without a government, without a legal system? They remain in our minds. Vague principles that we no longer know how to use. They seem to matter only to us Somalis, scattered all over the world. . . . I, too, was married once a long time ago, and I decided not to register my marriage. How could I trust a *system* that didn't recognize ours?" (29, emphasis added). The above quotation makes an interesting parallel to the epigraph I began this chapter with; Barni's statement that "we carry our home with us" becomes even more precarious as we see that laws and conventions, even languages and cultures often do not survive the journey. Further, *Little Mother* shows the reality of a dire situation in which many migrants and refugees leaving Africa do not survive the journey.

Migritude authors show that immigration is institutional, systemic, and that there are historico-structural causes that shape patterns of immigration in addition to psychological and identity-based effects. Yet this perspective is ontological (not causal), which for Heidegger is what marks the difference between existential and the solely ontic or individual. Heidegger analyzes Being with a capital "B" by assessing what he calls structures or modes of being that then make up Being-in-the-World. I suggest that, for our purposes, people who move do so within overdetermined structures of immigration including being subject to the symptoms and the ontological conditions it produces. Further, by approaching the structures and symptoms of immigration within a situated and postcolonial context, authors like Farah produce a timely phenomenology of movement. Immigration, like other institutions, is managed. Borders, checkpoints, passports, and so on are all symptomatic of larger modes of managing movement (such as questions of citizenship and nations wherein movement and territory are foundational concerns) and thus the construction and production of being immigrant. As *Little Mother* shows, checkpoints (which are crystallized symptoms of global apartheid) indeed impinge upon the being of migrants. This phenomenology of movement reveals the dialectic of the material and immaterial embedded, for example, in a checkpoint, border, or even a passport.

For Domenica Axad, "I do not deny that during my childhood [in Mogadishu] I had the most conflicted feelings for that armored fortress [Europe] where I imagined there was an abundance of delights and forbidden luxuries" (195). Once she has dual citizenship she is able to "pass-borders," as her mother is Italian. "At the airport, I went past the checkpoint walking backward. I could see Taageere frozen in that position, he who wanted so much to come with me. I and my pass for the fortress were going to meet Luul, who had arrived as an illegal immigrant" (118). Because Taageere does not have a European or American passport, he is unable to pass through security and into the fortress. Domenica Axad laments that "it's not easy to cross borders with Somali papers" (112). Further, she embarks upon a more existential take on the "value" of a European passport: "Do you know, Barni, what it means to possess something you take for granted? The idea that no one can refuse you entry to any country, that at most it's a matter of paying for a visa? A passport, a pass-borders. Without this thing that you take for granted, a journey over the desert or over the sea, a long and dangerous journey, is much more expensive than a full-fare airline ticket" (112). This passage both is suggestive of the asymmetrical value accorded certain passports in particular geographical locations and shows that migrating as an emigrant or refugee is much more costly than a plane ticket, both monetarily and in terms of physical safety. These global conditions, one more physically imminent than the other yet both dangerously effective, conscript in various ways, by shaping some routes, making others off-limits, deterring, detaining, pushing, propelling, deporting, categorizing, even shaping decisions to stay.

In *Little Mother* Barni tells the story of Luul, Taageere's sister, characteristic of many migrants' experiences, and shows the conditions subtending migration. For Luul, relatives finally arrange for her to come as their guest to Rome from the Italian island of Lampedusa and she is able to enter Italy, where she lives with other migrants. But once inside fortress Europe, she is subjected to its anti-immigrant apparatuses managing movement. For example, Barni considers sending her to the United States to join her brother Taageere but thinks better of it as "She would not have been able to pass the checkpoints. They would have checked her fingerprints and sent her back" (39). The fingerprinting and checkpointing of Luul is an example of biopolitical management of the movement of those excluded from the rights and protections of citizenship. At one point Luul lives in an abandoned warehouse with other Somali migrants and gives birth in an abandoned car, which later catches fire. Maxamad X "the mute" attempts to enter the burning car as he doesn't know Luul has escaped already and is badly burned, landing him in Barni's hospital, which begins Barni's narrative. It is stories like these in the novel that intertwine to illustrate the condition of immigration.

A Somali refugee, Luul "had come from the desert, from the sea" and "after having lived for years in a refugee camp in Kenya, after having tried her luck on a series of trucks, she got as far as Libya." As Mattathias Schwartz notes in his illuminating article on African immigration to Italy and the Lampedusa tragedy of October 2013, "In Libya, human smuggling is called 'the Lampa-Lampa business.'"[23] From Libya Luul finally lands on Lampedusa, an island off the coast of Sicily that has been a primary arrival and detention point for migrants (C. Farah 36–38). Lampedusa marks an interesting socio-geographical locale between Africa and Italy. Schwartz describes it as a kind of migrant purgatory with a colonial history:

Lampedusa is a seven-mile flyspeck of limestone and arid soil. Along with nearby Lampione, it is the last of Italy's footprints on Africa's continental shelf. Most of its southern shore is forbidding terrain, where the sirocco pushes breakers onto bare crags. In 1843, Ferdinand II claimed Lampedusa for the Kingdom of the Two Sicilies; during the Second World War, the Allies bombed it heavily. After the war, it enjoyed sixty years as a sleepy enclave of fishermen and tourists. . . . In 2009, as Italy's tolerance for new arrivals declined along with its economy, Silvio Berlusconi's government renamed Lampedusa's eleven-year-old reception facility the Center for Identification and Expulsion. Today, along with Spanish Morocco, Cyprus, Christmas Island, and Nauru, Lampedusa is a zone of global limbo, where developed nations decide who is most deserving of a new life on the other side of the wall. More than two hundred thousand people [coming from Africa] have landed on the island in the past fifteen years. (78)

Lampedusa as a zone of "global limbo" embodies an odd articulating link between a continent ravaged by colonial and neocolonial programs and Italy, one of the countries of the Global North benefitting from those programs, now a "destination." Luul's story is representative of thousands of other migrants caught between the Scylla of postcolonial Africa and the Charybdis of "fortress Europe."[24]

Little Mother, and migritude literature at large, attempts to negotiate the issues and challenges concerning global mobility and citizenship within what Emily Apter calls the "darker side of globalization." In *Against World Literature: On the Politics of Untranslatability* (2013), Apter discusses postcolonial authors and artists that challenge the violently nationalist and xenophobic nature of the checkpoint and who use something of a politics of untranslatability to reveal checkpoints, borders, and sovereignty as such (Azmi Bishara's novel *Checkpoint* is one example).[25] In a lecture and conversation with Senegalese philosopher Souleymane Bachir Diagne, Apter describes this "darker" side to globalization. *Africa Is a Country*'s Eliot Ross paraphrases her argument against "the bourgeois fiction that globalization has turned everybody into ultra-mobile cosmopolitans, a myth that's proved especially seductive to those involved in the project of writing and institutionalizing so-called 'world literature,' with its array of glamorous airport-hopping protagonists. Instead, Apter points to the phenomenon of ever-intensified 'checkpointization' (the word 'checkpoint' has been creolized into most languages) and the way in which so-called 'illegal' residents are harassed and deported even as 'multi-culturalism' is lauded."[26] The works assessed in this book challenge the bourgeois fiction that globalization has nurtured cosmopolitan movement (it has, but for the elite and for capital) by illustrating the "checkpointization" that the majority of the world's migrants face, the everyday racism they nego-tiate, while undermining governments' self-congratulatory "multiculturalist" rhetoric parroted in the media. Barni, for example, sees a story on the news that depicts the prejudicial nature of the Italian government and media. Barni recalls of the story that "they didn't really feature it much, something about two Egyptians arrested for suspected terrorism. They found a map of Rome in their pockets with all the most strategic spots circled in red . . . but there was hardly any mention at all of the fact that these circles indicated where the Caritas food distribution centers for the hungry were located . . . it was really ridiculous, that there was paranoia everywhere, that everyone had it in for the poor and that you could be sure the big shots would never get caught" (C. Farah 32–33). The "paranoia" that Barni picks up on indicates the national anxiety created via anti-immigrant fortress Europe and the checkpointiza-tion of the North. This illustrates that the checkpoint is not simply a literal location where immigrants or others are compelled to produce papers but a larger mode of societal control—a way of abstractly denoting "us/them" or "self/other." For these reasons, Apter argues, the checkpoint is a "figure of performative sovereignty" (106). That is, the checkpoint claims and demar-cates a specific geographical area while simultaneously inventing an inside and outside the nation, which then justifies repression, aggression, and, in terms of movement, the conscription of immigration.

The Body as a Checkpoint

Simon Faulkner reports that art curator, photographer, and filmmaker Ariella Azoulay's analysis of Israel's checkpoint system shows "that to suppress the possibility of a proper Palestinian border the [Israeli] occupation regime has created multiple points of division that often have the appearance of a border . . . that 'the border passes wherever a Palestinian body stands' . . . every time a Palestinian seeks to travel, Israel takes advantage of the opportunity to reassert its sovereignty" (Apter, 101). In the context of Israeli apartheid, then, the Palestinian's body itself becomes a checkpoint, through which it is tar-geted, harassed, and managed, which in turn, reasserts or "performs" Israel's sovereignty, much like the passbooks in South Africa under white apartheid rule or the ways in which "residence permits" [*permessi di soggiorno*] in Italy can be racialized via the differential ease with which they are obtained.

In the context of Italy, *Little Mother* provides something of a parallel argument by showing how Italian police target black men in Italy simply because they are black—their bodies become checkpoints upon which the border always falls. The Somalian Taageere describes one instance: "We were all sitting on a wall, me, the Sicilian, a Vietnamese friend of mine, and a Jamaican. Then along came an Indian, an old man, not a young one. The others were smoking a joint . . . The old Indian man, all happy took the first drag. We were ready to burst with laughter and, I swear, I've never seen anything like it. First his feet then his legs began to twist. Like someone doing a breakdance" (191). At that point the Italian police appear, accusing them of "unauthorized gathering . . . [and that they must leave, and] that these are the rules and that if we want to live in this country we have to abide by them" (192). In response Taageere shouts sarcastically that "This is the land of multiculturalism!" (192). Symptomatic of the insidious apparatuses that manage movement and thus the bodies of immigrants themselves, this "multicultural" group of men actually become checkpoints themselves as they are targeted and forced to move and disperse. In other words, wherever a nonwhite person stands, the border "passes over" them, justifying harassment by the police, which, in turn, reasserts (white) Italian sovereignty.

The above scene parallels Claude McKay's novel *Banjo* as it depicts a multiracial, multicultural gathering of diasporic men of color and the danger perceived by their levity and socialization by the police (see chapter 6). Interestingly, it would seem that these two moments separated by almost ninety years show that the treatment of immigrants has changed little from the colonial to the postcolonial period. One could parallel, for example, the treatment of young black males and females in the United States by the police—Ferguson, Missouri, and the resulting Black Lives Matter movement being one of many recent examples in a long history of racial targeting and abuse dating back to the institution of slavery. In other words, for American blacks in the twenty-first century, the body is a checkpoint (see United States–based rapper Jasiri X's "Checkpoint").

The passport represents another apparatus within the structural management of bodies, populations, and their movement. Axad in *Little Mother* again illustrates the valued hierarchy in which Northern passports are the gold standard against which those from the Global South become useless or even incriminating: "Libeen was traveling with fake documents and I wasn't supposed to think about it. My documents, Italian documents, were accepted anytime, anywhere. They are rock solid documents. Libeen? Different picture, different face. I kept thinking, they will notice. But to Customs officials black faces are all the same . . . try to imagine each border crossing. I was afraid as well" (89). Axad, who is lucky enough to have one white Italian parent and thus an Italian passport, highlights the embedded racism custom officials are socialized to perform as well as the hierarchy of passports, some providing fluid, cosmopolitan movement, and others its opposite, movement interdicted.

Souleymane Bachir Diagne's response to Apter's lecture on checkpoints parallels the arguments made in *Little Mother* above. "Diagne respond[s] by recounting his own experiences of many decades traveling under his Senegalese passport. His passport, he said, is 'a passport that does not pass ports'—it is a devalued document whose bearer is generally to be considered suspect."[27] Diagne and Libeen's shared experience shows simply that, contrary to making national borders more fluid and the world a more open place, globalization has actually generated the proliferation of borders, checkpoints, and apparatuses that (repressively) manage the movement of the world's poor, working-class, and nonwhite populations; that only global capital, information, and the elite roam the world more freely than in previous eras. The irony is that the material realities of twenty-first-century structures like fortress Europe, the US-Mexico border, the Wall in Gaza and Israel's apartheid, and the United States' consistent targeting of African Americans seem so out of place given the rhetoric of a more fluid, open world that proponents of globalization, and even world literature, have vaunted for the past few decades.

The reality is that capital in the Global North shores up its borders and walls, girds its markets, and exploits the markets and people it has not already drained of life, for example, immigrants and workers in the Global South, particularly women. Sonali Perera argues that "in the contemporary historical moment, the 'new proletariat' is best represented by the figure of the woman worker in the periphery. Separate from organized labor in industrialized countries of the North, the occluded agent of production in this 'postindustrial' age is the super-exploited worker in postcolonial, 'developing' countries with extraverted, rather than autocentric, economies" (79). Migritude literature uncovers the darker side of globalization under neoliberal capital and it does so by focusing on the hinge of movement and immigration, as well as gender, which I analyze subsequently.

Diagne's remarks above illustrate Apter's characterization of globalization and he continues by addressing the Lampedusa tragedy of October 2013, in which 300 migrants/refugees from Africa drowned not far from land and while boats patrolled the area. He is critical of the way African migrants are portrayed in the media and takes a pro-migrant stance.

> The story of African migrants entering the Eurozone by sea is basically indecipherable as it is told in global and national media reports, because they are described only as helpless victims, without taking into account the sophisticated understanding they have developed for negotiating international legal frameworks and European state bureaucracies. When you know long before you get there that the Europeans will want to deport you on arrival, it is imperative you do all you can to flummox them. Why risk the perilous crossing? Because if you come by sea there is no single national border across which to expel you. Why travel without papers? Because that passport won't pass ports; it will only answer the question of where you should be deported to . . . Why stand in silence when questioned by officials? Because the language in which you reply will give them a clue where you may have come from. If you speak a word of French you might be flown "back" to Niger even though you're from Mali. Say nothing at all and there is nothing to translate.[28]

Little Mother shares Diagne's assertion that not only does the media parrot problematic representations of immigrants, but contrary to these representations in the media and elsewhere, immigrants indeed have a sophisticated understanding of the global apparatuses managing movement and a technical understanding of how to negotiate them. For example, in *Little Mother* a friend of Domenica Axad, Saciid Saleeban, and his girlfriend demonstrate this working knowledge concerning levels of stringency and immigration policy between nations as they attempt to board in Bulgaria for strategic reasons: "They were planning on getting on a plane in Sofia, where it was rumored that immigration controls were less rigorous" (112). Migrants in *Little Mother* demonstrate, as Diagne has it, a sophisticated awareness of differences in the national apparatuses of Europe that manage movement. Later in this chapter I will analyze the ways in which Farah subtly shows that this "migrant awareness" of the fact that their own bodies can be conscripted as checkpoints can shift into a kind of solidarity; that her character Domenica Axad reclaims her self and her sanity by reclaiming her Somaliness within the Somali diaspora; and that it is the diaspora-community itself, the "protagonist" of the novel, that represents not only her ultimate psychological renewal but a mode of political and collective resistance. These migrant collectivities, however, are clearly gendered and thus differing in character, necessitating a closer look at Farah's project as it relates to women in the diaspora.

Gender as a Checkpoint

In her article "Beyond Words: Mirroring Identities of Italian Postcolonial Women Writers," Moira Luraschi describes migrant women's writing in Italy by identifying a combination of sociocultural and identity-based reflections in their work:

> The most striking characteristic of postcolonial literature written in Italian is the substantial presence of women writers. Their status, derived from their origins and gender, places them at the margin of any power position. . . . It is often women, among the post-colonized migrants, who begin speaking about their identity. This particular theme is one that brings literature and social sciences closer. In their work, these women authors define identity as mobile and negotiated. Obviously, this vision of identity comes from their personal experiences as migrants. (1)

This insightful remark is helpful in the description of migritude literature in the context of Italy. Gender roles, as Graziella Parati notes in the contemporary Italian context, are clearly visible as "men have migrated and become visible by selling in the streets. They have supported each other, living and travelling in communities. Women, who were among the first immigrants to Italy, responded to the need for domestic workers and caretakers and experienced migration dispersed in native familial spheres."[29] Barni is a "little mother," for example—a midwife and a nurse in a hospital. Despite Italy's increasingly restrictive immigration laws, Di Maio notes that there is "a large Somali community in Italy. Moreover, there is a recent group of Somali-Italian writers, many of whom are women, who have used their powerful voices to tell their often inconvenient stories" ("Black Italia," 136). These "inconvenient" stories are productive. Women's voices in particular can, as the inimitable Maryse Condé claims, "displease, shock, or disturb."[30] Migritude women writers like Igiaba Scego in the postcolonial Italophone context not only challenge and philosophize upon the conditions and structures of immigration, both in a materialist sense and a psychological one, but indeed speak to heteropatriarchal power and conventions symptomatic thereof in both host and home countries. Women's migritude writing shows that the biopolitical management of immigrants' bodies target and interpellate women's bodies in various and distinct ways, one could argue using gender as an extension of Azoulay's contention, as a checkpoint itself (remember Italy's refusal to recognize Shukri's divorce, for example).

If the protagonist of Farah's novel is the Somali diaspora, it is more narrowly about women in migration. Domenica Axad, Barni, Luul, Caasha, Shamsa, Ayan, and Aunt Xalima are all diasporic female characters in the novel. Farah situates her two main female characters within a feminist genealogy. Domenica Axad remembers her school in Somalia named after Xaawa Taka, heroine of the Somali independence movement: "As a child I attended Xaawa Taka Elementary School, one of the largest in the downtown area. Xaawa Taka, a heroine of the Somali independence movement, was famous for having convinced women to finance the League of Young Somalis through the sale of their jewels. This gave vital impulse to the struggle for autonomy" (195). Although the Somali Youth League, which was Somalia's first political party, was all male, Taka's organizing empowered women and thus provides something of a signpost for Domenica Axad as she wades through her identity and genealogy.

Yet, complicating the concept of the heroine, Domenica Axad sarcastically proclaims earlier in the narrative that "the woman who knows she has no value without a man is the best of heroines" (110). This is stated in the context of describing Caasha, another woman in the diaspora: "Caasha who never lost sight of her goal. Who walked from Mogadishu all the way to Kismaayo to flee from the killers. Who arrived in Nairobi by car, and who thanks to funds from her relatives, left for Syria a few months later. Caasha who, with a fake passport, flew to Germany with her four children, ages one, four, five, and six. Who was locked up in a German refugee camp and was able to escape thanks to a ruse. . . . Caasha who, adrift in the world, never forgot her husband and dedicated her life to rescuing him" (110). Caasha reunites with her husband after "eight years of sending him money," causing Axad to remark bitterly, "The woman who knows she has no value without a man," that is, the one who subscribes to this particular heteropatriarchal more, "is the best of heroines." Many women in the diaspora are unrecognized and devalued next to men, yet heroically survive anyway. Checkpoints are often used not only to silence those who would cross them with fear and intimidation; they also flatten heterogeneous and diverse identities into stereotypically boilerplate categories: terrorist, criminal, immigrant. Gender in motion then, in both global and local contexts, can be "checkpointized."

Condé's above point is illustrative. She adds that "Whenever women speak out, they displease, shock, or disturb. Their writings imply that before thinking of a political revolution . . . a psychological one" is needed (161). The patriarchy of the postcolonial era does not go unchallenged by Condé here nor by Farah above, since a psychological "disidentification" from patriarchy is necessary before "political revolution."[31] As a counterpoint to the unsuccessfully autonomous Caasha, Ayan represents a "liberated" Somali woman in *Little Mother*. Domenica Axad describes how Ayan's relationship with her fiancé changes after they get married: "Just imagine. After they got married he began to act like a traditional man. He had expectations. Ayan, an independent woman who supported herself, was supposed to wear a veil and have children. . . . She was a liberated woman; she enjoyed pleasure and her own body without any taboos. There was no vulgarity in her carefree lifestyle" (97–98). After they marry he reverts to a more traditional, patriarchal world view, conscripting her into a heightened patriarchal order. Much to the reader's joy, Ayan drops him as fast as she would a veil. Ayan disidentifies with intersecting patriarchal systems (at home and in the diaspora) that she exists within, resisting from the inside while providing a model for negotiating such a system (in this sense she circumvents one checkpoint). Although Caasha demonstrates true grit, she apparently does not disidentify with, or circumvent, the systems she works within but rather subscribes to those modes of relation (according to Axad, Caasha believes she has no value but in relation to a man). Patriarchal or misogynist checkpoints no doubt, are reproducible in unofficial, individual capacities, as Foucault's panopticon shows, and so Caasha, or anyone, can become and enforce checkpoint gender.

The bond between Barni and Axad is described as an "elective sisterhood" and is forged in movement. Sonali Perera describes the writings of working-class women in the Global South as something of a non-revolutionary socialism of the everyday. For Perera, "Too often, in literature and criticism alike, the working class is seen and represented as masculine, metropolitan, and revolutionary. Women's texts of nonrevolutionary socialism, however, present us with new figures and concepts for thinking unorganized resistance, everyday experience, and the shape of the ethical within globalization" (80). Perera's nonrevolutionary socialism seems conversant with migritude politics and *Little Mother*. Barni, for example states: "Because you see, for us women, in the end, those fixed points, our home, our daily life, motherhood, the intimacy of our relationships, they are like little signposts that save us from getting lost" (30). Just as women workers (including the care industry such as little mothers like Barni) in the global periphery are less visible than men, the idea of a politics of the everyday, or in Barni and Axad's case, an elective sisterhood, becomes a productive hinge toward collective autonomy, patriarchal critique, and the challenging of biopolitical apparatuses that manage movement. Farah above metaphorizes signposts as a way to describe women's everyday lives in the diaspora, but the word also functions as a metonym signaling movement and immigration—signs guide those who move. The signpost, then, is very different from the conscripting nature of the checkpoint—one provides valuable information while the other polices.

For Domenica Axad it is her elective sisterhood with Barni that allows her to begin to piece together her identity-in-migration via the reclamation of her Somali "half." She writes to her older cousin Barni, "I reclaimed Axad, the name that you, Barni, had picked for me, and every time someone pronounced it, I thought of you" (113). Referring to their childhood in Mogadishu, in which Barni acted as something of a guide and friend, she remembers her past as one that she erased early on after her move to Italy; as Barni describes it, she begins to "loosen some of the knots." Ironically, Axad finally returns to a Somalia that represents the becoming-whole of her self on the eve of the Somali civil war, a war that would tear the country apart. She becomes, like her compatriots fleeing the country, a refugee. This chaos of movement, however, allows her to reconnect with the Somali diaspora, to claim it in a way, and thus work toward "reconnecting the threads" of her identity: "As a refugee I followed the flow of a diaspora that was only marginally connected to me. I internalized its makeup, the absence of a vision, its lack of goals. I wandered around between Europe and the United States for almost ten years, following the trends that drove the masses of young people my age from one continent to the next, from a worse welfare system to a better one. . . . I became a polyglot; I exhumed my Somali and the ancient proclivity for the nomadic life. I reconnected the threads and strengthened them" (217). She is only "marginally connected" to recent waves of Somali refugees since she has lived in Italy for some time. Axad, however, "internalizes its makeup" as a nomadic and goalless mass surviving in movement (see chapter 6 for more on the aesthetic of nomadism). This passage is also suggestive of another kind of disidentification in which the forced movement (both on the individual level when police forbid public gatherings, and on the national level when people are deported to anywhere) is used to create a sense of identity, community, and knowledge production (the latter, for Axad, is represented in the effective understanding of which welfare systems are better or worse).

The word "system" here illustrates my general point about migritude literature and its structural, conditional, and systemic perspective on, and politics of, immigration. Axad re-valorizes the Somali part of her that she represses in Italy, among other reasons due to its racist discourse and laws targeting black immigrants, both women and men, in different ways. *Little Mother* is somewhat ironically about the continued process of becoming whole in fragmentation; of threading and unthreading ties in diaspora; of materially and psychologically negotiating systems aggregated into what I call immigration.

Fred Kuwornu's *18 Ius Soli* and Africa in Italy

As a diasporic refugee, Domenica Axad "wanders around and between Europe" attempting to find those missing threads that would strengthen her sense of herself. As I mention above, the goal that allows her to move forward parallels that of the conceit of Farah's novel itself—documenting the diaspora: "After London: a complex web of different places. Letting things go I lived . . . I met Saciid Saleeban in Germany. He was fixated on his video camera and an interesting project. The crazy idea of filming the Somali diaspora . . . Barni—how can I explain it—his project became my project" (107). For Axad, life would get in the way. She reflects, "My dream remains that of making a documentary about the Somali diaspora . . ." (222). Although the film does not get made in this novel, there is something akin to what it might have looked like in contemporary Afro-Italian filmmaker Fred Kuwornu's 2011 documentary *18 Ius Soli* (his title references the Ius Soli laws in Italy). His film documents the children of immigrants from Africa, Asia, and the Middle East born in Italy as well as young adults who, though immigrants, have grown up in Italy; it illustrates the daily challenges they face in a primarily anti-immigrant and racist society.

18 Ius Soli connects the colonial period to the twenty-first century. It opens with the sounds of a soccer match in 2010 in Italy. As Ghanaian-Italian superstar Mario Balotelli takes the field, fans begin to chant "there are no black Italians." It then segues into the experiences of second-generation children of immigrants and the daily repressions they deal with, including white racism, as above. A vignette follows, telling the story of famous Congolese-Italian boxer Leone Jacovacci, born in colonial Congo and raised in Italy by his father. After winning a title in 1928, Jacovacci was met with the following headline in the newspaper: "A negro cannot represent Italy" (Kuwornu, *18 Ius Soli*). The nearly verbatim slogans from 1928 and 2010 provide a haunting image of the similarities between colonial and postcolonial-era Italy, mobility, race, and citizenship. The film also provides another historical example in young Afro-Italian soldier in WWII, Giorgio Marincola, who was born in Somalia "at the height of the Italian Fascist colonial experience in Somalia" and who would grow up in Italy. Despite being treated as subhuman in Italy, he joins the Italian army. When asked about his seemingly contradictory decision, he states, "homeland doesn't mean a color on a map but freedom and justice for all the peoples of the World" (*18 Ius Soli*). Kuwornu here subtly provides an alternative world view to the racist-nationalist Italian one reflected in the above refrains from 1928 and 2010. And although African immigration to Italy does not begin en masse until the 1980s, these two early, colonial examples of African immigrants in Italy in a documentary focusing on twenty-first-century second-generation children of immigrants, their experience and treatment, showcases a striking illustration of the vestiges of colonial mentality in the structures and ideologies of contemporary Italy. These are the very "imperial formations" that Ann Stoler and others describe as the "imperial debris" of the past in the present and its active, ongoing processes. *18 Ius Soli* similarly explores the long history of the present by focusing on black Italia and the repressive techniques of power managing citizenship and movement.

The documentary includes a series of interviews with young second-generation children of immigrants from Africa, Asia, and the Middle East as well as with immigrants who have grown up in Italy. These young folks do not have equal rights and they daily struggle with life as second-generation or immigrant. *18 Ius Soli* also includes vignettes, as above, as well as musical interludes including "I Was Born Here," a song by Valentino, a young bio-technology student born in Rome to Nigerian parents and aspiring hip hop artist. This song near the end of the documentary details how Valentino and a number of other interviewed youth in the documentary are treated poorly, denied citizenship, and afforded few of the opportunities those children lucky enough to be born of (white) Italian parents have. The film's subjects relate how they are made to stand in long lines to re-up their residency permits, short term, which, along with other form of documentation, they must carry with them at all times, again similar to South Africa's passbooks under apartheid. Valentino tells an interesting story recounting his permit renewal: "They write 'born *at* Nigeria'" on his form when "in correct Italian they should write 'born *in* Nigeria' and anyway I wasn't born in Nigeria I was born in Rome" (*18 Ius Soli*, emphasis added). Ironically, the Roman with the better and native grasp of the Italian language is identified as Nigerian by the white, grammatically challenged government worker, when, by merit and by birth Valentino for all intents and purposes is or should be a citizen and afforded attendant rights.

The narrator of the film notes, near the opening, that "900,000 kids born in Italy are obliged to live with residence permits . . . Italian law doesn't permit their rights." The documentary shows how the permits "tie down" those able to get them and do not afford the same rights as citizens. Valentino states in the film that "having a residence permit means you're a 'third-class' citizen . . . it means you can't leave when you want," and if one cannot leave, if one must follow a different set of (often oppressive) laws and policies than those with white skin, then one is less a citizen than a conscript. Although Kuwornu's activist documentary does not solely document the Somali diaspora in Italy but the children of a much wider diaspora from the Global South born and raised in Italy, it converses with the Somali-diaspora film project in *Little Mother* in interesting ways. This is eerily suggestive of the ways in which nonwhite children born in Italy are held, both culturally and legislatively, in a migrant-like status.

18 Ius Soli therefore explores the *condition* of being migrant by exposing the multifarious (and nefarious, for that matter) apparatuses managing movement. Georgiana relates her experience of being fingerprinted, paralleling the almost biological management of Fatou Diome's protagonist at immigration control (see chapter 2) and Luul's in *Little Mother*; Valentino paints a picture of "third class" life with a residence permit, while Anastasio and Aziz relate the constant experience of having to renew their permits while being in long lines and how it is a demeaning experience that never ends. Dorkas and Georgiana also relate their fear of the ever-present threat of deportation, possibly "to some country you've never been." Deportations to anywhere regularly happen in Italy, throughout the Global North, and in Israel. Georgiana for example, in an interview about the precariousness of life as a second-generation child, muses that with the residence card regime "you'll always be terrified they'll deport you to some country you've never been to" (*18 Ius Soli*). A young Italian woman with parents from Sierra Leone named Dorkas remarks, "If someone asked me for example to go to Africa, I would be completely spaced out," as she has grown up in Italy and considers it home—in fact, she has never been to Africa. However, since Italy makes it nearly impossible for young adults like Dorkas and Georgina to gain citizenship and thus equal protection under the law, they are in constant fear of jail or deportation; and even though many have *permessi di soggiorno*, they are prevented from working. All these instances aggregate into a scary illustration of Apter's "checkpointization" of the Global North wherein the immigrants' and even the native-born children of immigrants' bodies are produced as a checkpoint, as a signifier of otherness and foreignness, despite all evidence to the contrary.

We will remember the contradiction Valentino deals with wherein, although he was born in Rome and not Nigeria, he is always already hailed as Nigerian. This attests to the varied biopolitical management of any non-white populations in "fortress Europe" or the United States and Israel: in the colonial period all Africans were hailed as black—often by worse epithet—whereas in the era of globalization racial categories have subtly proliferated, thus Valentino's interpellation as "Nigerian" or even the fact that "immigrant" itself is racialized in various ways. Both about the humanity of the individual subject and exclusionary immigration law, *18 Ius Soli* implicates the network of techniques of power used to "administer bodies" across various disciplines, disciplinary structures, political practices, and the production of an ideological anxiety among the "native" (white) section of the population which anxiety in turn appears symptomatically—the chanting of "there are no black Italians" in the soccer stadium in 2010, for example.

The documentary ends on a hopeful note: it highlights various multi-ethnic schools and the proposal of the "Modified Ius Soli" law that would empower second-generation children, and promotes a society where equal rights are better disseminated. However, according to Ashna Ali, my colleague in Italophone African and diaspora studies, this proposal died in 2018 after languishing for months through 2017, which is unsurprising in this era, yet saddening nonetheless. Italian professor of sociology Mauro Valeri remarks near the end of the documentary that "thanks to the second generation we'll have our pensions paid, we'll have a country that can develop, we'll have the capacity to deal with the challenge of global competition." Aziz essentially implores Italian society to change: "I'd like to make a contribution in any way I can"; however, if I am "always tied down to a residence permit," I will "not be allowed" to make that contribution. This both shows the willingness to invest in and contribute to Italy by the second-generation children of immigrants and more recent immigrants, and the corollary fact that repressive Italian laws and its racist and anti-immigrant zeitgeist continue prevent the realization of those contributions to Italian society—thus ultimately harming it.

∾

Contemporary Italy is an understudied site of black Europe, black and African diasporas, Italophone African literature, and black Italian literature. Alessandra di Maio points out that African immigrants in Italy have "inscribed Italy as a site of the African diaspora, offering new perspectives and directions to the field of Black diaspora studies" ("Black Italia," 119). Italy must therefore also be further studied as a site of migritude literature. Cristina Ali Farah's *Little Mother*, Marco di Prisco's digital quadriptych of African immigration in Italy, Fred Kuwornu's film locating a "black Italia," and others like Igiaba Scego and her novel *Adua* not only provide an illustrative window into issues of immigration in the geocultural and historical space of Italy showing how literature and art negotiate immigrant experiences, questions of home and movement, identity and gender; but also, as migritude texts they (ontologically) narrate and engage with larger structures, systems, and patterns of immigration. They assemble a phenomenology of conscription— of the networks of techniques of power used to produce and manage, thus conscripting in various ways, nonwhite populations in Italy via mobility. Valentino's statement in *18 Ius Soli* shows that under the residence permit regime he cannot leave when he wants to leave and thus the interdiction of and reeducation of his movement. *Little Mother* shows this as well via its illustration of the checkpoint system, as does di Prisco's piece "Men on a Wire" showing Africans moving across a tightrope, an almost impossible limitation of freedom of movement. Furthermore, migritude texts argue that the colonial system is organically antecedent and yet lives on in this global moment. That iterations of these formations are not only visible but have proliferated and shifted in various ways illustrates the tenacious temporality of these imperial *cum* global twenty-first-century formations, but illustrates my argument about the work of migritude literature, exposing the "imperial debris" of formations in the present by using immigration as a hinge through which to assess these socio-economic and historical configurations. As Nuruddin Farah suggests, one cannot look at the Somali diaspora in Italy, cannot read works like *Little Mother* without looking at the long durée or "slow violence" of imperial formations and their future in the present.

Chapter 5

"A MATTER OF TIMING"

Queer Diasporas and Heteronationalism in Diriye Osman's
Fairytales for Lost Children

In the Trump era, immigration has become more politicized, more draconian, and more punitive than in the past decade or more. From his "Muslim ban," which was upheld by the United States Supreme Court in 2018, to his "zero tolerance" policy regarding the US-Mexico border—which contributed to the separation from their parents and caging of more than ten thousand children—immigration in the present can undoubtedly be characterized in terms of crises. In an article for Center for American Progress published mid-2018, Sharita Gruberg joins a chorus of voices pointing out that LGBTQ migrants are disproportionately affected by ICE's policies (Immigration and Customs Enforcement).[1] She tells the story of Laura Monterrosa, a queer asylum seeker from El Salvador who sought refugee status in the United States after being targeted by homophobic street violence. She was detained by ICE and incarcerated at the T. Don Hutto Detention Center in Texas, a privately run prison complex that began under the Reagan administration and continues to profit off of imprisonment, where she was sexually abused multiple times by an ICE guard. Stories like Laura's are common. Gruberg reports that LGBTQ asylum seekers are also at greater risk since transgender women are "housed" with men (which is apparently against its own rules) ("ICE's Rejection of Its Own Rules Is Placing LGBT Immigrants at Severe Risk of Sexual Abuse"). This links heterosexism and transphobia on the one hand, because it espouses the view that transgender women are "men with dresses on" (this sinister variant of homophobia fuels legislation in the United States including recent "bathroom bills" or proposed reversals of bills protecting transgender people from discrimination), with immigration and the management of movement, on the other hand. This intersection begs a number of important questions.

Do migration and sexuality connect? If they do so, apart from the literal sense, wherein those who move surely have sexualities, how are they related? To understand either we must go beyond theorizing movement itself, or sex itself, and assess and historicize the ways and means in which both sexuality and immigration are conditioned, categorized, and even policed in various global, national, and local contexts. Why did the United States, for example, ban "homosexual" immigration in 1952, and then repeal that ban in 1990 (Tyson, 304)? Narratives of progress will often recite too simple a story—one told from the perspective of those least vulnerable in the world. Here, I look to contemporary global literature as it engages these issues, complicates misleading narratives of progress, and tells the stories of those subjected to—and who challenge—intersecting oppressions, showing, first, that migration and sexuality intersect in complex ways. Authors like Diriye Osman, Shani Mootoo, Makeda Silvera, and Thomas Glave, for example, write worlds wherein same-sex desire is central, not an aberrant anomaly as it is often portrayed; they show how the complex lives of those who desire alternatively are shaped, and how they are often on the move, intersecting with migration and the displacement of desires. This intersection, I suggest, is best theorized through the lens of conscription.

Second, non-normative sexualities and activisms on the one hand, as well as anticolonial thought and practice on the other, also intersect, challenging hetero-coloniality in the twenty-first century. For example, Nawo C. Crawford, one of the organizers of the first Paris Black Pride in 2016, describes their struggle: it is "not about gaining a few reforms of the modern/ colonial, western/Christian centric system but to be part of this larger network of LGBT of color who are fighting for a broader transformation of sexual, gender, race, spiritual, economic, political, and linguistic hierarch[ies] of power."[2] She argues that since the French colonial policy of "assimilation," not unlike the policies of other former colonial powers such as the U.K. and United States, is a "form of oppression that considers 'whiteness' as the model, the universal model of humanity . . . LGBT people of color are [therefore] not meant to question the Eurocentric notions of sexuality" (Crawford, xiv). Scholars like David Eng, Judith Butler, Jasbir Puar, and Laura Westengard have indeed made similarly convincing arguments. This indicates not only that the ways and means of policing or managing sexuality itself has a history in the Global North's imperial adventures, but that it is also mediated in and through various heteronormativities of the nation-state. Following the now foundational work of Kimberle Crenshaw and others, it is important to address oppression as multiple and intersectional.[3] Darren Rosenblum argues that queer identity itself is intersectional, "since most queers face multiple aspects of discrimination, as women, as people of color, as poor people, as [trans]people," and so on.[4] Diriye Osman's *Fairytales for Lost Children* poetically yet critically enacts this intersectional critique through his geography of identity since he, and the majority of his characters are black, gay, and Muslim. Furthermore, these identities intersect in motion and are therefore refracted through immigration as both a process and an identity. Heteronormativity, often racialized, certainly crosses cultures, races, nations, and religions, yet voices of resistance negotiating and challenging it also span the global and the local, intersecting critiques of racial capitalism, sexism, homophobia, neoliberalism, pinkwashing, and so on.

Heterocoloniality erupted once again in Africa, for example, with the passage of two laws. Sokari Ekine, in "Beyond Anti-LGBTI Legislation: Criminalization and the Denial of Citizenship," notes that it was about a month between the passing of the Nigerian Same Sex Bill (NSSMB) and the Ugandan Anti-Homosexuality Bill (AHB) in early 2014, which declared "LGBTI persons illegal, [and has] made them non-citizens and bait for sexualized violence—rapeable, beatable, and killable."[5] LGBTQI persons are not only denied the protections offered other citizens but targeted as well. This duality of dispossession and oppression parallels the status of immigrants in some ways, particularly those without white skin. Immigrants of color who also happen to be visible sexual minorities are most vulnerable. Alisa Solomon's "Trans/Migrant: Christina Madrazo's All-American Story" details the multiple rapes of a trans woman from Mexico at the infamous Krome Detention Center in Miami. Like Monterrosa, she was simply seeking asylum in America.[6] Solomon begins by asking: "Why are asylum seekers—people fleeing persecution in their homelands for freedom in the United States—locked up in detention centers?" (4). Why are they targeted, stripped of human rights, and locked away when they seek help? Despite differences in legal language—"refugee," "immigrant," "asylum seeker," "illegal alien," "*sans papiers*," each representing a distinct category—there is one commonality they share with sexual minorities, with those who have, metaphorically or not, been deported or expelled, from citizenship or from their families by law or otherwise: dispossession. In the past two decades or more, the burgeoning fields of queer diaspora and queer migration studies has broached this shared dispossession between immigrants or refugees of color and sexual minorities.[7]

These particular forms of dispossession and oppression have a historical antecedent in Western imperialism. Ekine reminds us that the anti-homosexuality bills passed in 2014 "were built on existing laws which were part of the civilizing mission of colonialism, reinforcing heterosexuality as the natural order" (19). Contemporary immigration laws and modes of policing migrants, as I have shown throughout this book, harbor echoes of the colonial management of movement. If colonialism polices both sexuality and immigration, it is important to draw upon both anticolonial and queer critiques of the nation, citizenship, movement, and normativity, not to mention intersections of race, class, and gender, to adequately understand our contemporary moment. There was a global outcry, for example, shortly after the Nigerian and Ugandan passage of the anti-homosexuality bills, including well-known African and African diasporic authors like Chimamanda Ngozi Adichie, Jackie Kay, and Helon Habila (Nigeria) and Binyavanga Wainaina (Kenya). Many critiqued African leaders' intolerance and homophobia while others challenged the hypocrisy of those like Museveni and Mugabe who loudly decry imperialism and the West while accepting and reproducing European and United States–style religious imperialism. Further, Ekine perceptively notes that "the hypocrisy is not limited to African leaders. For example, [then] President Obama on the one hand evokes LGBTQI rights whilst on the other failing to hold US evangelical organizations to account for their role in exacerbating homophobia in the US and across the Global South. The duplicity is being spun on both sides of the Atlantic" (20). Certainly things have worsened under the Trump administration. With all this in mind, I pause on Binyavanga Wainaina's response to the bills, "I am a homosexual, mum," published in *Africa Is a Country* shortly after they passed, because he directly intersects sexuality and migration.

It is important to read texts like "I am a homosexual, mum," for the ways in which they not only tell us about the tyranny of heteronormativity, but the incisive ways movement, diaspora, or migration become important contextual modes of disclosing various heteronationalisms within global contexts and imperial histories. There are two sections in Wainaina's short prose piece (about three or four pages total), revolving around the death of his mother in Kenya in 2000. "This is not the right version of events," begins the first section:

I was putting my head on her shoulder, that last afternoon before she died. She was lying on her hospital bed. Kenyatta. Intensive Care. Critical Care. There. Because this time I will not be away in South Africa, fucking things up in that chaotic way of mine. I will arrive on time, and be there when she dies.[8]

In this version of events, Wainaina is able to travel to Kenya from South Africa to be with his mother before she dies, whispering to her finally, "I am a homosexual, mum," which would be the first time he speaks those words out loud to anyone. He would return home and accompany his mother as she prepares to travel to her next world. However, this is not what would happen:

> July, 2000. This is the right version of events. I am living in South Africa, without having seen my mother for five years, even though she is sick, because I am afraid and ashamed, and because I will be thirty years old and possibly without a visa to return here if I leave . . . my uncle calls me to ask if I am sitting down. "She's gone, Ken." (Wainaina)

Since Wainaina cannot risk "illegal deportation" and "lose everything," he does not, in reality, see his mother before she dies, nor attend her funeral. In other words, if he leaves South Africa, it would be unlikely that he could return to his life there since he is unable to obtain the correct papers or documents. How many families has immigration law the world over kept apart, alienated? Wainaina reflects upon the unspoken fact that he has "known that [he] is a homosexual since [he] was five," and that he would not even be able to "say the word gay until [he] is thirty nine," ten years after his mother's death. He ends the short piece addressing not his mother but an unknown person or audience: "I am a homosexual." Given the timing of this "lost chapter" of his 2011 autobiography *One Day I Will Write about This Place*, it appears to respond to or challenge the two anti-homosexuality bills passed early in that same year, joining the necessary chorus of voices condemning the bills. Yet what is singularly interesting about Wainaina's piece is that, in addition to engaging sexuality and the effects of oppressive heteronormativity, it also engages the structures of immigration as another important antagonist. If Wainaina's move is not purely coincidental, what is its import?

Wainaina's painfully intimate prose asks us to consider the ways in which discourses and material laws structuring immigration and sexuality indeed overlap. They intersect within what queer Kenyan writer Kegura Macharia calls heteronationalism, or, I might otherwise call it, simply nationalism (*Decolonizing Sexualities*, 20). Nationalism excludes and includes based on race, origin, sexuality, and other markers as it attempts to produce and reproduce the normative citizen. For Wainaina is both a sexual minority and a "foreigner" in what was and is a particularly xenophobic South Africa. For those around the world in precarious situations in which they are denied the proper papers or documents or passports, or are too afraid to apply for them because they are officially targeted populations, they may leave, but might not be able to return to the new life they have built and to the country they have supported in various ways, from paying taxes, filling jobs, to simply promoting cultural diversity, to name just a few.

Neelika Jayawardane and Ainehi Edoro argue that African writers have long been in the business of representing same-sex love. Yet, until recently, these depictions have caricatured, vilified, or portrayed same-sex desire as a kind of un-African or Western perversion ("Gay Sexuality and African Writers"). Guilty parties include Wole Soyinka (in his classic *The Interpreters*), Yambo Ouloguem, Ayi Kwei Armah, and Ama Ata Aidoo. Jayawardane and Edoro correctly point out that conversely, a cohort of younger writers like Adichie, Wainaina, and Diriye Osman (the latter two themselves gay), have "moved on from resorting to such ridiculous, caricatured depictions of gay people" ("Gay Sexuality and African Writers"). Chinelo Okparanta's 2015 novel *Under the Udala Trees* is an example of a complex and sympathetic portrayal of lesbian life in Nigeria, while Kenyan South Asian and lesbian writer Shailja Patel's *Migritude* deals with these issues and language (there is no word for lesbian in Gujarati, Patel points out) in "Dreaming in Gujarati" (*Migritude*, 51). Diriye Osman is a queer Somali writer born in 1983 who grew up in diasporas in Kenya and later Britain after the Somali civil war broke out in the early 1990s. He is gay, black, and Muslim, and various migrations mark an undercurrent in his life. His 2013 collection of short stories brilliantly narrates these intersections; indeed, he fashions (he is also a fashion designer) a queer diasporic philosophy of identity, existence, and time in *Fairytales for Lost Children*.

In this chapter I show how Osman's *Fairytales* represents a keen existentialist intervention into theories and experiences of diaspora, sexuality, and modes of racialization. As a counterpoint, I conclude by examining instances of queer liberalism and liberal (in)tolerance of queerness in Somali writer Nurrudin Farah's *Hiding in Plain Sight* (2014). Building on Eve Kosofsky Sedgwick, Robert Reid-Pharr, and David Eng, I argue that neoliberal globalization and the management of movement—immigration—cannot be disentangled from heteronationalist discourses and laws conscripting sexuality, whether they be conservative or liberal, and that queer liberalism and liberal toleration of queerness both practice and promote intolerance in terms of their inherent racialization and homophobia, respectively. These claims are made visible precisely through the study of systems of immigration as conscripting forces themselves and the concomitant treatment of immigrant populations.

"A Matter of Timing":
Temporality and Same-Sex Love in Migration

Diriye Osman's collection of short stories *Fairytales for Lost Children* (2013) pictures life in twenty-first-century *banlieues*—or racialized "ghettos"—in South London and Nairobi for Somali "lost children," those who have grown up as diasporic subjects peopling transnational flows both on the continent and between African and Europe. He follows gay and lesbian refugees, international students, and economic migrants. At the heart of these narratives lies the being-in-the-world of African immigrants who desire alternatively and for most of whom Islam is an abiding element of their identities. Osman struggles with the complexities of both external and internal negotiations of home and freedom in the lives of his queer diasporic subjects in postcolonial Kenya and the U.K. Further, he tracks the ways in which neocolonial-global structures of immigration, heteronationalism, and racialization temporally and materially condition processes of self-making for his cast of characters.

There are eleven short stories in Osman's *Fairytales*, each followed by an illustration along with Arabic script created by the author. All but the first story focus on the lives of gay or lesbian Somalis who have migrated to either Kenya or London, and their experiences in these transnational diasporas. The first, "Watering the Imagination," is the only story set in Somalia; it frames the collection by introducing themes of migration and displacement, same-sex desire, home, and freedom. The narrator is a Somali mother who loves and supports her lesbian daughter (she is the only parent in the book who accepts her/his gay child). "I respect her privacy," she muses, "and I allow her to live."[9] Like Osman himself, this Somali mother is a storyteller. "While the boat people, those who are hungry for new homes in places like London and Luxemburg, risk their lives on cargo ships, I stand firm on this soil and I tell stories" (3). Osman's *Fairytales* refashions notions of home and freedom through his project of "mattering" diasporic lives and alternative sexualities. Osman suggests, for example, that black gay migrants can be "homed" in their own bodies, constituting something like a self-materializing in movement (Jayawardane and Edoro, "Diriye Osman"). Processes of "homing" in this transnational and queer context, as we will see, are generally unfaithful to various heteronormative and neocolonial techniques of power and intolerant traditions. Alternatively, "queer," in terms of elite white gay/lesbian capital, for example, can be conventional, repressive, racializing, or nationalist.

Osman's penultimate story in *Fairytales*, "The Other (Wo)Man," illustrates the ways in which narratives of non-normatively desiring subjects in diaspora critically examine the intersection of immigration and sexuality. The short story follows Yassin, a young Somali immigrant living in an impoverished South London neighborhood, who meets an older Jamaican-British gentleman on the dating site "Gaydar." "The Other (Wo)Man" speaks to conditions of immigration in terms of geography, institutions, discourse, and migrant subjects. Geographically, for example, Osman illustrates the segregation of immigrant neighborhoods and the denial of rights and resources to those populating them. Yassin lives in Peckham, the site of 2011 "riots," which, though differing in context and location, parallel the Clichy-DuBois uprising in Paris 2005 and Ferguson 2014 in the United States.

Yassin's neighborhood is impoverished yet vibrant: "One could hear an imam's call to prayer at the local mosque or high-life blaring from Nigerian barbershops. There was a startling contrast between poor minorities and rich white folks, and even though the physical distance between their worlds was small, that proximity only served to emphasize the larger social and cultural divisions between them" (128). Osman here describes a de facto apartheid in which poor and racialized neighborhoods border and exist in tense and unequal relationship with wealthier white neighborhoods. *The Economist* describes Peckham as an "intensely African neighborhood," which Osman's prose illustrates from that "intensely" African perspective ("Race and Immigration"). *The Economist*'s tone represents the characterization of neighborhoods like Yassin's by both conservative and liberal media and political discourse—racialized, foreign, other.

He describes the diverse and bustling Peckham in dystopian terms: his "estate was an ugly mass of greyness and rot. Outside the windows of each flat deteriorated drainage pipes dripped nastiness onto the heads of pedestrians passing below" (132). By describing the conditions of immigrant life in dystopian terms, Osman discloses the neocolonial order of things. Salman Rushdie similarly uses a dystopic tone to describe British immigrant neighborhoods as akin to a "new colony" (132). For these "citizens of the new, imported Empire," as Rushdie calls them, and "for the colonized Asians and blacks of Britain, the police force represents that colonizing army, those regiments of occupation and control" (132). Although Osman and Rushdie importantly depict and characterize this new apartheid, it is not a new idea. The Black Panthers in the United States in the mid-1960s, and later, Stokely Carmichael and Charles V. Hamilton described the lived experience of black Americans in a similar way as early as 1967. "Black people are legal citizens of the United States . . . Yet they stand as colonial subjects in relation to the white society. Thus institutional racism has another name: colonialism" (5). Osman's description of the structural inequalities in Britain between "poor minorities and rich white folks," along with his dystopian *mise-en-scène*, underscores Carmichael's and Rushdie's commentaries about ghettos, banlieues, and immigrant neighborhoods as a kind of colony for nonwhite folks.

As Rushdie, Stuart Hall, Paul Gilroy, and others have shown, Britain has a track record in denying its black British citizens and its immigrant and second-generation populations equal rights. As Rushdie notes, in London even native-born blacks "are thought of as people whose real '*home*' is elsewhere" (132, emphasis added). As Yassin watches Somali cab drivers chewing khat in Peckham, they remind him of his present dystopic reality, out of which utopic "other ways of being" can be imagined and practiced: "He was reminded that his people were a traumatized community who didn't realize they were traumatized: by war, dislocation, poverty, miseducation and a general rift between young and old; by the tear between the past and future. It was a kind of collective psychosis, each sufferer oblivious to the fact that they were paying for the sins of their fathers and father's father . . . Yassin would not make the same mistake they had . . . he would find other ways of being" (138). Although Yassin seemingly misplaces blame on migrant individuals, the "father's fathers," rather than on an intolerant and (neo)colonial British society, he incisively calls out the temporal "collective psychosis" of the community, the rift between past and future, as well as the need to "heal" and to organize and advocate for change.

This is connected to the concepts of home and freedom for Osman, arguably the two most important in the book. Rahul K. Gairola insists that we must engage questions of sexuality in the frame of home, and that to erase questions of sexuality from notions of home risks naturalizing heterosexuality as the natural sexual paradigm of home and nation (*Homelandings*, 73–120). *Fairytales* foregrounds explicit erotic and loving same-sex sexuality within its diasporic collection of narratives. In an interview with Neelika Jayawardane for *Africa Is a Country*, Osman describes the process of writing about home in migration:

When I was writing the book, I was engaged in the kind of magical thinking that arises out of trauma and dislocation . . . Ultimately, I realized that I am my own home. Everything [in my home] is minimalist and basic because I'm satisfied with the fact that I'm "homed" within my own body. That's the ultimate gift. I have found the freedom to be comfortable within myself . . . We can't choose the families we're born into but we can choose the families we decide to make our own. ("Diriye Osman on being Gay, Muslim and African")

The kind of "magical thinking" that arises out of "trauma and dislocation" also harkens back to the tradition of magical realism in the Global South and Négritude. Osman assembles these accoutrements in something like a curation of home embodied. If Osman's practice of homing himself within his own body leads to the discovery of "the freedom to be comfortable within myself," it also must necessarily point to myriad processes of alienation that he is subject to, from systems of immigration and their racializing techniques of power to the heteronormative scripts that marginalize and dematerialize gay and lesbian lives both at "home" and in diasporas. Finally, Osman's point about choosing families echoes queer diaspora studies' argument regarding the promise of affiliation over filiation, against its ties to blood, the nation, and heteropatriarchy.

These points are reflected in Osman's story "Ndambi," which opens with the narrator Samira in London on the phone with her sister in Somalia, their birthplace. Samira is black, Muslim, and lesbian, the latter being, for her sister, sinful: "'Walaahi, I pray that you see the light,' she says with the faux-sympathy of the faux-pious. 'I pray that the shatan leaves your spirit; I pray that you find a man because lesbianialism can be cured'" (69–70). Like the forced assimilation of the immigrant into the culture of the host country, heteropatriarchy and its constituents police the borders of sexuality, perhaps most ardently by, the pious. Samira muses:

> The prophet once said that dreams are a window into the unseen. I have been told many times by family, friends, colleagues and strangers that I, a black African Muslim lesbian, am not included in this vision; that my dreams are a reflection of my upbringing in a decadent, amoral Western society that has corrupted who I really am. But who am I, really? Am I allowed to speak for myself or must my desires form the battleground for causes I do not care about? (73)

Samira's "lesbianialism" is ironically blamed on the West, which was, through colonization and the missionary regime, the source of religious homophobia in Africa (Murray and Roscoe). Samira describes her lesbian desire and identity as a battleground for "causes" outside herself illustrating the ways in which structures and discourses of "tradition," and heteronormative national identity, operate to "manage," in Foucauldian terms, or conscript, her sexual and religious practice in both racialized and gendered ways.

Black gay migrant existence becomes a "battleground" both in the home and host country as well as in the in-between spaces of immigration. As a mode of identification and survival, Samira creates home in ways that differ significantly from conventional ways of making a home:

> Sometimes home takes the shape of my ex, Adrienne. I like to think that the memory of her beautiful Afro, spiky attitude and sweetness is sacred, that I worship at her altar. Other times, I regard Somalia, my birthplace, as home, as the land where my soul will be laid to rest. Many times home is Kenya or London. But none of these places or people truly embody home for me. Home is in my hair, my lips, my arms, my thighs, my feet and hands. I am my own home. And when I wake up crying in the morning, thinking of how lonely I am, I pinch my skin, tug at my hair, remind myself that I am alive . . . Remind myself that it's all about forward motion . . . change . . . that elusive state. Freedom. (74)

Initially, home is represented by Samira's lover Adrienne in terms of her recognition and reciprocation of Samira's desire, her "spiky attitude" or way of being in the world, and her beauty—described through her Afro. Home is also described in terms of place. First, Somalia as homeland, then Kenya, a site of Somali refugee camps and Somali diasporas, and finally London. Yet, as none of these locales "*embody*" home for Samira, they are perhaps substantial markers on her temporal journey toward the construction of self and home, represented by her statement "I am my own home." However, Samira's statements at the end of the above section indicate that her bodily home is structured by that "elusive state," that is also perpetually in "motion"—"freedom."

Osman connects freedom with the struggles inherent in being gay, Muslim, and African in London. "The crux of the book is about sexual identity, within the context of being gay, Muslim, African. It is fundamentally a book about freedom" (Jayawardane, "Diriye Osman on being Gay, Muslim and African"). To put it another way, freedom itself must fundamentally include rather than exclude other ways of being. Interestingly, the epigraph preceding "The Other (Wo)man" cites French existentialist philosopher Jean-Paul

Sartre's adage "freedom is what you do with what's been done to you," which suggests that being is also shaped by conditions (including societal structures and institutions), or matters of existence. Sartre might have been most influenced by Martin Heidegger, who argued that being itself is constituted by temporality, and so Samira's home is both a matter of timing and an always already temporal making. In other words, it is always in time and through time that Samira must circumvent the violence and microaggressions of both heteronormativity and anti-immigrant patriotism; she must, to use a migrant metaphor, stay one step ahead of the forces that would un-home her—the cultural version of deportation. Yet, since these conditions generally shape her world, circumvention is never an endpoint but a process, a struggle toward freedom, as her reflections suggest.

Osman fashions a black diasporic literary genealogy by both extending conversations about race, home, and freedom, on the one hand, and reshaping them on the other. In addition to engaging these concepts philosophically in his stories and interviews, he cites Sartre, Audre Lorde, and Alison Bechdel. And interestingly, mid-twentieth-century African American writer Richard Wright (who has been called existentialist by some) makes a hauntingly similar statement about fashioning home. In 1957's *White Man, Listen!* Wright muses that although "I am a rootless man . . . I can make myself at home almost anywhere on this earth" (647). Yet, he cannot, or chooses not to, make a home in the context of the United States' racial apartheid. For Wendy W. Walters, Wright's rootlessness is "one born of the experiences of racial exclusion . . . Wright thus locates the very source of his global wandering in the psychological distance, the political exclusion, and the racial violence he experienced growing up in the United States" (24). Diasporic subjects are often met with apartheid-like conditions in Northern metropolitan centers. Brian Keith Axel's foundational work on diaspora argues that it is always already predicated upon violence. His model of theorizing diaspora "is intended to foreground violence as a key means through which the features of a people are constituted" (412). Wright's capacity to make a home almost anywhere and Osman's process of making *himself* a home, are constituted not just through diasporic movement but of the undergirding violence of diaspora.

Though Wright's and Osman's phrases defining home are strikingly similar, there is a key difference between them. Wright "can make myself at home almost anywhere" while Osman is "'homed' within [his] own body," presumably anywhere. Wright seems to suggest that home is exterior and can be made outside of one's self while Osman implies the opposite, that home is on the inside. Inasmuch as they both share the experience of existing in a world conditioned by white supremacy, Osman connects the intimacy of sexuality and gender to being itself. Wright's experience of institutionalized racism in the United States, and Osman's experience of the Somali civil war as well as racial and sexual violences in the diaspora (Kenya and London), shape their experience of home on the move.

Epigraphs can frame works thematically or philosophically, yet they can also clue readers in to the ways in which an author crafts a kind of genea-logical kinship with other writers, thinkers, or artists—think of diasporas of ideas or stories and textual landscapes with their own borders and flows. The first of two epigraphs beginning *Fairytales* quotes Audre Lorde, one of which reads: "When I dare to be powerful, to use my strength in the service of my vision, then it becomes less and less important whether I am afraid" (front matter). Osman's citation of Lorde here is suggestive of his own self-crafted conversation with a black diasporic LGBTQ genealogy in terms of both home and freedom. It is important here to mention Lorde's 1985 *Apartheid U.S.A.*, an example of her black internationalist writing wherein she compares black existence in America with black South Africans struggling under apartheid. She argues: "the connection between Africans, and African Americans, Afri-can Europeans, African Asians, is real, however dimly seen at times, and we all need to examine without sentimentality or stereotype what the injection of Africanness into the socio-political consciousness of the world could mean" (12). Calling out American apartheid while protesting the situation in 1980s South Africa represents both Lorde's global understanding of black-ness and oppression as well as her particular pan-African politics or ethics of "injecting" Africanness into the consciousness of the world.

Lorde's *Zami: A New Spelling of My Name* would have spoken to Os-man since it is both a diasporic text and one that theorizes home. As a second-generation child of Caribbean immigrants, Lorde begins *Zami* by illustrating structures of immigration shaping her parents' experience. "My mother and father came to this country in 1924 [from Grenada and Barbados respectively], when she was twenty-seven years old and he was twenty-six . . . She lied about her age in immigration because her sisters had told her that americans wanted strong young women to work for them, and Linda was afraid she was too old to get work" (*Zami*, 9; note that Lorde does not capital-ize "American"). Here, she situates being and existence in terms of African diasporic communities, particularly women. She observes: "Grenadians and Barbadians walk like African peoples. Trinidadians do not. When I visited Grenada I saw the root of my mother's powers walking through the streets.

I thought, this is the country of my foremothers, my forebearing mothers, those Black island women who defined themselves by what they did" (9). For Lorde, temporal agency—acts of doing—indeed constitutes oneself. This Caribbean iteration of existentialism's "existence is essence" relates to conceptions of freedom and home as a (collective) self-making from the perspective of black women.

When Lorde was a child, her mother's island of Carriacou was still not on American maps and "*home* was still a sweet place somewhere else which they had not managed to capture yet on paper, nor to throttle and bind between the pages of a schoolbook" (14). Black history, and by extension black home, would be throttled by Apartheid U.S.A.'s system of education. Lorde comes to realize though, as would Osman, that home is not necessarily a place. In the epilogue of *Zami*—the word "Zami" describes groups of women in Carriacou who worked and loved together—Lorde reflects: "once *home* was a long way off, a place I had never been to but knew out of my mother's mouth. I only discovered its latitudes when Carriacou was no longer my home" (256, emphasis in original). Lorde's "biomythography" shows how she makes a home of herself with others, particularly meaningful as a black lesbian writer, where American racial and heteronationalist apartheid invest in freedom for a few and deny it to many others. What then is the link between home and freedom?

In an interview with the BBC upon the publication of *Fairytales for Lost Children*, Osman suggests that although "the crux of the book [is] about sexual identity, within the context of being gay, Muslim, African[,] it is fundamentally a book about freedom" (Jayawardane). *Fairytales* provides an alternative to, and challenges, abstract and Western conceptions of freedom, often mobilized at the very moment of the enslavement or colonization of Africans, Muslims, immigrants, or gay subjects. Orlando Patterson argues in "Freedom, Slavery, and the Modern Construction of Rights": "the social construction of freedom was made possible by the relation of slavery. Slavery had to exist before people could even conceive of the idea of freedom as value, that is to say, find it meaningful and useful, an ideal to be striven for" (117). Susan Buck-Morss reminds us that "by the eighteenth century, slavery had become the root metaphor of Western political philosophy, connoting everything that is evil about power relations. Freedom, its conceptual antithesis, was considered by Enlightenment thinkers as the highest universal political value. Yet this political metaphor began to take root at precisely the time that the [European] economic practice of slavery was intensifying" (21). Further, "the paradox between the discourse of freedom and the practice of slavery marked the ascendancy of a succession of Western nations within the early modern global economy" (23). This marks a peculiar contradiction in Western universalism that indeed refracts into contemporary discourses like neoliberalism and tolerance.

Osman uses Sartre's phrase "freedom is what you do with what's been done to you" as an epigraph for the penultimate story in the collection (119). Sartre's formulation has a temporal quality as it points toward the fashioning of being in time and in the context of material reality. Sartre's phrase comes out of the existentialist tradition, following Heidegger, and Sartre vocally supported Négritude and anticolonial movements in the Third World. He was an ardent critic of European colonialism and, I think suggestively, described Négritude as the "Being-in-the-World of the black man" ("Black Orpheus," 314). However, received moments of racialism seep into Sartre's philosophy and politics. Robert Reid-Pharr critiques Sartre's misrepresentation of black Americans, for example, as a "mass" whose grandparents had "no hand in their own manumission," a belief that Du Bois's *Black Reconstruction* shows to be incorrect (Reid-Pharr, 97). Reid-Pharr argues that Sartre "simply reiterates the centuries-long tradition of writing black individuality out of narratives of Western modernity" (97). Frantz Fanon also takes umbrage with Sartre's totalizing and somewhat patronizing view of the Third World, as well as his relegating of Négritude, and by extension blackness, to the "antithesis" of colonialism, only to be swept away in the syntheses of dialectical historical movement (*Black Skin White Masks*, 132–33). Yet, for Reid-Pharr, "by rejecting the racialism that invades the existentialist project we might just gain access to the radical humanism" of Sartre, de Beauvoir, and others, that has yet to come (98). There is indeed a kind of existentialism or "radical humanism" in Diriye Osman's *Fairytales for Lost Children*, necessarily refracted through the lenses of diaspora, queerness, and being Muslim (which becomes doubly precarious as same-sex desire is forbidden within the religion, and secondly, Osman and other immigrants are continually targeted by the Islamophobia of the West). Osman's text, then, gets to the being-in-the-world of queer and Muslim immigrants, not as a totalizing characterization but one that engages everyday existence while foregrounding black individuals. It pushes into the realm of alternative desires and the subsequent repression of being via heteronormative conditions as a reconfiguration of home and freedom in the context of the neocolonial and neoliberal world order.

Yassin's story, for example, discloses the hidden privileges within heterosexual migrant narratives that rely on normative notions of gender, the family, and the domestic sphere, while critiquing the racialization of immigrants: "In Somalia and Kenya, the countries he was born and raised in respectively, homosexuality was something to be hidden for fear of violence. . . . After immigrating to London he had slowly allowed the mask to slip as he became more comfortable in his new surroundings. But despite the city's myriad possibilities here he was, four years later, lonelier than ever" (127). The question becomes, what is the constitutive difference between East Africa's conventional intolerance of same-sex love and London's ostensible liberal "tolerance"? For Yassin as a nonwhite, non-elite immigrant subject, the question becomes complex and illustrates that London's claim of tolerance or multiculturalism is questionable.

Yassin therefore takes to Gaydar and eventually meets Jude, an older (married) Jamaican-British man. They meet in a café in South London, where Jude brings Yassin a plant. Eventually Yassin invites Jude back to his apartment. Tension arises when Jude wants Yassin to dress up in women's underwear during foreplay. An offended Yassin exclaims, "So now you want me to dress up like a woman for you? . . . You don't want a man and you certainly don't want a woman. You just want someone inbetween who you can foist your fantasies on. Well that's not me alright? You need to get the fuck out of my house!" (136). Eventually Yassin decides to try on the role Jude asks him to play, donning panties and silk during sex. Although he is curious and feels "free" in the stockings, Yassin is also "slightly repulsed by it all" (140). Yassin's ambivalence here, in terms of the complexities of gender identity and sexuality, is symbolically constructed in the title of the story, "The Other (Wo)Man," where Osman parenthetically sections off the feminine prefix while still keeping the sum of its parts. This is suggestive of the fact that, at this point, Yassin is still unsure of his own desires, and so he decides to try on the identity Jude has fashioned for him.

Before a night at a local gay bar, Yassin buys an outfit from the women's section at a nearby store and wears women's makeup. "Yassin felt he was creating himself, bending the pages of the rulebook back until the spine split and the leaves came loose" (144). As he applies his makeup he muses, "With a few deft strokes of a brush he hoped to unshackle the person locked in his head who was no longer a slave to social convention" (144). The constricting rulebook that he attempts to bend back until the spine splits is of course the gender and heteronormative "script" embedded in various societal structures and discourses around the world. Yet the script for Yassin is not something that he wants to completely reject *tout court*, given that, he feels somewhat comfortable in his "male persona." In this sense he is both conscripted and is the orchestrator of his own conscription, script, or play (at the same moment, he *plays with* normative scripts by showing their very instability, contradictions, or play).

However, "for this night at least he was willing to erase his male persona and squeeze into the butterfly jeans and tight blouse to complete his transformation into a (wo)man" (145).

> He didn't just want to become a (wo)man, he wanted to become a Muslim (wo)man, or at least his playful idea of a Muslim (wo)man. It was ironic that for all his wanting to break free of social strictures he should choose to wear a garment that embodied the very essence of fitting into the mould. He felt that since he was a Muslim he would retain the most conspicuous marker for women of his faith but use it to his own subversive ends. (145)

Initially he feels reticent to wear a headscarf, which seemed for Yassin, to represent tradition-as-homophobia, and yet in wearing it he finds it represents something else, something subversive. In Western metropoles the headscarf is frowned upon by conservative anti-immigrant sentiment. It has even been banned in France, as it had come to signify "improperly" assimilated populations and thus does not represent the ideal (meaning white) national citizen. In this context—one predicated upon migration—Yassin's Muslim headscarf becomes subversive, doubly so on a gay black man in drag as he represents multiply intersecting improprieties. Yassin is therefore "unfaithful" to the strictures of normative racial, gender, sexual, and religious practice. With a quick reference to *Paris is Burning* no less, Yassin heads out on the town for a night of dancing at a lesbian bar. Unfortunately the night does not end well. And, although it does not end in the normative national-individual self-fashioning of the *bildungsroman* but rather with the deferral of what Yassin calls "true liberation," it does not end hopelessly (151).

On the dance floor, Yassin is hit on by "one of the pimp-looking young men he had seen by the bar," who after dancing somewhat intimately with Yassin, is angered upon realizing that Yassin is "a fucking bloke" (151). "I don't know what *you're* chatting about," retorts Yassin, "'You're a straight guy fishing for chicks in a dyke bar!' 'You arsehole,' said the guy in his prepubescent voice before lifting his T-shirt to flash a firmly-bandaged chest that showed the faintest outline of flattened breasts. 'I *am* a fucking dyke!'" (151). Ashamed, Yassin storms out and tears off some of his more feminine garments in an alley, asking himself what he had hoped to gain from this most recent "experiment of the body" (151). "Such experiments," he philosophizes, create "a desire for something more fulfilling. It was a hunger born of rootlessness but he couldn't see that. He couldn't see that true liberation was a strictly DIY process, frightening in both its intensity and limitless scope" (151). Yassin's "rootlessness" is not solely due to his gender-sexual positionality, unmoored from traditional social structures but to his immigrant status as well. Alternative desires can themselves be viewed as migrations since they require leaving normative avenues of sexuality. And just as outside forces impinged upon Yassin, so "his interior landscape was in transition" (152). Perhaps Yassin's queer DIY version of Richard Wright's "rootlessness" represents the possibility of "true liberation," one that is fashioned and remade in context like Sartre's "freedom is what you do with what's been done to you." It is the practice of doing it yourself, a phrase with punk-rock and alternative connotations, both against and with repressive societal rules and repressions, that represents "true liberation" or freedom. The short story itself enters and exits *in media res* highlighting Yassin's struggles to fashion a home *of* himself, armed not just with conceptions of freedom, but its practice.

As Yassin leaves the bar ashamed, not necessarily of his failed "disguise" but of his sense of homelessness, he grapples with the fact of being excluded from various communities given his sexual orientation: "He didn't belong to just one society: he was gay, Somali, Muslim, and yet all these cultural positions left him excluded. It was Somaliness, the pure beauty of being a part of a proud, distinctive, culture that glued all his other selves together" (137). Osman's use of Somaliness as a "proud, distinctive culture" to glue himself back together is not a nationalism that celebrates ethnicity at the often brutal expense and construction of others, but one that is DIY, punk rock, and "radically" queer. Yassin uses the terms "hierarchy" and "timing" to describe his identity. This reconfigures the ways in which materiality and temporality situate identities particularly in regard to immigration and alternative sexualities. Yassin states that he "was Somali first, Muslim second, gay third. But perhaps that hierarchy was a matter of timing: born Somali, raised Muslim, discovered gay" (137). "Hierarchy" calls to mind "structure" or "condition," on the one hand, while "timing" denotes temporality on the other, suggesting that it takes time to come to one's self. Temporality conditions both Yassin's experiences and his struggle to fashion a sense of himself as he negotiates the meaning of his own being as an immigrant in London—a place in and through which his various subject positions battle. Structures constellating the immigrant condition indeed shape or route Yassin's experience: from anti-immigrant laws and rhetoric to the apartheid-like life in immigrant neighborhoods in the West, to the continued marginalization of gay subjects. The word "matter" in Yassin's phrase is suggestive of an "issue," as in "a matter of timing"—as well as materiality itself. It also signals that which is worthwhile or important, as in #Blacklivesmatter.

It is here, at the end of the story, that he inaugurates a phenomenology of time and being. "He was Somali first, Muslim second, gay third . . . And now he was venturing out into the world without a sense of his place within it and this frightened him" (137). Home, and by extension freedom, is deferred. Perhaps for Osman, home is created through the act of writing itself, which is always already a process of critical thinking, reading, and revising. And perhaps it is Osman's incisive pairing of home and freedom within his queer migritude cache of fairytales that represents a new phenomenology of movement as he delineates the world of objects that, both materially and discursively, repress or alienate him while others sustain or shape his self-fashioning. The final words of the short story read: "This night had been a dystopian fairytale but now the spell had been broken and he had awoken. He licked his wounds and started walking home" (152). Facing an abyssal homelessness, Yassin, Like Domenica Axad in *Little Mother*, tactically owns his "Somaliness," as a way to reassemble his other selves, shattered in and through the system of immigration and institutional and epistemic responses to desiring otherwise, back together. Again, this is not nationalist, given that he is exiled in part from Somali national culture due to his sexuality (as are the other characters in *Fairytales*, whether in Kenya or London). The Somaliness he utilizes is rather a queer "DIY process," a temporal and spatial making a home of himself as a *practice*—rather than an achievement—of freedom. I close with a brief reading of queer liberalism and liberal toleration in Nuruddin Farah's 2014 novel *Hiding in Plain Sight*.

Subjects of Toleration:
"Our Hearts Are Not Where Our Papers Are"

The title of Nuruddin Farah's *Hiding in Plain Sight* refers both to closeted "homosexuality" in Africa as well as to invisible Somali refugees in Kenya. In the novel, Valerie and Padmini are two bourgeois lesbian characters, one white and British, the other South Asian–Ugandan. I read them as, among other things, representing a variant of "queer liberalism" (Eng). Another character, Bella, is straight but polyamorous, and demonstrates a kind of "tolerant" liberalism toward queerness. Farah portrays both of these mechanisms of liberalism as ultimately problematic despite apparently positive elements.

Farah touches upon queer sexualities in Africa, racialization of Somali immigrants in the Kenyan diaspora, colonial histories, and the neocolonial present. *Hiding in Plain Sight* does not, however, represent a queer diaspora narrative like Osman's *Fairytales*, which celebrates migrant queerness as a practice of freedom and home, but rather paints an incisive picture of the casual racism of queer elite subjects (Valerie and Padmini), and the problematic "tolerance" mobilized within liberal attitudes toward queerness (Bella). Finally, like Osman's narrative, it indeed engages questions of freedom and home in diasporas.

The novel begins with a Somali man named Aar who has two children, Salif and Dahaba, with a white British woman, Valerie. Aar and the children live in Kenya, while his twin sister Bella lives in Italy. Aar is killed in Somalia by Al Shabab terrorists who deem his work with the United Nations in Somalia undesirable. Bella must return to Kenya to care for her niece and nephew while dealing with Aar's erstwhile ex-wife Valerie, who is now in a relationship with Padmini, a South Asian–Ugandan woman who Valerie meets in Britain. As Bella and Valerie vie for guardianship of the children, Farah illustrates the experience of poor and middle-class Somali refugees in Kenya.

Salif, Aar and Valerie's teenage son, meditates upon his condition as a diasporic subject in another nation: "Our father obtained Kenyan citizenship through bribery after living here for decades as an undocumented refugee . . . [Somalis] were declared stateless when they first arrived, along with all the other Somalis fleeing the civil war [1991]. Eventually, they got Kenyan papers, but I do not think of myself as a Kenyan since I am not welcomed as such."[10] Like Osman's depiction of the Somali diaspora in London and Kenya, Salif paints a picture of immigrant life in a society that "tolerates" but does not welcome its guests as such, and where toleration can include various repressions and discriminations. Salif responds, as if speaking to Kenya, with the defiant "our hearts are not where our papers are" (173). This could perhaps become a migritude rallying cry, mirroring Shailja Patel's oft-cited description of "migrants with attitude," or those that speak out against multiple injustices. But interestingly, Salif's "hearts" in "our hearts are not where our papers are" can also indicate those *who* we love and *how* we desire, which, must also not be documented or categorized as a means of repression. To translate it another way: police not our movement, our sexualities, nor our being, no matter who we love or where we come from. Through that promising phrase, "our hearts are not where our papers are," we can productively map out migration and sexuality at the intersection of conscription.

Bella documents the being of Somali diasporic subjects in Kenya: "Kenyan Somalis, who account for nearly six percent of this country's population, have remained third-class citizens here, disenfranchized and marginalized. If they behave badly, that is undoubtedly in part a result of their poor treatment by other Kenyans" (173). Bella seems to imply that anti-immigrant rhetoric elides the repressive conditions of reality producing "bad behavior," instead exhuming and endlessly recycling tired stereotypes as if to confirm its own dusty colonial ideas. Similarly, migritude writer Fatou Diome defamiliarizes the concept of "toleration" as naturally positive. Her cast of African characters in France, as I show in chapter 3, "managed to forget that no one ever spoke of gratitude towards them or even simply citizenship, but only of tolerance and integration into the mould of a sieve-society in which they are the lumps" (172). Here, being subject to toleration is both alienating and fundamentally bereft of both gratitude and citizenship, which implies that toleration and its twin, intolerance, are mutually constitutive for a variety of reasons, not least due to the ways in which formerly colonial powers grasp the formerly colonized.

Indeed, an underlying yet fundamental condition of reality that shapes immigrant existence is marked by various colonial pasts that haunt the present whether in Britain, France, Italy, Kenya, or Somalia. For example, in *Hiding in Plain Sight* Bella notes: "Nairobi has never enjoyed much stability; right from the get-go, a concentration of British colonists occupied the best land and the Africans were pushed into the slums to live in shanties knocked together out of sheets of zinc, earning no standing in the colonial scheme as the city became a hub for business and, eventually, international organizations. The instabilities, which are of a piece with the African neocolonial city, have continued till this day, making Nairobi one of the most violent cities on the continent" (66). In addition to connecting the future of colonial pasts to neocolonial presents, Farah pays homage to urban African fiction, from Mongo Beti's 1954 *Cruel City* to Chris Abani's 2005 *Graceland* and Lauren Beukes's 2011 *Zoo City*. The devastating effects of neoliberal economic policy on places like Somalia and Kenya, marshalled in by the Global North (IMF, World Bank, etc.), have direct links to colonial policy. Both Diriye Osman's work and Nuruddin Farah's novel speak to these issues, yet through the prism of immigration and alternative sexualities.

How then are liberalism, neoliberal globalization, and the management of sexuality and immigration connected? Citing Jodi Melamed, David Eng outlines this question: "Today, under the shadows of a U.S.-led globalization—capitalist development as freedom—the politics of colorblindness employs the depoliticized language of what Jodi Melamed describes as 'neoliberal multiculturalism.' . . . In the final analysis, neoliberal multiculturalism portrays racism as nonracialism and neoliberalism as the key to a multicultural, postracial world order of freedom, opportunity, and choice," while naturalizing systems of global capital accumulation that "grossly favor the Global North over the Global South" (9). Neoliberal "freedom," or capitalist development, means the freeing *up* of formerly colonized peoples in the Global South (or the North) for direct or indirect exploitation (structural adjustment programs or free-trade zones, for example), all while lauding abstract values such as the free market, privatization, even individualism (none of which represent much value for those unlucky enough to be on the wrong side of capital). Similarly, Lauren Gantz elaborates Eng's queer liberalism as "a form of neoliberalism that allows for the enfranchisement of certain homosexual citizen-subjects. This enfranchisement manifests itself within the realm of the domestic, via increasing rights to sexual privacy, adoption, and same-sex marriage. While such developments have been greeted as progressive, Eng urges his readers to be circumspect about queer liberalism's hidden costs" ("On the Feeling of Kinship"). For Eng, the hidden costs are uncovered by assessing processes of the reeducation of queer subjects in and through enfolding them within the heteropatriarchal institution of marriage, capitalist consumerism, and its attendant racisms (often anti-immigrant or refugee).

I read Farah's *Hiding in Plain Sight* as illustrating the racialization of Bella as an apparatus of queer liberalism. Valerie and Padmini, for example, though queer subjects, adopt a kind of casual racism as members of an upper middle class that happens to look down upon (and refuses to understand) Africa. In a conversation about sex with Bella, a Somali woman, "Padmini asks, 'Do you enjoy sex?' 'What a stupid question to ask,' says Bella. 'Haven't they chopped yours off?' Valerie adds, 'That genital thing, she means'" (132). After Bella answers no, Valerie states, "I thought you were . . . I imagined every Somali woman underwent infibulation" (134). At the same dinner, a Kenyan waiter is surprised Bella, as a Somali woman, even goes out to restaurants, a practice that does not conform to his notion of what a Somali woman does. A resigned Bella is not surprised about both European and Kenyan "generalizations about Somalis . . . After all, Valerie, who was married to a Somali man and gave birth to children who are part Somali, has just demonstrated that she knows next to nothing about Somalis" (135). After Valerie commends her son Salif for learning to speak Somali (Valerie has been absent for many years, having "abandoned" Aar and the children for Padmini), Dhaba remarks, "'Our best friends are Somali.' . . Valerie responds 'I hope your

Somali friends here do not teach you to use guns and stuff!' Bella recoils at the stereotype, but Dahaba says only, 'Actually, they're very nice'" (151). The narrator of *Hiding in Plain Sight* problematizes Valerie's stereotyping as we are made to "recoil" along with Bella. Further, these conversations represent a kind of retained cultural chauvinism constituting liberal colonial racism, yet in the neoliberal era. The Hollywood blockbuster *Black Hawk Down* and the Tom Hanks film *Captain Phillips* do similar colonial-neoliberal work, for example, with reference to Somalia, by wielding the specious whites-as-saviors and Somalis-as-barbarians narrative. Historically speaking, from devastating colonial to neocolonial policies, whites have been the driving force behind the destabilization of Somalia (see chapter 4).

Conversely, however, Bella, who is also middle class, demonstrates a problematic liberal "toleration" toward queerness (particularly toward Valerie and Padmini). It is ambiguous as to whether or not the reader should identify with, or "recoil" from, Bella's (in)tolerance, as the following passage in particular is ensconced within seemingly progressive statements: Bella "knows that Aar, unlike most Somalis raised in the urban centers in the south of the country, had no issue with male homosexuality and couldn't be bothered about lesbianism. As for herself, while the platitude is true—many of her best friends are gay, and some are in openly gay marriages—she acknowledges that maybe she is not quite as advanced in her attitudes as she likes to think. But with her three lovers, she knows that she lives in a house of glass and cannot afford to throw stones at anyone in a similar position" (156). Bella only accepts gay and lesbian desire and practice because of her own polyamorous "derivation" from normative proscriptions of domestic decorum, not as an ally, and further, she admits that maybe she isn't "quite as advanced in her attitudes as she likes to think."

And herein lies the point: whenever tolerance is evoked, particularly within various strands of liberal discourse, its relationship to *intolerance* is uncomfortably closer to it than proponents admit. Tolerating something is not to love it or even like it, but, at best, to put up with it. To put it another way, putting-up-with and the acts of shunning, casual repression, and hate are not mutually exclusive. The next sentence in the novel, interestingly, finds Bella lauding both the liberal notion of freedom and a more socialist or populist one: "Freedoms are a package deal, she thinks, useless unless you value them all. Freedom of expression, freedom of religion, freedom of association with whom you please—all of these are as important as the right to education, to food, to clean water" (156–57). The first three, liberal notions, are followed by the last three, a more progressive or socialist triptych. These notions of freedom are put, by either Bella, Nuruddin Farah, the narrator, or all three, into conversation with alternative sexualities in Africa generally speaking: "In Africa, gay men and women are seldom open about their sexual preferences. In many countries homosexuality is a crime, and even where it is not, people talk as if it were alien to the culture, even though, of course, there are gay people in every society everywhere" (157). Although the tone is a bit didactic, it was at the time a relatively rare occasion in African literature (there are more and more exceptions) to find gay or lesbian protagonists, and so it is nonetheless an important intervention that Farah makes in broaching these topics.

To further unpack these characters and statements in Farah's *Hiding in Plain Sight* and to connect them to Osman's *Fairytales for Lost Children*, I cite David Eng and Eve Kosofsky Sedgwick. In *The Feeling of Kinship*: *Queer Liberalism and the Racialization of Intimacy*, Eng states:

> To take a critical page from Eve Kosofsky Sedgwick's monumental book on the persistence of homophobia in the age of sexual toleration, contrary to popular opinion, "advice on how to help your kids turn out gay, not to mention your students, your parishioners, your therapy clients, or your military subordinates, is less ubiquitous than you might think. On the other hand, the scope of institutions whose programmatic undertaking is to prevent the development of gay people is unimaginably large." In a similar vein, while the law no longer criminalizes interracial marriage, advice on how to promote interracial union is less ubiquitous than our colorblind pundits would have it. (7)

This insightful critique uncovers the intolerant material institutions (homophobia and racialization) that subtend liberal notions of "sexual toleration" and "multiculturalism." Undoubtedly, Valerie would have benefited from the latter form of advice (on antiracist interracial union), as she, a white British woman, is ignorant of her own husband's (and children's) Somali culture and subscribes to racial stereotypes, while Bella, on the other hand, might have benefited from the former (on how to *create* alternative desires rather than suffocate them), as she is "not quite as advanced in her attitudes as she likes to think," despite her protestations of "tolerance," and the platitude of "I have gay friends." I am inclined, then, in comparison with Bella, Valerie, and Padmini, to call Diriye Osman's queer migritude narratives radically democratic; or, to reiterate Robert Reid-Pharr's important term, suggest that they embody a radical humanism.

In the last short story of Osman's *Fairytales* "My Roots are Your Roots," for example, the ownership of lives and bodies is announced through prosaic yet poetic transnational black gay love:

> I am Jamaican and Korfa is Somali. Neither of our families knows that we're two men who love each other . . . I forget that by loving Korfa my life is in danger. In those sticky summer nights in South London our windows stay open and our tiny apartment becomes our secret garden . . . no limits no borderlines. The secret garden leads to the marigolds of Mogadishu and the magnolias of Kingston and the heat turns us sticky and sweet and unwilling to be claimed by defeat[;] we own the night. We own our bodies. We own our lives. (156)

The final two lines of *Fairytales for Lost Children*, "We own our bodies. We own our lives," are really quite radical given that the preceding stories are populated by gay and lesbian African Muslim individuals who have immigrated to London or Kenya from Somalia, and who are not elite, nor are they jet-setting Afropolitans, or even "liberals" in the above senses—queer or otherwise. They are workers, students, refugees, dancers, writers, artists, and lovers; they are those for whom merely being tolerated is simply not enough. Furthermore, Osman intersects migration and sexuality, as there can be no "borderlines" in their secret garden—the implication being that, if there were borders, they would not own their own bodies or lives. This indicates the ways in which the policing of both movement and sexuality conscript people rather than free them.

I have shown that national and international systems of immigration and various national policies, discourses, and treatment of immigrants are not only racial, gendered, and classed in nature, but heteronormatively constituted as well. Like other scholars working within the burgeoning fields of queer diaspora and queer migration studies, I attend to the matter of whether or not heterosexual immigrants have different experiences from those diasporic subjects who desire alternatively and practice same-sex love. Global black LGBTQ authors and artists like Diriye Osman, Thomas Glave, Audre Lorde, and Shani Mootoo, as well as those with queer diasporic affinities like Maryse Condé, indeed picture a different kind of immigrant experience in addition to differential repressions in movement and in migrant communities elsewhere. I have detailed the ways in which Diriye Osman not only illustrates queer migrant experiences but, in doing so, rearticulates conceptions and practices of home and freedom that can reshape Western notions from within by drawing upon black radical and international writers from previous generations. I have also shown how contemporary African literature, including Osman's text and Nuruddin Farah's novel, speak to and challenge queer liberalism and liberal notions of toleration. Osman's *Fairytales* does indeed *matter* "the lives that have not mattered," as Judith Butler speaking on the #Blacklivesmatter movement puts it, and it names those who struggle "to matter in the way they deserve" ("What's Wrong with 'All Lives Matter'?").

ON THE IMPERIAL ORIGINS OF IMMIGRATION IN NADIFA MOHAMED'S *BLACK MAMBA BOY* AND CLAUDE MCKAY'S *BANJO*

"A hyena-rich darkness covered the town and Jama could feel Jinns and half-men at his back stalking the alleys, making the hairs on his neck stand on end. . . . Jama felt the impending bloodshed sizzle in the air and rubbed down the tiny hairs on his lower spine as they nervously stood up, as if they were frightened conscripts standing to attention before a bloodied old general" (Mohamed, *Black Mamba Boy*, 58). As I mention in chapter 1, these sentences highlight the tension in the Horn of Africa during its colonial period and portend the bloodshed on the African continent by a European war. They foreshadow Jama's own conscription by the Italian army in Somalia as an "askari" or black soldier, so it is no accident that Mohamed uses the term *conscript* metaphorically. In this chapter I show how Jama is already conscripted by colonial structures and systems of immigration in the high imperial era. I reveal how imperial systems of immigration and its apparatuses like passports, documents, or checkpoints, interdict, redirect, and reeducate that very dispersal of people in and through colonial technologies managing movement. Mohamed's narrative indeed unfolds upon the very conditions set by the Berlin conference in the late nineteenth century, where heads of Europe divided up Africa amongst themselves, imposing arbitrary borders and building the infrastructures that would manage those borders and the people who would cross them: "His land had been carved up among France, Italy, Britain, and Abyssinia . . . The British had built the road to ease their passage into and out of their possession, and now Jama trundled along it, making slow progress toward the artificial border between Somaliland and Djibouti" (77–78). Here, British roads, borders, and infrastructure, all imposed or "artificial," shape Jama's movement. Again Jama is not simply a conscript of the Italian colonial army; he is a conscript of migration.

Mohamed's novel is a semi-biographical account of Mohamed's Father—Jama—as a young boy and his journey to find *his* father, taking him across and between the Horn of Africa, the Middle East, Sudan, North Africa, and Europe, including a brief sojourn in Palestine. The narrative begins in tandem with the rise of Italian colonialism in Africa and its invasion of Ethiopia in 1935. Jama's mother migrates from Somalia to work in a coffee factory in Aden, Yemen, after Jama's father, her husband Guure, leaves for Sudan to find work as a driver for the "ferengis"—an Arabic term for white Westerners—referring to white British colonial soldiers. The novel opens in Aden, Yemen, a diasporic port city and nodal point of colonialism and global capitalism. As the itinerant Jama wanders into the coffee factory that his mother works in, "the smell of tea, coffee, frankincense, myrrh swept up the hill and swathed him in a nauseating, heady mix" (9).

> As Jama reached the first warehouse, bare-chested coolies chanted while they pushed heavy wooden crates onto the backs of lorries. After standing outside Al-Medina Coffee Stores for a moment, Jama walked through the stone entrance and peered into the darkness. Sunlight splintered through the roof, illuminating the dust rising from the coffee beans as they were tossed to loosen the husks. A field of underpaid women in bright, flowery Somali robes were bent over the baskets full of beans, spreading them on a cloth and removing stunted ones before the coffee was exported. (9)

South Yemen had been a British colony since 1839 and thus Aden would have still been under British rule in *Black Mamba Boy*'s 1930s. The British East India Company, also present since the seventeenth century, would have installed coffee factories like the one Jama's mother works in.[1] Although it is unclear as to whether Ambaro, Jama's mother, is employed in a British-controlled coffee factory, her workplace represents a microcosm of the imperial order of things and cannot be disentangled from the colonialism's global project or its vast reach regarding international trade and conquest. Aden was a port city partly because it represented a halfway point between Britain and its "crown jewel" colony, India; it was therefore one of many centers on a grid of global capital.[2]

There are three important points in the above passage that illustrate Mohamed's phenomenological descriptions of movement and migration in the novel: 1) The passage describes commodities to be exported from the Global South (a context narrated from the perspective of Africa and Yemen), to the North via colonial structures already in place, such as factories exploiting labor like the one above, or shipping routes and roads (both economic and military). Here, the conditions producing the possibilities of the narrative cannot be separated from the never-setting sun of colonialism. 2) The workers' bright flowery robes metonymically represent the Somali diaspora in Yemen—Mohamed had already described the port city as fundamentally diasporic: "Market boys of all different hues, creeds, and languages gathered at the beach to play, bathe, and fight" (7). In this way the narrative takes the condition of diaspora as its object. And, finally, 3) more specifically Mohamed's picture of the coffee factory is gendered as she describes fields of "underpaid women" providing the labor and surplus value upon which world capitalism thrives. This representation of women in the diaspora not only corrects the absence of women from colonial histories and male-centered literature, it also strategically gestures toward our contemporary context of globalization in which workforces in the sweatshops of the Global South for example—neatly erased from filiation with transnational corporations in the North via creative use of subcontracting—are predominantly young women.

Movement indeed guides the passage: from the winnowing of the coffee beans that will then be moved to the port by the "bare-chested coolies" from India, where they will enter into the global circulation of commodities and capital, to the diasporic communities themselves having moved from Somalia or India to Aden and perhaps back again, always producing for the Global North, to Jama's own itinerant circulations around the city as the novel progresses. It is this kind of movement that Mohamed maps in her novel, what she elsewhere calls the "violence of dispersal,"[3] picturing not solely individuals who cross borders, the products of their labor, and the circulation of commodities but also and necessarily the technologies of power producing and managing migrant movement. For example, Mohamed embeds checkpoints, borders, and passports into her novel as a way to tell the story of imperial-era black migrants.

Mohamed's passage above demonstrates the articulation between the warmth and vibrancy of the diasporic port-city-slum and the violence of the global system constitutive of it. The "bare-chested coolies" slave away for the Global North pushing "heavy wooden creates on the backs of lorries." The picturesque description of Somali coffee women in bright flowery robes belies the execrable conditions under which they toil. The centripetal force of the colonial system holds Aden in its constellation just as the poetry of the passage itself is held together by the pull of the sentences describing the oppressing global forces at play—most immediately in terms of exports and "underpaid women" in Aden's "port the world goes through," to borrow Claude McKay's phrasing (*Banjo*, 46). In this chapter I argue that the aesthetic of nomadism in *Black Mamba Boy* offers a migrant-centered engagement with colonialism and pan-African communities that link the Horn of Africa to its points of contact in Africa and the world. Interestingly, Nadifa Mohamed weaves Claude McKay's wandering protagonist Banjo from his 1929 novel of the same name into her own twenty-first-century migritude novel; she harnesses his pan-African politics of vagabondage into an aesthetic of nomadism that, like *Banjo* before her, challenges the colonial management of immigration. I reveal the reason why she finds *Banjo* so important, arguing that it has something to do with McKay's own anticipation of migritude.

Urban Colonial Aden and Home to Hargeisa

The book opens with "the black planets of Jama's eyes [roaming] over Aden—industrial Steamer Point; Crater, the sandstone old town, its curvaceous dun-colored buildings merging into the Shum volcanoes" (*Black Mamba Boy*, 3). Aden's beauty exists in a tense relationship with its abject poverty, as Mohamed documents the working-class and poor in Aden's urban context. Jama and his friends as well as their parents are in many ways representative of those who live and move across the Global South: economic migrants, sailors in the port, the un- or underemployed, and those living in or between the shanty-towns, townships, or slums. Mohamed's Somali coffee women who migrate to Aden for economic reasons, illustrate urban entanglement with movement and the world. Ashley Dawson argues that "postcolonial scholars have been slow to address issues relating to urban space and society in the Global South," specifically slums that make up the mega-cities in the Global South like Lagos or Kolkata.[4] It is therefore necessary to delineate this first section of Mohamed's novel in Aden not just in terms of diaspora and movements of people between nations but as representing the patchwork of slums providing the backdrop to a narrative in which the movements of people are embedded within processes of colonialism, global capital, and urbanization. Slums across the Global South are a designed effect of the geography of colonialism and global capitalism, thus its subjects are already conscripted by particular conditions before they decide to move or not move; they are variously pulled or pushed, in other words.[5]

Transnational and diaspora studies emphasize travel or displacement across national boundaries, all too often at the expense of *intra*national movement. The translocal tableau opening *Black Mamba Boy* is devoted to Jama and his multiethnic and multicultural band of fellow perambulatory street urchins, some homeless, all poor. Picturing Aden's port neighborhood, the narrator describes "the black lava of the Shum Shum volcanoes loom[ing] over them when they reached the beach. Market boys of all hues, creeds, and languages gathered at the beach to play, bathe, and fight. They were a roll-call of infectious diseases, mangled limbs, and deformities" (7). The bustling multicultural beach is tempered by the persistent symptoms of poverty: disease, deformations, and mangled limbs. Somali migrant children make up the most impoverished and thus voiceless of the Yemeni population. "Indian kids, Jewish kids, and Yemeni kids all lived with their parents, however poor they might be. It was only the Somali children who ran around feral, sleeping everywhere and anywhere. Many of the Somali boys were children of single mothers working in the coffee factories, too tired after twelve hours of work to chase around after boisterous, hungry boys" (31). These vagabonds are "feral," boisterous, yet, as subalterns, voiceless and powerless. Jama's aunt, for example, persecutes her "guests" when she finds that, after taking them in, they would not be her servants as she had expected. "I'm not surprised Somalis have a bad reputation, the way some of these newcomers dress, all naked arms with their udders hanging out the sides" (12). Mrs. Islaweyne, despite being a distant relative, wields her "superior" class position as a weapon against her "dirty Somali" guests.

Jama responds by taking flight, living out-of-doors, sleeping on rooftops, and running with the other "little vagrants" of Aden. He also dreams of literal flight: "I would buy an airplane so I could fly through the clouds and come down to earth whenever I wanted to see a new place, Mecca, China, I would travel even farther, to Damascus and Ariwaliya, and just come and go as I wanted" (25). Like his erstwhile Father Guure, Jama has caught the spirit of the vagabond, and in Claude McKay's words again, was "gripped by the lust to wander."[6] Although the first section of Mohamed's novel in Aden merely sets the stage for Jama's epic journey to follow, it does the important work of connecting migration and movement to urban centers and to the global nodal points of capitalism and colonialism in the inter-war and World War II eras.

Jama returns to his aunt's house in Aden after hearing his mother has taken ill, only to find Ambaro on her death bed. His aunt refuses to pay for a doctor and so his mother dies after giving Jama her meager savings, which he promises he'll use to find his father in Sudan. He lives on the streets of Aden until he is called home to Hargeisa, Somalia, by his great aunt on his mother's side. Jama's "homecoming"—the shortest chapter in the novel—is not a modernist-return-from-exile narrative like those produced by earlier generations of African authors and their contemporary counterparts. From Chinua Achebe's *No Longer at Ease*, to Nuruddin Farah's *Links*, to Chimamanda Ngozi Adichie's *Americanah*, these authors focus on the pain of exile and the unease of return. Though Jama is too young to really know Hargeisa before he and Ambaro leave, there is an affective reaction to Somalia when he returns, whether generated through actual or imaginary connection to his homeland:

> Jama looked around him. Somaliland was yellow, intensely yellow, a dirty yellow, with streaks of brown and green. A group of men stood next to their herd of camels while the lorry over-heated, its metal grille grimacing under an acacia tree. There was no smell of food or incense or money drifting in the air as there was in Aden, there were no farms, no gardens, but there was a sharp sweetness he breathed in, something invigorating, intoxicating. This was his country, this was the same air his father and grandfathers had breathed, the same landscape that they had known. (48)

As in other returning-exile narratives, "home" is both foreign and familiar. Somaliland is not an urban center and so for Jama it doesn't smell like Aden, with its requisite smells of the compact lives of millions of people; foods, fish, incense, bodies, animals, and so on. But it is familiar, as it represents the land of Jama's ancestors; it is a place in which he breathes the same air as his family. However, Jama's homecoming is conspicuously brief (under twenty pages in the novel). This choice sets Mohamed's novel apart from a substantial number of works of African literature written in the past half century as it does not center upon a single return or exile. It also departs from other works as movement within Africa accounts for the majority of the novel whereas others like Imbolo Mbue's *Behold the Dreamers* focus on life in United States or European cities. Migration itself becomes the subject of her project and it is almost objectified as a matter of perception; Jama above provides almost a phenomenology of movement in miniature.

There is no homecoming, per se, in Hargeisa. Jama is alienated amongst his mother's clan, by whom he is viewed as an uncouth street urchin; and, despite finding thankless work carrying cow carcasses for a slaughterhouse, he is again forced leave his homeland after a dispute with his second cousin. Although Jama has made the decision to leave, "he only [knows] to walk away from Hargeisa . . . the desert terrified him, the silence, the boulders marking nomad's graves, the emptiness" (72). In lieu of a narrative of return, Mohamed writes a pan-African migritude novel narrating the reeducation of movement upon a hierarchical and global colonial grid while documenting the relationships between various and shifting groups of colonized people (she completed years' worth of research for the novel). Rather than the pain of one exile, the process of multiple and collective exiles are woven into her tapestry of movement. Take for example her portrait of Assab, Eritrea, an African port city in the novel. "The people were a ragbag of wanderers: Abyssinians looking for work, Yemeni fisherman following the shoals of the Red Sea, nomadic Afars with their teeth filed to points, Somalis on their way to somewhere else" (104). Mohamed's ragbag of wanderers illustrate the conscripted globality of the black migrant inextricable from the repressive colonial material conditions of reality they daily meet, and the burgeoning pan-African relationships fomenting between them often in response to the exploitative processes of European colonialism and racialized capitalism.

Conscripts of Migration

Black Mamba Boy shows that the anarchy of movement is traced upon the anarchy of empire. The majority of the novel tells the story of Jama's peripatetic journey (beginning in tandem with the 1935 Italian invasion of Ethiopia), around the Horn of Africa, Sudan, Egypt, then on to Palestine, France, Wales, and finally, the end of the novel leaves Jama on the cusp of a return to Eritrea. So Jama "only knew to walk away from Hargeisa." The narrator describes a post-Berlin conference scene subtending the first footsteps of Jama's journey as "his land had been carved up among France, Italy, Britain, and Abyssinia" (77). Italy had claimed Southern Somalia while Britain claimed the section above that. France took what is now Djibouti while Ethiopia (Abyssinia) conquered the ethnically Somali Ogaden area. But we will remember that new colonial roads reshape migrant routes. As Jama hitches a ride on a British lorry headed to Djibouti after leaving Hargeisa, the narrator again traces Jama's diasporic paths stenciled upon colonial routes: "the British had built the road to ease their passage into and out of their possession, and now Jama trundled along it, making slow progress toward the artificial border between Somaliland and Djibouti" (77–78). Evoking founding Négritude author Léopold Sédar Senghor's statement that "all borders are artificial,"[7] Mohamed meditates upon what she calls the violence of dispersal, begging the questions: To what extent does the violence of colonialism create dispersal? To what extent does the colonial interdiction of that very dispersal of peoples and things at or across borders represent a structure of violence?

The violence of colonialism creates dispersal, and in the same moment interdicts, redirects, and reeducates that very dispersal of peoples in and through technologies managing movement. My reading of the novel reveals this conscription. For example, as Jama rides on the lorry to Djibouti in the hopes of eventually getting to his father in Sudan, Mohamed pictures the structural colonial violence in the following passage in terms of the materiality of borders and European infrastructure, itself "picked up and dropped" onto its colony: in French Djibouti "European soldiers manned a checkpoint and were nearly taking apart the vehicles in search of smuggled goods . . . This town was conjured up from the fantasies of its conquerors, a home away from home despite the anti-European sentiment; a provincial French town picked up and dropped into the hottest place on earth" (81). Karim Mattar and David Fieni argue that "the checkpoint functions not only to control the flow of migrants, illicit goods, and insurgents/terrorists, but also to divide contiguous lands and to reproduce politically and legally encoded distinctions between 'us' and 'them.' Thus performing sovereignty, the checkpoint appears to be symptomatic of fears of catastrophe, whether economic, political, or social, in various national and global contexts" (qtd. in Apter, 106). If the colonial and postcolonial checkpoint is symptomatic of national anxiety about the Other beyond the pale, then borders themselves are symptoms of the European nation-state picked up and dropped onto "the hottest place on earth"—in this case, colonial Africa. Throughout the novel Mohamed depicts not only national borders and checkpoints in this sense but segregated cities and towns as well, such as the neighborhoods in Djibouti with French quarters and black shantytown counterparts. This follows for Italian- and British-controlled states.

National borders are striated by internal borders and checkpoints, shantytowns against neighborhoods, that under colonialism emit an apartheid-like hue. In French (read white) Djibouti, "palm trees grew by the side of the street, evenly placed out like guards. Buildings stood in the distance, with a style at odds with Somali or Adeni construction; they were curvaceous and tall, and built to last much longer than the edifices of the British in Hargeisa" (81). As Jama walks on and continues out of the pristine and "provincial" French neighborhood, which is interestingly "at odds" with

African architecture, he finds an entirely different scene: "the street came to life, market boys argued and fought, young mothers with chains of copper coins over their foreheads sat outside chatting as their babies slept. Old women shuffled around barefoot, discreetly begging . . . Jama sat under a palm tree and scanned around for another lorry, but he was in the heart of a vast shantytown" (81). Later in the narrative, for example when Jama reaches Asmara, Eritrea, the colonial Italian iteration of partition is pronounced. "After a few hours they finally reached the manicured avenues of Asmara. Everywhere new houses sparkled, the paint on them barely dry. Large Italian villas were painted in mouthwatering reds, corals, pinks, yellows . . . Jama looked around and all the shops were run by Europeans, the town seemed to belong to the fat-bellied men with upturned moustaches sitting outside the shops . . . The only Africans he could see were street cleaners" (109). One can imagine young Jama's wonderment at an Africa without Africans. And yet, that is precisely the contradiction that Mohamed's geography of apartheid shows.

Michela Wrong describes the violence of the colonial nation-state in Eritrea: "In Asmara, pride of Benito Mussolini's short-lived second Roman empire, the architects of the 1930s unleashed the full, incongruous force of their Modernistic creativity."[8] From Art Deco cinema "palaces" to "petrol stations that looked like aircraft in mid-flight," Asmara represented the folly of Italy's nation-building project in Africa that would culminate in apartheid (5). "In modern-day Eritrea," Wrong continues, "popular memory tends to divide the Italian colonial era into two halves; the Martini years, time of benign paternalism when Eritreans and Italians muddled along together well enough; and the fascist years, when the Italians introduced a series of racial laws as callous as anything seen in apartheid South Africa . . . the assumptions of biological determinism that came to form the bedrock of both Fascism and Nazism were present from the first days of the Italian presence in Africa," and one could argue, all nineteenth- and twentieth-century colonialism to a greater or lesser extent (45).

Black Mamba Boy chronicles colonial apartheid from Jama's and other Africans' perspectives, revealing a system in which its subjects are already conscripted: "The driver found the way to the African reservation and slowed down. 'Where do you want me to drop you off?' he asked. 'Farther down, where the Somalis are'" (110). The term "reservation" eerily suggests the non-humanness of Africans from the perspective and practice of the colonists. Like the British concentration camps in Kenya during "the Emergency" poignantly depicted in Ngũgĩ Wa Thiong'o's *A Grain of Wheat*, *Black Mamba Boy* echoes Fanon's description (and Césaire's before that) of colonialism itself as Manichean. The violence of colonialism interdicts, reifies, and hierarchizes sociality, as seen above, and at the same time creates dispersal and migration, while redirecting and revaluing the movement of peoples and things. In this way, colonialism in the high-imperial era can be analyzed as a structure of violence whose function, above all, is the production and management of movement. It is through movement itself that Jama becomes a conscript of migration, yet, these conditions prefigure his movement.

Although Jama's geographical errantry provides narrative thrust to the novel, it is precisely those things that stop him—borders, lack of papers or passports, and always already segregated colonial infrastructures—that proffer a postcolonial perspective. After being conscripted as an askari in the losing Italian army, under which he is consistently subject to racism and squalid conditions at the hands of the ferengi soldiers, he sets off again toward Egypt in search of more gainful employment as a sailor on British ships. As Jama travels north through Sudan toward Egypt, he is met with the contradictory materiality of the artificial constructs called borders: "Crowds were walking toward the station, where uniformed policemen stopped and searched them. Jama had never needed identification before, he had no paper saying who he was and where he belonged, but from now on, his abtiris would not be enough to prove his identity. In this society you were a nobody unless you had been anointed with a stamp by a bureaucrat" (215). His abtiris, a list of his grandfather's names—a sort of memorized genealogy of kinship—no longer suffices as an identity marker within Fanon's Manichean world of the colonizer and colonized, which prescripts Jama as an Other, a non-citizen, and thus a criminal to be deported.

Though Jama circumvents the police and Wadi Halfa terminal by walking into Egypt along the banks of Lake Nasser, he is soon caught in Alexandria: "At the end of the interrogation the policeman told Jama that he would be deported back to Sudan and banned from entering Egypt again. . . . the whole carriage was full of Somalis who had also entered Egypt illegally, all roamers who had known only porous insubstantial borders and were now confronted with countries caged behind bars" (225). Jama is furious at this construction of otherness and remarks that "he hadn't left Gerset just to be treated like dirt again," as they are deported to a Palestinian border town (225). Jama's bewilderment in the passage above intimates the imaginariness of the nation form mapped onto the geographical area of North Africa, while his anger announces the violent materiality of borders, passport checks, and imprisonment or deportations that Africans are subjected to. What is interesting about this description is that it not only asks us to question the supposed "illegality" of diasporic movement, insofar as the narrative names a foreign legal structure arbitrarily imposed upon a peoples and their geographical area, but also metaphorizes the concept of the nation itself as a "cage . . . behind bars."

The narrative therefore produces a transnational phenomenology of the nation. It historicizes and problematizes the violence of both the nation form as well as its concept and the ways in which it produces subjects via structures of immigration—exclusion, inclusion, citizenship, right to mobility, etc. It accomplishes this through assessing Jama's own affective perception of the nation, and its objects that press upon him, as an object of analysis itself (what Husserl calls the mental content of perception, which is always directed at something). A town crier in Omhajer, Eritrea, for instance, calls into question colonial property rights as shaping the being-in-the-world of the colonized, which in this context essentially sweeps away any native rights, expropriating resources, land, and even animals for the Europeans. This creates dispersal, refugees, and catalyzes economic migration, at the same moment that it legislates not just property, but the right to move. The town crier laments to a crowd that, "'all possessions held by the natives of Italian East Africa will be adjudicated by colonial legislators . . . O people hear me, they are telling us we own nothing, and we cannot kill a thing for our mouths without asking them first.' The crowd laughed uncertainly" (147). European liberal property rights, beginning with John Locke's statement that land or raw materials mixed with labor equal property, are only observed in the African context with an absolute bias toward Europeans, illustrating the arbitrary and violent dispossession of human rights afforded natives causing, as the novel shows, almost chaotic transmigrations.[9]

The following passage, however, narrativizes black resistance to white power, showing that white power constructs itself dialectically in terms of masters and slaves, which then creates migration: "A group of [askaris] disguised themselves as Sudanese traders and snuck off in a truck, pissed off with the Italians and their stupid white-man, black-man laws. They want you to step into the gutter when they approach, say master this, master that . . . The longer you stay the less of a man you become" (123). We will remember Fanon's statement that "the 'thing' which has been colonized becomes man during the same process by which it frees itself" from colonial apartheid.[10] As soon as the askaris toss away the racist labels of colonialism and leave—"the longer you stay the less of a man you become"—human being and anti-colonial resistance become possible. The thematic of anti-colonial resistance is situated within the larger context of migration and movement, highlighting the ways in which the colonial production and management of movement variously conscripts its African subjects.

The Practice of Diaspora

Mohamed's book is a sophisticated anti-colonial critique of the violence of dispersal. But in addition, *Black Mamba Boy* shares a certain "diaspora-ness" with 1920s and 1930s pan-Africanist writers, Négritude authors, and specifically, Claude McKay's wandering protagonist, the eponymous Banjo from his 1929 novel *Banjo*, which I detail at the end of the chapter. Migration, diaspora, errantry, and nomadism constitute an identity for Jama, helping him negotiate questions of Somaliness. Jama's friend Jibreel relates to Jama later in the narrative that "Everywhere I go I meet Somalis, always from the north, standing at the crossroads, looking up to the sky for direction . . . I think there are more Somalis at the bottom of the sea or lost in the desert than there are left in our land" (281). On October 30, 2013, eighty-seven sub-Saharan African migrants perished in Niger's Sahara desert. They were heading either to Europe or North Africa, most likely as economic migrants.[11] Just a few weeks before this incident, on October 3, 2013, a ship carrying Eritrean migrants ("refugees," to be more specific in this case) capsized near the small Italian Island of Lampedusa. This is a regular occurrence if one pays attention to international news. Over 350 people drowned that night. Matthias Schwartz, reporting on the "Lampedusa Tragedy," notes that what was exceptional about this case was not the number of dead migrants, since "in the past twenty years, more than twenty-thousand immigrants have died on their way to Europe," but that the ship sank just over 1,000 yards from land. An Eritrean priest named Father Mussie Zerai muses sadly that the tragedy "seemed like a manifestation of Europe's approach to African migration—a hardening of its borders coupled with a disturbing indifference to human life" (qtd. in Schwartz, 78). Jibreel's description above of Somalis in movement, whether migrants or refugees, is not simply a romantic metaphor for those wayward souls who cross borders, but an accurate and tragic depiction of the everyday material realities for those Somalis and African migrants from the greater Global South who move due to various colonial, postcolonial, and global factors. In this sense the violence of dispersal is literal. And yet dispersals, diasporas, and the nomadic also figure dialectically into identity formation.

In response to Jibreel's musings, Jama responds: "It's because we are no-mads, land is the same to us everywhere we go, we only care if there is food and water to be found" (281). Somali writer Yasmeen Maxamuud's recent novel narrating the Somali diaspora in America during and after the Somali civil war is called *Nomad Diaries*, which is suggestive of both narration (the writing of a diary) and Somali identity in movement (the nomadic). At a reading in New York, Nadifa Mohamed characterized Somalis as nomadic and, albeit somewhat facetiously, quipped "[we're] not used to borders and passports" ("Black Mamba Boy: Reading and Discussion with Nadifa Mo-hamed"). Mohamed's remark might be read as an essentializing yet strategic move that offers a nomadic alternative to colonial Being.[12] For Jama, Somali-ness is movement, necessarily antithetical to the cage-like state formations endemic of European colonialism.

The concept-aesthetic of nomadism Mohamed adopts as a challenge to the colonial management of movement and its geography is paralleled by one of her contemporaries, Djiboutian migritude writer Abdourahman A. Waberi. Waberi reframes pan-Africanism and Négritude within his own meditations on the violence of dispersal in the Horn of Africa in his 2003 novel *Transit*, which was translated from its original French in 2012. One of the central narrators, Alice, mobilizes nomadism as a response to police brutality during independence struggles of the 1970s and beyond: "It is impossible for the police to contain the movement, its life, its protuberances, its transformations, its desires and its new needs, which come from afar, from very far. Silence, exile, and cunning. Crossing and re-crossing borders that make no sense for anyone; a surge of nomadic life, mobility, cooperation, exchange, sharing, the power to annoy" (77). In addition to *the* movement, movement itself subtends challenges to state power. The surge of nomadic life in this sense exists in excess of, and as a challenge to, the violence of imposed colonial borders that "make no sense for anyone." Perhaps taking up a nomadic critique of the United States might offer an alternative mode of being and a challenge to the hardened borders of white nationalism, Islamophobia, and anti-immigrant rhetoric and discourse in the Trump era.

Waberi's *Transit* opens present-day in Roissy Airport in France as the main characters—also from Djibouti—witness a sort of African deportation pipe-line from France to Africa: "ROISSY. Air France. Daily flight to Saint-Denis de la Réunion [on the island of Réunion next to Madagascar], via Cairo and Djibuti" (5). The flight from France to its former colony (which became an "overseas department" in 1946) enacts the quotidian condition of postcoloni-ality for migrants in France and shows how structures of immigration work.

Our narrator notes that it is "boarding time for the Africans being deported 'of their own free will'" (5). The ironic French double-speak in this passage, representing official French language on immigration policy, mirrors the colonial discourse represented in *Black Mamba Boy* couching oppression in terms of freedom. "Today's deportee is a Congolese, supposedly a shopkeeper from Pointe Noire, and his fate seems to be sealed" (6). However, the well-worn routine reenacted is this: the deportees create a scene on the plane, which makes the tourists uncomfortable, which in turn causes the pilot to ask security to escort said deportees off the plane and back to the "retention center in the waiting zone of the airport. At least he's alive," muses our narrator, he is "luckier than the ones who die of dehydration in the Arizona desert or freeze to death inside the undercarriage of some cargo plane" (5). Here, Waberi references the publicized story of two young Guinean boys who died in the undercarriage an airplane headed from Africa to Brussels in 1998 and a note found on one of their bodies pleading for European aid to Africa.[13] This heartbreaking image, however, becomes symbolic of the everyday dangers and death that migrants and refugees face. In addition, Waberi references the US context and the border between the United States and Mexico—migrants dying in the "Arizona desert." The US border was a crisis well before Trump's both maligned and celebrated policy of separating children from their parents beginning mid-2018, which drew comparisons to both Nazi prison camps and summer camps for migrant children. Like Teju Cole's interactive Twitter poem about the border and Mexican immigration to the United States titled "A Piece of the Wall,"[14] Waberi parses global systems managing movement to and from the Global South pointing toward the violence of dispersal. To reiterate an earlier point, these stories differ somewhat drastically from elite cosmopolitan or Afropolitan narratives of travel, race, and identity.

Waberi's identification of nomadic identity—always already "mixed"—challenges the white supremacist rhetoric of apartheid, Brexit, and Trump's Muslim ban, which was upheld by the US Supreme Court in June 2018. Abdo-Julien again muses: "All blood is mixed and all identities are nomadic, Maman, would have said, talking about me, Papa, herself, or the whole wide world. This business of mixed blood is a very old story, she would add, raising her voice—so old the first traces of African migration in the Italian peninsula, to give just one example, date from the conquest and the fall of Carthage" (*Transit*, 26). Like Mohamed's nomadic wanderers in *Black Mamba Boy*, Alice's (Maman's) use of nomadism does not align simply with the ethnic nomads wandering the Horn of Africa but the wandering and mixing of "blood" itself, of movement.

In Mohamed's novel, when Jama and his fellow travelers meet an old Somali man at a bus station in Gaza, the narrator describes a shared sense of physiognomy as markers of movement: "They shared with him the same mishmash of features, an awkward alchemy of eyes, noses, mouths, hair textures, and skin tone that belonged to different continents but somehow came together. Their faces were passports inscribed with the stamps of many places but in their countenances was something ancient, the variety of those who went wandering and peopled the earth" (232). Jama and the old man share a kinship in the textures of their faces, signifying their Somaliness, yet it is just as symptomatic of Somaliness that they meet outside of Somalia, that they are of those variety of people who "went wandering." Further, it is important to mark Mohamed's complex distinction between faces and countenances, passports on the one hand, and the ontological genealogy of those nomadic souls, the nomads' abtiris, on the other. Faces here signify an external map weathered upon the traveler's face telling a story of his or her journey. This is contemporary and ontic, to use Heidegger's terminology. Passports are a symptom of colonialism and the modern nation-state. Countenance, by contrast, which expresses mood or character, is temporal and ontological, and indicates the being and temporality of those who went wandering and their diasporic genealogy. Countenance in this sense contrasts the shallowness of a passport in that it represents an ontology or way of being-in-the-world.[15]

Although Somali features can be recognized, Mohamed's biological metaphor in terms of shared facial features suggests that what makes Somalis Somali is not a unique biological origin of sameness but, like Waberi's nomad in *Transit*, mixing and difference (sameness *in* difference). In other words, the alchemy of features from different continents and different peoples constitutes what is shared between Jama and the old man, not a shared set of nationally recognizable features corresponding to the geographical location of the state (the ideal of the nation-state). Somalia is relatively unified in terms of culture and language, but this passage does not (nor does the novel) suggest that national chauvinism therefore follows. Mohamed's face/countenance complex marks an implicit critique of the ideal of the nation-state and an explicit engagement with the being-in-the-world of the black nomad via her literary phenomenology of movement.

Countenance can also denote a facial expression or meaning disseminated by the arrangement of features, a kind of expression *of* something, not in terms of voice but of communication, signification, or meaning-making. Here, it is the representation of "something ancient," something ontological. Countenance as described by the narrator in *Black Mamba Boy* represents the bringing into being of the black migrant, already conscripted by colonialism, through the genealogy of "those who went wandering," the "contemporary nomad" or vagabond, who exists in Mohamed's novel in a both locally specific and transnational way. In other words, the *Somali* nomad, moving upon colonial routes and global structures, bears the mark of both symptoms of colonial structures of violence identified upon the face as well as the more ontologically deep affective *abtiris* or genealogy subtending, and expressed through, countenance.

Brent Edwards has also theorized movement and diaspora in terms of the body, specifically the African diaspora and constitutive difference, using the joint as a metaphor for the ways in which difference actually constitutes the diaspora and allows for its movement: "But the joint is a curious place, as it is both the point of separation (the forearm from the upper arm, for example) and the point of linkage . . . it is exactly such a haunting gap that allows the African diaspora to 'step' and 'move' in various articulations."[16] Though Edwards's object here is black internationalism in the twenties and thirties and the various translations between groups and languages therein, his notion of articulation and difference helps unpack Mohamed's literary depictions of Somaliness in *Black Mamba Boy*. There is a linkage between the three Somalis, the mishmash of features making a distinctly Somali face, and a difference or separation—that the *métissage* of features cull from different continents. To this transnational play of sameness and difference, consider also Awrala's statement earlier in the novel. Awrala is a Somali woman living in Eritrea who houses Jama at one point during his journey. When Jama asks her if she will return to Somalia; she replies: "Why should I? I'm not Somali anymore. The place where you are born is not necessarily the best place for you, boy. I've got too used to the rain, hills, and cool air of Asmara. I'll be buried here" (113). Nationality is seemingly conflated with place, and being buried after one's death represents the ultimate bodily identification with land and place (if one is lucky enough to have a choice in the matter). Perhaps Awrala's leaving Somalia is indeed what contradicts her statement that "I'm not Somali anymore" since movement itself, nomadism, and leaving in *Black Mamba Boy*—and much of Somalian literature itself—is often what *is* Somali.

Yet Awrala's narrative suggests a postcolonial critique of the nation-state, identity, and the violence of dispersal. Awrala is a migrant coming to Eritrea as a young girl from Somalia with her father. She farms with him and, as happened to many during the colonial period, they are subsequently dispossessed of their land by the Italian colonists. She is now "cleaning Italian villas" (112). Though she remains connected to and invested in the Somali diaspora, as evidenced in her care for and interest in the itinerant Jama, she adopts Asmara as home. Further, she expressly disidentifies with the Somali nation or motherland—"I'm not Somali anymore"—reflecting not simply a separation but a link as well. Also consider the moment in prominent Somali author Nuruddin Farah's novel *Maps* in which protagonist Askar's uncle Hilaal philosophizes on identity and the Ogaden war: He tells Askar that "Somalis went to war in order that the ethnic origin of the people of Ogaden would match their national identity . . . Imagine, Askar. A nation with a split personality!"[17] Using (regrettably) pathological terms, Hilaal essentially describes the ideal of the nation-state in which a people who share a language, culture, and ethnic origin also share a political entity in which borders represent an outward manifestation of essential geographical boundaries. Imperial Ethiopia, in this case, colonized the Ogaden area of Somalia (not to mention Eritrea). Since the people of Ogaden are ethnically Somali, for Hilaal, they should not be governed by the "foreign" Ethiopian state. This appears to be an argument against all colonization, yet it is one that accepts the (European) structure and idea of statehood *tout court*.

Awrala would experience cognitive dissonance, holding two or more contradictory beliefs or values at once, since the "national identity" of Eritrea (ethnically Tigrinyan) does not match up with her Somali ethnic origin. Yet she immediately discards this framework as she implies that one can, and sometimes should, cross into or between national identities: "The place where you are born is not necessarily the best place for you," the "you" here seemingly movable as she identifies as Eritrean. Asmara's transnational *you* proposes the following question: if the nation-state itself is a colonial construct and thus imposed from the "outside," wouldn't it always create dissonance in the colonized or formerly colonized world both structurally and psychically? What does it do to the colonizers, as Frantz Fanon once asked? Jama's own luck with borders, themselves predicated upon the violence of exclusion, illustrates the not always salutary machinations of the nation. Riffing on Fanon's work analyzing the psychological alienation stemming from what he calls the violence of the Manichean and compartmentalized colonial world Farah, Mohamed, and Waberi extend this critique to the idea and practice of the nation resonant in both the colonial and postcolonial world. Awrala's affective identification echoes Fanon's own adoption of, and identification with, Algeria—though originally Martiniquean, he proclaims "we Algerians" in *Wretched of the Earth*.

A dissonant subject-position or ontology such as Askar's or Awrala's, or even Fanon's, if we can call it that, although a "nervous condition" seems promising as it denotes an ontological positionality that precludes the violence of ethnic nationalisms or chauvinisms—what Ray in *Banjo* calls "the poisonous seed" of patriotism—and promotes an openness to others and other places as well as movement: "The vagabond lover of life," muses Ray, "finds individuals and things to love in many places and not any one nation . . . patriotism hides the beauty of other horizons" (*Banjo*, 137). But what it also suggests is that modernity (and its Western emblem, the nation-state), is predicated upon managing and reeducating—conscripting—the movements of the colonized, people of color, or more generally the peoples of the Global South. It illustrates the creation and production of what has come to be termed the "immigrant" in the world.

Like McKay's *Banjo*, Mohamed's *Black Mamba Boy* illustrates and interrogates the being-in-the-world of the migrant, laying bare the assemblage of structures conditioning and producing the "immigrant." Passports, borders, checkpoints, moments of exclusion and inclusion, and nationality itself are each tied not only to the machinations of capitalism and empire, but to the production of the immigrant. In the following scene, Jama is finally granted a passport near the end of the narrative. And though it affords him slightly better opportunities, it illustrates his embeddedness within this global and asymmetrical system. Again, his "abtiris was no longer sufficient":

Name: Jama Guure Mohamed
Date of Birth: 1/1/1925
Eyes: Brown
Hair: Black
Complexion: Man of Colour
Nationality: British
Place of Birth: Hargeisa (242)

"This thin description of Jama in the dark green passport was all the Western world needed to know about him; he was subject of the British Empire. The passport determined where he could go and where he couldn't, the ports where his cheap labor would be welcome and where it would not" (242). Jama's nomadic narrative shows that the materiality of immigration in laws, passports, checkpoints, etc., are tightly interwoven with the production of cheap labor through colonialism and racial capitalism—"his cheap labor" is welcome in certain places and not in others. His body is monitored, categorized, and his movement biopolitically reeducated through colonial structures and routes. That he is *subject* indeed shows his subject-position which, like other black migrants and nomadic wanderers, is monitored and policed in terms of movement, where he can go is based upon where his cheap labor is needed; where it is not, he is not. Like his unlucky friend Mahmoud, who gets deported from Port Said, Egypt seven times—"each time I walk they pick me up, I walk, they pick me up; my feet were cut to shreds!"—Jama is subject to national rules managing movement and populations not their own.

But conscription is never absolute. Shadowing, yet marking an alternative to, colonial structures of movement and interdiction are indeed what Mohamed's narrator calls "old nomad's network[s]" where in the urban center of Alexandria, Egypt, groups of Somali diasporics help each other out in terms of finding work or shelter. Like the Somali "coffee women" in Aden, these groups exist within colonial structures but on the margins, unofficial, beneath or above, and liminal. In some ways these groups are formed specifically to circumvent colonial structures such as borders by using fake passports or papers; denizens circulate knowledge in terms of how to negotiate various systems, or who to seek out or not, and so on. This nomadic network represents organic resistance arising out of and against the violence of dispersal and containment—of conscription.

From *Banjo* to *Black Mamba Boy*

In New York City in 2012, Nadifa Mohamed gave a reading celebrating the release of her most recent work *Black Mamba Boy*. Interlocutor Peter Hitchcock asked the Somali-British writer about her reference to Claude McKay's *Banjo* in the acknowledgments to her novel, and she responded that for her, *Banjo* represents the black pan-African experience during the colonial era of her father and other black nomadic working-class seamen, drifters, and immigrants. Indeed McKay's classic text, set in the "Ditch" area of the "great port" city Marseille, is thoroughly pan-African and yet migrant, as evinced in the following passage: "All shades of Negroes came together there. Even the mulattoes took a step down from their perch to mix in . . . But the magic had brought them all together to jazz and drink red wine, white wine, sweet wine. All the British West African blacks, Portuguese blacks, American blacks, all who had drifted into this port that the world goes through" (45–46). In the Senegalese-owned bar in the Ditch, the eponymous Banjo strums an old "Aframerican" tune on his banjo, Papa Charlie Jackson's "Shake That Thing," and dreams of starting a "black orchestra" with his fellow black diasporic vagabonds.[18] What McKay ultimately suggests is that it is not "magic" that brings this transnational community of blacks together (though magic is created there) but the global system of racialized capitalism, particularly as it is subtended by institutions controlling migration: passport control, documentation, imposed borders, and the construction of citizenship, each element skillfully embodied in McKay's "port the world goes through."

Toward the end of the narrative of *Black Mamba Boy*, Jama, after having lived through the perils of immigration and war in in the 1930s and 1940s, receives a British passport and finds work as a stoker on a British steamship. Jama stops in Marseille, France and is subsequently thrust into McKay's world of "the Ditch" where, in a particularly joyful intertextual move, McKay's characters from *Banjo* appear in Mohamed's novel. The narrator of *Black Mamba Boy* describes Jama and his friends as they end up

> in the seedy Ditch, in an African bar run by a Senegalese man. An American named Banjo sat by them and played wild songs, "Jelly Roll," "Shake That Thing," "Let My People Go." Jama danced Kunama-style to the strange music and the bar filled with black sailors from the West Indies, United States, South America, West Africa, and East Africa. Banjo introduced them to his friends Ray, Dengel, Goosey, Bugsy, and a pretty Abyssinian girl called Latnah, and Jama smiled as he shook their hands, wondering if Bethlehem would believe that there were Habashi girls in France. (254)

Here Mohamed recalls the promise of black transnational relationships in the 1920s and 1930s, that "magic" that McKay evokes opening *Banjo*. These relationships were forged upon and against the structures or paths of colonialism and thus constitute a politics as well as an affiliation, also depicted in *Banjo*. Interestingly, Mohamed adds to the musical repertoire of *Banjo*'s beach boys in *Black Mamba Boy*, as they do not play "Let My People Go" in McKay's original. This signifies not a misremembering but a strategic illustration of *Banjo*'s emancipatory politics by using a placeholder in the African American spiritual, working here as a nodal point anchoring the discourse of black liberatory struggle. That is, "Go Down Moses" becomes a trope or image in the black diaspora easily mobilized as an emancipatory gesture. Mohamed's pan-African "(mis)translation" indeed shares the emancipatory spirit of McKay's original while updating it, in one way, by connecting the Horn of Africa to radical African American liberation struggles.

Furthermore, Latnah in McKay's version is not Ethiopian but ethnically indeterminate. She has olive skin, and Malty, a West Indian, confesses: "I don't know if she is Arabian or Persian or Indian. She knows all landwiges" (*Banjo*, 10). McKay's Latnah was born in Aden to either a Sudanese or Ethiopian mother and an unknown father, likely Middle Eastern or South Asian. So why does Mohamed place McKay's prostitute polyglot's origin squarely in Ethiopia, which on the surface appears to limit the import of McKay's original racial creolization? For one, it is possible that Mohamed gestures toward another black transnational nodal point in Ethiopia which, from Blyden's citation of the biblical "and Ethiopia shall stretch out her hand unto God" as a pan-Africanist rallying call, to Haile Selassie and the outcry in the African diaspora against the Italian invasion of Ethiopia beginning *Black Mamba Boy*, represents another meaningful discursive marker in the black diaspora and Africa.

For Europeans in the pre-colonial epochs, Ethiopia represented all of Africa and all Africans were called Ethiopians, while in the colonial and post-colonial eras Ethiopia symbolized anti-colonial African struggle. However, early on in the narrative of *Black Mamba Boy*, Somalis in Aden discuss African American reactions to Italy's invasion of Ethiopia in seemingly startling ways: "'Colored Americans raise money in churches but the rest of the world looks on' . . . [exclaims one Somali] 'Good! They turned their gaze when the Abyssinians stole our land in Ogaden, handed over to them by the stinking English. If the Habashis can take our ancestral land then let the Ferengis take theirs'" (33). Far from an aggrandizement of Ethiopia as representative of "Africa" in anti-colonial struggle, Ethiopia gets called out, from a Somali perspective, as the semi-imperial power that it is.

Perhaps more importantly, Mohamed's depiction of Latnah conforms to her political and aesthetic project of representing African women in diasporas. Therefore it becomes important that, among McKay's cohort of transnational black males, the lone woman in his text be recuperated as an African migrant woman in hers. Mohamed's text indeed represents communities of African migrant women in diaspora, from the Somali coffee women in Aden, to migrant women like Awrala, to her iteration of Latnah and the other "Habashi girls" in France. And her more recent novel, *The Orchard of Lost Souls*, tells the stories of three Somali women from three different generations. The subtle shift in focus or meaning, from *Banjo* to *Black Mamba Boy*, is suggestive of the ways in which migritude writers both borrow from the politics of early twentieth-century-century pan-Africanist thought and literature and depart from it, shift, or mistranslate its meanings for tactical effect, essentially updating the black radical and transnational politics of that epoch to their own, or again as Dongala phrases it, from Négritude to migritude.

One final moment of (mis)translation stands out: On a British ship Jama notices that Sidney, a fellow working-class seaman, who is white, has a picture of a "yellow hammer and sickle on a red background" in his cabin in addition to posters of naked women (264). "'It means,'" Sidney explains to Jama referring to his communist flag, that "'I believe workers like you'—he poked his finger in Jama's chest for emphasis and then pointed at himself—'and me should unite, together, understand?' His fingers were now knotted, caressing one another. The smile fell from Jama's face. The intertwined fingers meant only one thing and he didn't want that, but what about the naked women, perhaps they were just to disguise Sidney's real intention?" (264). This comical moment of cultural mistranslation in which a white Marxist friend's political ideals signified in his gesture of "uniting" workers is misunderstood by Jama, who takes them as sexual in nature and as a possible romantic advance upon him by Sidney. The white sailor's interracial internationalism is clearly aligned with the ideology set forth in the novel, as *Black Mamba Boy* represents poor, working-class, migrant, and refugee populations (specifically African) instead of bourgeois, wealthy, or Afropolitan classes. However, there is a gap or *décalage*, to use Edwards's term, as Sidney's meaning wanders in translation and ultimately eludes Jama. But for Edwards this mode of articulation as misunderstanding is representative of colonial-era black internationalism between black groups and black and white groups, not exceptional. Internationalism, particularly African internationalism, indeed works this way in stops and starts, with breaks in the flow of meaning. And although Jama misses this particular radically internationalist signifier as a suspiciously sexualized gesture, for him there are "enough humane ferengis to make life interesting" (264).

Black Mamba Boy, like *Transit* and to a lesser extent *Banjo*, can be read as a refugee narrative. The Somalis in Aden, displaced black soldiers of all armies, dislocated villages, towns and cities ruined by the violence of colonialism and war, or the Somalis at the bottom of the sea, are refugees in one way or another. But what is perhaps most interesting given its cultural and geographical coordinates is that Nadifa Mohamed also tells the story of the Jewish refugees of *Exodus 1947*. Jama's ship docks just offshore of Palestine in 1947: "Five hundred gunners of the British marines stood longside tanks, trucks, military jeeps, their guns aimed at a broken-down steamship renamed *Exodus 1947* and the unruly Jews on board it. Four thousand refugees were trying to force open the British quota into Palestine and were in sight of the promised land" (247). The narrator's *mise-en-scène* pictures the treatment of the refugees by the British: "Jama came on deck during this festival of violence, and he had never believed white people could treat each other with such open violence" (261). I am interested not so much in the historical details of whether the *Aliyah Bet* ("illegal immigration fleet") was warranted or not—given Israel's abominable treatment of Palestinians and African refugees, essentially creating its own apartheid—but rather the fact that the reader is made to empathize with refugees and immigrants of all races, and that this scene is narrated from the particular perspective of a colonized African. I also suggest that this is a pan-Africanist move, like one that had been made by Olaudah Equiano much earlier in and through his paralleling of the African and Jewish diasporas. In his 1789 *The African: The Interesting Narrative of the Life of Olaudah Equiano* he sees a "strong analogy" between his native countrymen of West Africa stolen from their homes during the reign of the transatlantic slave trade and the Jewish diaspora. This analogy "even by this sketch imperfect as it is, appears to prevail in the manners and customs of my countrymen and those of the Jews, before they reached the Land of Promise . . . an analogy which alone would induce me to think that the one people had sprung from the other."[19] E. W. Blyden also uses this comparison. For Equiano and Blyden, this association with the Jewish diaspora gives weight to the African one in a biblical-liberal humanist sense and creates new resonance with Mohamed's use of "Go Down Moses."

Mohamed's 2010 text indeed humanizes dehumanized groups: black migrants, refugees, African women in the diaspora, nomads, and other groups. Somalis themselves have been dehumanized historically and in the present: from United States military interventions to depictions of starving children and Somali pirates or the most recent attempt by the Trump administration to smear Somali immigrant communities in Minnesota, and his "Muslim ban" which excludes everyone from Somalia. On the same day that saw the election of Donald Trump, Ilhan Omar was elected as the first-ever Somali-American legislator in that selfsame Minnesota. Mohamed's picture of Somalis is a sympathetic and realistic one, an answer perhaps to the latest Hollywood engagement with Somalia (after *Black Hawk Down*) in Tom Hank's 2013 *Captain Phillips*, a grossly ignorant picture of Somalia. But the nomadic humanism in *Black Mamba Boy* is also an engagement with the project of Somali literature itself. Consider Nuruddin Farah's *Links*, which in the following passage also pictures conquest from the perspective of Somalis:

It was from the ocean that all the major invasions of the Somali peninsula had come. The Arabs, and after them, the Portuguese the French, the British, and the Italians, and later the Russians, and most recently, the Americans—here, Jeebleh remembered how the U.S. intervention to feed the starving Somalis became an invasion of a kind, hence the term 'intravasion,' frequently used at the time. In any case, all these foreigners, well-meaning or not, came from the ocean.[20]

This mirrors Mohamed's own attempt to counter US and European illusions or stereotypes about Somalia by linking the history of the multitude of white conquering nations who colonized Somalia at various moments to their aide and foreign intervention in Somalia in recent decades. The Euro-American equation of Somali=terrorist is quite reversed.

After McKay's "vagabondage,"[21] nomadism is another capacious term signaling movement and moving populations in general, as it is specifically associated with "Somaliness." British anthropologist Ioan Lewis notes: "It cannot be emphasized too strongly that pastoral nomadism constitutes the economic base of the vast bulk of the Somali population, and manifestations of the nomadic lifestyle and traditions pervade almost all aspects of Somali life."[22] In addition, "Some 60 to 70 percent of the population [of Somalia] are nomadic or have nomadic affiliation, even though many today live in urban centers part of the time" (3). This orientation, though not absolute, is reflected in literature as well. Yasmeen Maxamuud's epic 2009 novel *Nomad Diaries*—Somalia's twenty-first-century answer to *War and Peace*—narrativizes the Somali diaspora in the United States. Nuruddin Farah, perhaps the most well-known Somali writer in English, "writes of a society in which nomadic values seem to been strongly enshrined as central to the national self-image."[23] Somali poet and scholar Ali Jimale Ahmed's most recent book of poetry names the first section of *When Donkeys Give Birth to Calves: Totems, Wars, Horizons, Diasporas* "Nomadic" and includes a poem of the same name.[24] In *Black Mamba Boy*, Jama mulled over the trope of nomadic Somaliness: "we are nomads, land is the same to us everywhere we go, we only care if there is water and food to be found" (281). Yet, rather than overdetermining nomadism as "essential" to Somaliness, which elides the complex cultural and material histories of the region, I argue that Somali writers utilize nomadism as a hinge through which to figure movement. It provides a way of negotiating the complexities and nuances of Somalia's fraught history of foreign colonization and neo-colonization (neoliberal globalization), which substantially contributed to the civil war and the atrocities committed therein, the Somali failed state itself, and Somalia's multiple and thriving and struggling diasporas the world over.

For Mohamed, the phenomenology of movement is a way to tell multiple stories: a Somalian story, a story about the European colonization of the Horn of Africa, and another of global capitalism and the movement of people in the early to mid-twentieth century. *Black Mamba Boy* is both about Jama becoming nomad due to a confluence of outside forces and a pan-Africanist challenge to a colonial world. In many ways he is a refashioning of McKay's itinerant character Banjo. The authors Mohamed quotes in the epigraphs to her novel (Maxamed Cabdulle Xasan and Rabindranath Tagore) attest to this engagement with movement and/as historical context as both were early to mid-twentieth-century opponents of imperialism.[25] Anti-imperialism, then, undergirds the choice of poems speaking to movement; the juxtaposition of these two poets suggests in some ways that, for Mohamed, movement and colonialism are linked in complex ways—Tagore's "vagrant" may have spoken to Mohamed's desire to write a pan-African figure of the "nomad" as surly McKay's "vagabond" did. Thus the politics of vagabondage reemerges as the nomadic in *Black Mamba Boy*. Yet the contemporary import of the novel is that it reconfigures the ways in which we understand immigration. Jama, and many others like him, are already conscripted by colonial structures and systems of immigration in the high imperial era, which, in turn, reflects our own twenty-first century and the global violence that the policing of movement and people inflicts.

The novel ends with Jama on a ship as he begins to make the long journey back to Africa from Wales as fellow seamen dance to Louis Armstrong's "Let My People Go." "They would pack up their bags," muses Jama as he imagines his future with his wife Bethlehem, "and move like nomads over Africa, over Europe, discovering new worlds, renaming them Jamastan and Bethlehemia if they wanted" (284). On the deck of the *P&O*, the African American protest song furnishes the diasporic notes and movements upon which Jama's imagined nomadic futures travel, between Africa and Europe, Jamastan and Bethlehemia. Echoing the reverberations of *Banjo* one final time, "Jama let his legs move to the swinging jazz, let his hips whine a little, his shoulders shimmy, anything to free the music trapped within his soul" (284).

~

Immigration in the era of neoliberal globalization is transnationally constituted, institutional, and historical. It is not simply about moving here or there, since racial capitalism, imperialism, neoliberal globalization, and now a resurgent xenophobic nationalism all continue to shape the conditions within which we choose to move or not and that movement itself. The dehumanizing designation and construction of immigrants as such, as refugees or "illegals" and so on, is also shaped by received notions of race, gender, and sexuality, which constellate and shore up relative national normativities. This marks not an exception to modernity as such, but its rule. In fact, as this book has attempted to show, the production, management, and policing of the movement of people on the one hand, and of capital on the other, represents the fundamental ground upon which modernity was built and is sustained. This includes processes of racialization, the production and maintenance of economic and social class, gendering mechanisms, and sexual normativity (heteronationalism).

If nothing else, this book warns that if we do not seriously rethink immigration itself, both in terms of defining and enforcing it, we will ultimately fail as a country and as a world. We will continue to see humanitarian crises regarding human movement and the rise in isolationist xenophobia, so antithetical to simple inclusive morals and ethical values. There is a long history, however, of activism that speaks out for immigrant and refugee rights, most recently (at the time of writing this book) in the #AbolishICE movement. This should be seen as parallel to the Movement for Black Lives and for trans lives. Migritude authors indeed double as activists (see Fatou Diome and Shailja Patel), while migritude cultural production and the literatures of new African diasporas provide an important complement to that activism by creating and circulating the narratives of those who move and yet who continue to be silenced. The constellation of these narratives embody a particular politics, ethics, and philosophy, that is, what we might call migrant humanism. This humanism, as opposed to other humanisms that would privilege Euro-American or white humans, is so important now, given that environmental destruction, climate change, global warming, global wars, and other crises will significantly change the habitable world in the next few hundred years, suggesting that our present may be one of the human species' last few chapters.[26] How do we want these chapters to read? This is an existential-collective question and one that surely cannot be answered through the lens of neoliberal racial capitalism or nationalism.

NOTES

Chapter 1

1. Stephen Castles and Mark J. Miller, *The Age of Migration* (New York: Palgrave Macmillan, 2003). ` o Quebec mosque attack," *BBC News*, March 28, 2018. Web. *http://www.bbc.com/news/world-us-canada-43564126*. Accessed May 2, 2018.

5. Edward Said, *Culture and Imperialism* (New York: Vintage Books, 1994), 8.

6. Eric J. Hobsbawm, *The Age of Empire: 1875–1914* (New York: Vintage Books, 1989), 62–64.

7. Michelle M. Wright, "Pale by Comparison: Black Liberal Humanism and the Postwar Era in the African Diaspora," in *Black Europe and the African Diaspora*, 271.

8. Although the actors and theories that would beget neoliberalism certainly predated the 1970s, for this book I use the decade of the 1970s to mark the period of neoliberal globalization affecting the Global South as it directly follows the era of independence movements across the South in the 1960s.

9. Quinn Slobodian, *Globalists: The End of Empire and the Birth of Neoliberalism*, (Massachusetts: Harvard University Press, 2018) 16, 6.

10. Fatou Diome, *The Belly of the Atlantic*, trans. Lulu Norman and Ros Schwartz (London: Serpent's Tail, 2006), 130.

11. See Myron Echenberg, *Colonial Conscripts: The Tirailleurs Sénégalais in French West Africa 1857–1960* (Portsmouth: Heinemann, 1991), 2.

12. See Christian Koller, "Colonial Military Participation in Europe (Africa)," *International Encyclopedia of the First World War*, 1–2. Web: https://encyclopedia.1914–1918-online.net/home/.

13. Gebreyesus Hailu, *The Conscript: A Novel of Libya's Anticolonial War*, trans. Ghirmai Negash (Athens: Ohio University Press, 2013).

14. Jenna Loyd, Matt Mitchelson, and Andrew Burridge, "Borders, Prisons, and Abolitionist Visions," in *Beyond Walls and Cages: Prisons, Borders, and Global Crises*, eds. Jenna Loyd, Matt Mitchelson, and Andrew Burridge (Athens: University of Georgia Press, 2012), 1.

15. Donald Carter, "Navigating Diaspora: The Precarious Depths of the Italian Immigration Crisis," in *African Migrations: Patterns and Perspectives*, eds. Abdoulaye Kane and Todd H. Leedy (Bloomington: Indiana University Press, 2013), 64.

16. Paul Gilroy's classic *The Black Atlantic: Modernity and Double-Consciousness* was followed by important works like Susan Buck-Morss, *Hegel, Haiti, and Universal History*; David Scott, *Conscripts of Modernity: The Tragedy of Colonial Enlightenment*; Lisa Lowe, *The Intimacies of Four Continents*; and most recently, Robert Reid-Pharr's wonderful book *Archives of Flesh: African America, Spain, and Post-Humanist Critique*.

17. By "national normativity" I do not so much mean a single nation's norms (though they are relevant here) but the normative idea of the "nation" as conceptualized through a global neoliberal imaginary as well as the history of that imaginary.

18. David Eng, "Transnational Adoption and Queer Diasporas," *Social Text* 21, no. 3 (2003): 4.

19. Nadifa Mohamed, *Black Mamba Boy* (New York: Farrar, Straus and Giroux, 2010), 58.

20. Claude McKay, *Banjo: A Story Without a Plot* (New York: Harper & Brothers, 1929), 146.

21. Talal Asad, "Conscripts of Western Civilization?" in *Dialectical Anthropology: Essays in Honor of Stanley Diamond*, vol. 1, Ed. C. Gailey (Gainesville: University Presses of Florida, 1992), 333–51.

22. Stanley Diamond, *In Search of the Primitive: A Critique of Civilization* (New Jersey: Transaction Publishers, 1974), 204.

23. David Scott, *Conscripts of Modernity: The Tragedy of Colonial Enlightenment* (Durham: Duke University Press, 2004), 106.

24. John Torpey, *The Invention of the Passport: Surveillance, Citizenship, and the State* (Cambridge: Cambridge University Press, 2000), 3–19.

25. *Fatal Journeys: Tracking Lives Lost in Migration*, International Organization for Migration (Geneva: International Organization for Migration, 2014), 15.

26. "MSF: 29 dead bodies found on crowded refugee boat," *Al Jazeera*, October 27, 2016. Web.

27. Abu Bakr Khaal, *African Titanics*, trans. Charis Bredin (London: Darf Publishers, 2008/2014), 3–4.

28. Chinua Achebe, "An Image of Africa," *Research in African Literatures* 9, no. 1, Special Issue on Literary Criticism (Spring 1978): 2.

29. "Series Editors' Foreword," Glenda Garelli and Martina Tazzioli, *Tunisia as a Revolutionized Space of Migration*, eds. Glenda Garelli and Martina Tazzioli (New York: Palgrave Macmillan, 2017), v.

30. Salman Rushdie, "The New Empire Within Britain," in *Imaginary Homelands: Essays and Criticism 1981–1991* (London: Granta Books, 1991), 132.

Chapter 2

1. Bernard Binlin Dadie, *One Way: Bernard Dadie Observes America*, trans. Jo Patterson (Urbana and Chicago: University of Illinois Press, 1994), 1.

2. Cristina Ali Farah, *Little Mother*, trans. Giovanna Bellesia-Contuzzi and Victoria Offredi Poletto. Introduction by Alessandra Di Maio (Bloomington and Indianapolis: Indiana University Press, 2011), 1.

3. "The Africans gave [Ray] a positive feeling of wholesome contact with racial roots." Claude McKay, *Banjo*, 320.

4. "Too often, in literature and criticism alike, the working class is seen and represented as masculine, metropolitan, and revolutionary. Women's texts of nonrevolutionary socialism, however, present us with new figures and concepts for thinking unorganized resistance, everyday experience, and the shape of the ethical within globalization." Sonali Perera, *No Country: Working-Class Writing in the Age of Globalization* (New York: Columbia University Press, 2014), 80.

5. Tidiane Kasse, "Africa and its diaspora in migration dynamics," *Pambazuka News: Pan-African Voices for Freedom and Justice*, Issue 684, June 26, 2014, 1.

6. Shailja Patel, *Migritude* (New York: Kaya Press, 2010), 19.

7. Jacques Chevrier, quoted in Dominic Thomas, *Black France: Colonialism, Immigration, and Transnationalism* (Bloomington and Indianapolis: Indiana University Press, 2007), 5.

8. Emmanuel Dongala, "From Négritude to Migritude: The African Writer in Exile," conference presentation, Exil: mode(s) d'emploi—Experiencing Exile in Literature and the Arts, University of California Los Angeles, 2005.

9. *Paris, Capital of the Black Atlantic: Literature, Modernity, and Diaspora*, eds. Jeremy Braddock and Jonathan P. Eburne (Baltimore: Johns Hopkins University Press, 2013).

10. *Black France/France Noire: The History and Politics of Blackness*, eds. Tricia Danielle Keaton, T. Denean Sharpley-Whiting, and Tyler Stovall (Durham and London: Duke University Press, 2012).

11. "Being-in-the-world" is Heidegger's term used to theorize what all humans have/are ontologically, marking a departure from Cartesian metaphysics. I appropriate this term as well as the philosophical vocabulary of Heidegger, Sartre, and the Négritude poets' ontological phenomenology. Martin Heidegger, *Being and Time*, trans. John Macquarrie and Edward Robinson (San Francisco: Harper, 1962).

12. See Edmund Husserl, *Ideas: General Introduction to Pure Phenomenology*, trans. W. R. Boyce Gibson (London: Collier, 1956), 105; *The Essential Husserl: Basic Writings in Transcendental Phenomenology*, ed. Donn Welton (Bloomington and Indianapolis: Indiana University Press, 1999), 66.

13. See Sara Ahmed's *Queer Phenomenology: Orientations, Objects, Others* (Durham and London: Duke University Press, 2006), 27–28.

14. Étienne Balibar, "Toward a Diasporic Citizen? From Internationalism to Cosmopolitics," in *The Creolization of Theory*, eds. Francoise Lionnet and Shu-Mei Shih (Durham and London: Duke University Press, 2011), 217.

15. Mahmood Mamdani, *Define and Rule: Native as Political Identity* (Cambridge: Harvard University Press, 2012), 1–2. Further, Mamdani argues that "apartheid, usually considered unique to South Africa, is actually the generic form of the colonial State in Africa." See Mahmood Mamdani, *Citizen and Subject: Contemporary Africa and the Legacy of Late Colonialism* (Princeton: Princeton University Press, 1996), 8.

16. Abdourahman Waberi, "Les Enfants de la Postcolonie: Esquisse d'une Nouvelle Génération d'écrivains Francophones d'Afrique Noire," *Notre Librairie* 135 (1998): 8–15. Print.

17. There is some debate regarding the French term *banlieue*, which literally translates as "suburb" but has much different connotations in the French context, where it is suggestive of diverse black and immigrant neighborhoods or housing projects that are usually

impoverished. See Dominic Thomas, *African and France: Postcolonial Cultures, Migration, and Racism* (Bloomington and Indianapolis: Indiana University Press, 2013); Alec Hargreaves, "Banlieue Blues," in *The Cambridge Companion to the Literature of Paris*, ed. Anna-Louise Milne (Cambridge: Cambridge University Press, 2014), and others.

18. Lisa Lowe, *The Intimacies of Four Continents* (Durham and London: Duke University Press, 2015).

19. Shailja Patel, "Shailja Patel: Migritude," Interview by KQED Public Television. San Francisco, March 2007.

20. Vijay Prashad, "Speaking of Saris," in Shailja Patel, *Migritude*, ii.

21. Khainga O'Okwemba, "Kenya: Migritude—a Revelation of Migrant Mysticism," *AllAfrica*, May 2013, *http://allafrica.com/stories/201305310461.html*. Web. Emphasis added.

22. See T. Denean Sharpley-Whiting, *Négritude Women* (Minneapolis and London: University of Minnesota Press, 2002).

23. Interestingly, this reflection comes from a later section in the book called "Shadow Book," in which she analyzes her own performance of the texts onstage. Patel, *Migritude*, 85.

24. Noam Chomsky, *Year 501: The Conquest Continues* (Chicago: Haymarket Books, 2015), 16.

25. Karl Marx, *Dispatches for the New York Tribune: Selected Journalism of Karl Marx*, ed. James Ledbetter (New York: Penguin Classics, 2007), 215.

26. Michel Chossudovsky, *The Globalization of Poverty: Impacts of IMF and World Bank Reforms* (London: Zed Books, 1997), 55.

27. Joseph Kipkemboi Rono, "The Impact of Structural Adjustment Programmes on Kenyan Society," *Journal of Social Development in Africa* 17, no. 1 (January 2002): 96.

28. Folasade Iyun, "The Impact of Structural Adjustment on Maternal and Child Health in Nigeria," in *Women Pay the Price: Structural Adjustment in Africa and the Caribbean*, ed. Gloria T. Emeagwali (New Jersey: Africa World Press, 1995), 31.

29. Michelle M. Wright, "Pale by Comparison," 271.

30. See, for example, works like Sidonia Alenuma-Nimoh and Loramy Christine Gerstbauer, "Gendered Globalization: A Re-examination of the Changing Roles of Women in Africa," in *Critical Perspectives on Neoliberal Globalization*, ed. Dip Kapoor (Rotterdam: Sense Publishers, 2011); and Grace Change, *Disposable Domestics: Immigrant Women Workers in the Global Economy* (Cambridge: South End Press, 2000).

31. John Torpey, *The Invention of the Passport: Surveillance, Citizenship, and the State* (Cambridge: Cambridge University Press, 2000), 3–19. Emphasis added.

32. Paul Gilroy, *There Ain't No Black in the Union Jack: The Cultural Politics of Race and Nation* (Chicago: University of Chicago Press, 1987), 11.

33. Thatcher's speech quoted in Rahul K. Gairola, "A Critique of Thatcherism and the Queering of Home in *Sammy and Rosie Get Laid*," *South Asian Review* 32, no. 3 (2011): 124.

34. Chinua Achebe, "An Image of Africa," *Research in African Literatures* 9, no. 1, Special Issue on Literary Criticism (Spring 1978): 13.

35. Cedric Robinson, *Black Marxism: The Making of the Black Radical Tradition* (Chapel Hill and London: University of North Carolina Press, 1983), 9.

36. Eric Williams, *Capitalism and Slavery* (Chapel Hill and London: University of North Carolina Press, 1994), 7–19.

37. Eric J. Hobsbawm, *Nations and Nationalism since 1780* (Cambridge: Cambridge University Press, 1990), 10.

38. " . . . in its modern and basically political sense the concept *nation* is historically very young. Indeed, this is underlined by another linguistic monument the *New English Dictionary* which pointed out in 1908, that the old meaning of the word envisaged mainly the ethnic unit, but recent usage rather stressed 'the notion of political unity and independence.'" Hobsbawm's emphasis, 18.

39. Ernest Renan: "Forgetting, I would even say historical error, is an essential factor in the creation of a nation and it is for this reason that the progress of historical studies often poses a threat to nationality. Historical inquiry, in effect, throws light on the violent acts that have taken place at the origin of every political formation, even those that have been the most benevolent in their consequences. Unity is always brutally established." Ernest Renan, "What is a Nation?," text of a conference delivered at the Sorbonne, March 11, 1882, in Ernest Renan, *Qu'est-ce qu'une nation?* (Paris: Presses-Pocket, 1992). (Translated by Ethan Rundell.)

40. Étienne Balibar and Immanuel Wallerstein, *Race, Nation, Class*, trans. Chris Turner (London and New York: Verso, 1991), 93–96.

41. Save for fringe migrant activist movements, theorists of immigration, and migritude literature itself.

42. Saskia Sassen, *Guests and Aliens* (New York: The New Press, 1999), 155.

43. Pap Khouma, *I Was an Elephant Salesman*, trans. Rebecca Hopkins (Bloomington: Indiana University Press, 2010), 7. Emphasis added.

44. *Globalisation, Migration, and the Future of Europe: Insiders and Outsiders*, ed. Leila Simona Talani (London and New York: Routledge, 2012), 2.

45. Gloria Emeagwali, "The Neo-Liberal Agenda and the IMF/World Bank Structural Adjustment Programs with Reference to Africa," in *Critical Perspectives on Neoliberal Globalization, Development and Education in Africa and Asia*, ed. Dip Kapoor (Rotterdam: Sense Publishers, 2011), 10.

46. Alenuma-Nimoh and Gerstbauer, "Gendered Globalization: A Re-examination of the Changing Roles of Women in Africa," 89.

47. Aviva Chomsky, *"They Take Our Jobs!" and 20 Other Myths about Immigration* (Boston: Beacon Press, 2007), 152.

48. For example, see Grace Chang, *Disposable Domestics: Immigrant Women Workers in the Global Economy* (Cambridge: South End Press, 2000); or Jamaica Kincaid, *Lucy: A Novel* (New York: Farrar, Straus, and Giroux, 1990).

49. Léopold Sédar Senghor, "Négritude: A Humanism of the Twentieth Century," in *Colonial Discourse and Postcolonial Theory: A Reader*, eds. Patrick Williams and Laura Chrisman (New York: Columbia University Press, 1994), 27.

Chapter 3

1. Leonora Miano, *Ecrits pour la parole*, trans. Régine Jean-Charles 2013 (French and European Publications, 2012).

2. Achille Mbembe, *Critique of Black Reason*, trans. Laurent Dubois (Durham and London: Duke University Press, 2017), 38.

3. Rosemary Haskell, "Senegalese Migrant Novelist Fatou Diome Is Now the Militant Marianne," *World Literature Today,* October 4, 2017. Web. https://www.worldliteraturetoday .org/blog/cultural-cross-sections/senegalese-migrant-novelist-fatou-diome-now-militant -marianne-rosemary.

4. Only two other African teams have made it to the FIFA World Cup Quarterfinals: Cameroon in 1990 and Ghana in 2010.

5. Diome's phrase in the original French. Fatou Diome, *Le Ventre de l'Atlantique* (Paris: Le Livre de Poche, 2003), 240.

6. The term *Afropean* is Leonora Miano's. See *Afropean Soul et autres nouvelles.*

7. Isaie Dougnon, "Migration as Coping with Risk and State Barriers: Malian Migrants' Conception of Being Far from Home," trans. Helene Gagliardi. *African Migrations,* 50.

8. Gary Wilder, *The French Imperial Nation-State: Negritude and Colonial Humanism Between the Two World Wars,* (Chicago: University of Chicago Press, 2005), 140–41.

9. I include under the banner of "African literature" literature by Africans living elsewhere as well as second-generation African immigrants born outside the continent but for whom Africa (and the experience of being African or immigrant) is significant. I define African literature, then, broadly.

10. Amy Marczewski and Julie Nack Ngue, "Exil: mode(s) d'emploi: New readings, new endings." *Paroles gelées,* 22(1), 2006. http://escholarship.org/uc/item/14f349×5

11. Alain Mabanckou, *Blue White Red,* trans. Alison Dundy (Bloomington: Indiana University Press, 2013), 107.

12. Michel Foucault, *The History of Sexuality Vol. 1: An Introduction* (New York: Random House, 1978), 140. Emphasis added.

13. Michel Foucault, *Security, Territory, Population,* trans. Graham Burchell, ed. Michel Senellart (New York: Palgrave, 2007), 1.

14. Abdourahman A. Waberi, *Transit: A Novel,* trans. David and Nicole Ball (Bloomington and Indianapolis: Indiana University Press, 2012), 74.

15. Jim Wolfreys, "Making Racism Respectable: Islamophobia in Sarkozy's France," *Global Social Justice Journal* 1, no. 1. Published by the Centre for International Studies at Cape Breton University, 2013.

16. Myron Echenberg, *Colonial Conscripts: The Tirailleurs Sénégalais in French West Africa 1857–1960* (Portsmouth: Heinemann, 1991), 5.

17. Elisa Camiscioli, *Reproducing the French Race: Immigration, Intimacy, and Embodiment in the Early Twentieth Century* (Durham and London: Duke University Press, 2009), 156.

18. Pius Adesanmi, "Redefining Transmodernity," in *Paris, Capital of the Black Atlantic,* 326.

19. Stephanie Bosch Santana, "Exorcizing Afropolitanism: Binyavanga Wainaina explains why 'I am a Pan-Africanist, not an Afropolitan' at ASAUK 2012," *Africa in Words,* February 2013. Web. https://africainwords.com/2013/02/08/exorcizing-afropolitanism-binyavanga -wainaina-explains-why-i-am-a-pan-africanist-not-an-afropolitan-at-asauk-2012/

20. Faïza Guène, *Kiffe Kiffe Tomorrow: A Novel,* trans. Sarah Adams (Orlando: Harcourt, 2006), 142–43.

21. Mehdi Charef, *Tea in the Harem,* trans. Ed Emery (UK: Serpent's Tail, 1989), 62.

22. Ayo A. Coly, *Pull of Postcolonial Nationhood: Gender and Migration in Francophone African Literature* (Pennsylvania: Rowan & Littlefield, 2010), 99.

23. Manthia Diawara, "Toward a Regional Imaginary in Africa," in *The Cultures of Globalization*, eds. Frederic Jameson and Masao Miyoshi (Durham and London: Duke University Press, 1998), 104.

24. Folasade Iyun, "The Impact of Structural Adjustment on Maternal and Child Health in Nigeria," in *Women Pay the Price: Structural Adjustment in Africa and the Caribbean*, ed. Gloria T. Emeagwali (New Jersey: Africa World Press, 1995), 31.

25. Léopold Sédar Senghor, *Prose and Poetry* (Oxford: Oxford University Press, 1965), 74.

26. Léopold Sédar Senghor, *On African Socialism*, trans. Mercer Cook (New York: Fredrick A. Prager, 1964), 80.

27. Souleymane Bachir Diagne, *African Art as Philosophy: Senghor, Bergson, and the Idea of Negritude*, trans. Chike Jeffers (London: Seagull Books, 2011), 190.

28. Ousmane Sembéne, *La Noire de*, (film, France and Senegal), *Filmi Domirev* and *Les Actualités Françaises*, 1966.

29. Ashley Dawson, *Mongrel Nation* (Ann Arbor: University of Michigan Press, 2007), 2.

30. Mabanckou, *Blue White Red*, 107. Also see the 2005 Clichy-DuBois protests in France regarding treatment of black and immigrant communities.

31. Haby Assevero, "Black Blanc Beur: A French story," Esports Media Group, November 9, 2005. http://www.e-sports.com/articles/959/1/Black-Blanc-Beur-A-French-story/Page1.html.

32. Eliot Ross and Sean Jacobs, "The Banana that Revealed Europe's Persistent Racism," Al Jazeera America, April 30, 2014. http://america.aljazeera.com/opinions/2014/4/dani-alves -bananafootballbarcelonaracism.html.

33. *Le Ventre de l'Atlantique*, 88. Author's emphases.

34. Chinua Achebe, *Things Fall Apart* (New York: Anchor Books, 1994), 53.

35. James Ferguson, "Seeing Like an Oil Company: Space, Security, and Global Capital in Neoliberal Africa," *American Anthropologist* 107, no. 3 (2005): 379.

36. Stephen Ocheni and Basil C. Nwankwo, "Analysis of Colonialism and its Impact in Africa," *Cross-Cultural Communication* 8, no. 3 (2012): 48.

37. Christopher Ian Foster, "Towards a Caribbean Migritude? Immigration, Sexuality, and the Gendered Caribbean Body," *Small Axe Salon* 18 (February 2015).

38. Achille Mbembe, "Africa and the Future: An Interview with Achille Mbembe," Thomas M. Blaser, *Africa is a Country*, November 20, 2013. http://africasacountry.com/ africa-and-the-future-an-interview-with-achille-mbembe/.

Chapter 4

1. "While Italy's colonial past in East Africa has meant that some Afro-Italians have lived in Italy since the immediate post-Second World War period, a wave of new immigration into *lo stivale* (the boot, as the country is often nicknamed) followed crushing postcolonial and often political persecution in North, West, East and Central Africa." Christopher Hogarth, "Afro-Italian Literature: From Productive Collaborations to Individual Affirmations," in *Africa in Europe: Studies in Transnational Practice in the Long Twentieth Century*, eds. Eve Rosenshaft and Robbie Aitken (Liverpool: Liverpool University Press, 2013), 162.

2. "Free-market policies might may be associated with democracy in the United States and elsewhere in the industrialized world, but in the Third World, they more commonly come

with the disappearance of democratic rights, as in Pinochet's Chile." Aviva Chomsky, *"They Take Our Jobs!" and 20 Other Myths about Immigration* (Boston: Beacon Press, 2007), 152.

3. Graziella Parati notes that over the past thirty years, "Italy and other Southern European countries have experienced immigration." Graziella Parati, "Introduction," in *I Was an Elephant Salesman* by Pap Khouma, trans. Rebecca Hopkins (Bloomington and Indianapolis: Indiana University Press, 2010), xi.

4. See http://www.africandigitalart.com/2014/03/digital-artwork-that-portray-african -immigration/. Cristina Ali Farah, *Little Mother*, trans. Giovanna Bellesia-Contuzzi and Victoria Offredi Poletto, Introduction by Alessandra Di Maio (Bloomington and Indianapolis: Indiana University Press, 2011), xv. Originally published 2007 as *Madre piccola*.

5. Pap Khouma, *I Was an Elephant Salesman*, trans. Rebecca Hopkins (Bloomington and Indianapolis: Indiana University Press, 2010), 4

6. Aviva Chomsky notes that, in the United States for example, "in every generation, people have found rationales for systems of social and legal inequality. Native Americans had no rights in the new country, so their land could be taken for white settlement. Africans had no rights, so it was all right to enslave them. Women had no rights, and their labor was generally unpaid. Contract workers had few rights so their labor was underpaid. Immigrants, as well as workers in other countries, have also been deprived of rights—yet their low-paid labor provides the cheap products that our economy depends on . . . a large and growing portion of our population [as in Italy] lives without the full rights of citizenship." Aviva Chomsky, *"They Take Our Jobs!" and 20 Other Myths about Immigration*, xiii.

7. It was reported in January 2010 by Al Jazeera that "Immigrants work in the area as day labourers picking fruit and vegetables, with some 1,500 living in squalid conditions in abandoned factories with no running water or electricity. Human rights activists say they are exploited by organised crime groups." http://www.aljazeera.com/news/eu rope/2010/01/20101812051648430.html. "At least 300 African migrants have been transported out of a southern Italian town rocked by two days of clashes between the migrants, police and local residents. Eight buses transferred the African fruit pickers on Saturday from Rosarno to a temporary shelter elsewhere in Calabria . . . Migrants blamed the attacks on racism and groups of protesters stoned police, attacked residents and smashed shop windows and cars." http://www.aljazeera.com/news/europe/2010/01/20101918461937126.html. January 2010.

8. In an email to me, Di Prisco confirmed that he had been thinking about the Nigerian workers in the orange orchards in Rosarno as he began envisioning his piece.

9. As migrant laborers in the orchards are primarily male, I use the possessive pronoun "his"; however, the gender of the figure in *Postcard* is ultimately unclear.

10. Kamau Edward Brathwaite, *Contradictory Omens: Cultural Diversity and Integration in the Caribbean* (Kingston: Savacou Publications, 1974), 64.

11. Alessandra Di Maio, "Black Italia: Contemporary Migrant Writers from Africa," in *Black Europe and the African Diaspora*, 119.

12. See scholars like Alessandra di Maio, Graziella Parati, Moira Luraschi, and Eleanor Paynter's recent article on Igiaba Scego, "The Spaces of Citizenship: Mapping Personal and Colonial Histories in Contemporary Italy in Igiaba Scego's La Mia Casa È Dove Sono (My Home is Where I Am)," *European Journal of Life Writing* [S.1.], v. 6 (July 2017): 135–53.

13. "There is no formal forum in Africa specifically for the discussion of migration matters by all stakeholders—in particular the media and the public—as a continuous process, in order to avoid the misrepresentations, ignorance and xenophobia that currently surround the issue of migration. Discourses on migration, especially from the receiving end, are full of anxiety, misconceptions, myths and prejudices, and are often fed on xenophobia." Aderanti Adepoju, "Rethinking the Dynamics of Migration Within, from, and to Africa" in *International Migration: Within, To, And From Africa*, ed. Aderanti Adepoju (Lagon, Ghana: Subsaharan Publishers, 2009), 22. Also see Alessandra Di Maio: "The media [in Italy] promoted new terms and definitions, not infrequently revealing racialist overtones." Di Maio, "Black Italia: Contemporary Migrant Writers from Africa," in *Black Europe and the African Diaspora*, 124.

14. "In Somalia, Italian was the main language of instruction in the colonial system and remained so for many years after decolonization, even after Somali (until then an oral language) was finally transcribed in 1972," one year before Cristina Ali Farah was born. Alessandra Di Maio, "Introduction: Pearls in Motion," in Cristina Ali Farah, *Little Mother*, trans. Giovanna Bellesia-Contuzzi and Victoria Offredi Poletto (Bloomington and Indianapolis: Indiana University Press, 2011), xviii.

15. Nuruddin Farah, *Yesterday, Tomorrow: Voices from the Somali Diaspora* (London: Cassell, 2000), v.

16. Nega Mezlekia, *Notes From the Hyena's Belly: An Ethiopian Boyhood* (New York: Picador USA, 2000), 195.

17. Stoler's nuanced and temporal perspective is important for postcolonial studies and this project in particular: "Our focus is less on the noun *ruin* than on 'ruination' as an active, ongoing process that allocates imperial debris differentially and *ruin* as a violent verb that unites apparently disparate moments, places, and objects." Ann Stoler, *Imperial Debris: On Ruins and Ruination*, 7.

18. For more on postcolonial Italy and its relation to Somali-Italian literature, see Eleanor Paynter, "The Spaces of Citizenship: Mapping Personal and Colonial Histories in Contemporary Italy," in Igiaba Scego, "La Mia Casa È Dove Sono (My Home Is Where I Am)."

19. *18 Ius Soli*, dir. Fred Kuwornu (Rome and New York: Struggle Filmworks), 2011. Film.

20. Alessandro Dal Lago, *Non-Persons: The Exclusion of Migrants in a Global Society*, trans. Marie Orton (Italy: IPOC Press, 2009), 12.

21. I do not mean "humanity" or "humanism" in terms of liberal concepts inherited from the Western tradition, which, for Talal Asad, "emerged in the nineteenth century with the consolidation of European nation states, the expansion of European colonial empires and the global development of capitalism" and that "the exercise of violence is intrinsic to the modern concept of the human . . the motives of humanitarians must traverse through imperial structures." Talal Asad, "Reflections on Violence, Law, and Humanitarianism," *Critical Inquiry* 41, no. 2 (Winter 2015). What I mean is postcolonial cultural production that *rehumanizes* in response to dehumanization.

22. See Moira Luraschi, "Beyond Words: Mirroring Identities of Italian Postcolonial Women Writers," *Enquire* 3 (June 2009); Lucie Benchouiha, "Hybrid Identities?: Immigrant Women's Writing in Italy," *Italian Studies* 61, no. 2 (Autumn 2006).

23. Mattathias Schwartz, "The Anchor: Letter from Lampedusa," *New Yorker*, April 21, 2014, 78.

24. Michelle M. Wright states that "some will be familiar with the phrase 'fortress Europe,' which refers to the explicit attempt to ahistoricize Europe as a 'whites-only' enclave that must protect itself against the 'invasion' of non-white hordes [similar to] increasing hegemonic aggression espoused and practiced by the United States." Michelle M. Wright, "Pale by Comparison: Black Liberal Humanism and the Postwar Era in the African Diaspora," in *Black Europe and the African Diaspora*, 271. Further, in the Mediterranean context, Alessandro Dal Lago notes: "An eloquent illustration of the closing of Europe's borders to foreigners is evident in the migration politics of the new countries of immigration, Spain, and Italy, who, together with Greece, have played the role of sentinels for the Mediterranean in the 'fortress Europe' codified by the Schengen agreement . . . For Southern European countries, closing their borders to migrants is undoubtedly a prerequisite for being accepted into the European club politically and financially dominated by France and Germany." Dal Lago, *Non-Persons*, 29–30. *Little Mother* describes and therefore challenges Europe in these terms.

25. Emily Apter, *Against World Literature: On the Politics of Untranslatability* (New York: Verso, 2013).

26. Emily Apter. Paraphrased in "The Passport that Does Not Pass Ports," by Eliot Ross, *Africa is a Country*, March 2014. http://africasacountry.com/the-passport-that-does-not-pass-ports/.

27. Souleymane Bachir Diagne, paraphrased in Ross, "The Passport that Does Not Pass Ports."

28. Diagne, Souleymane Bachir. Response to Emily Apter. "Translation, Checkpoints, Sovereign Borders." Lecture, Columbia University, October 24, 2013.

29. Graziella Parati, *Migration Italy: The Art of Talking Back in a Destination Culture*, (Toronto: University of Toronto Press, 2014), 67.

30. Maryse Condé, "Order, Disorder, Freedom, and the West Indian Writer," *Yale French Studies* 97, 50 Years of Yale French Studies: A Commemorative Anthology. Part 2: 1980–1998 (2000), 161.

31. I analyze the term "disidentification" in the Caribbean context, though relevant here, in Christopher Ian Foster, "The Queer Politics of Crossing in Maryse Condé's *Crossing the Mangrove*," *Small Axe* 43 (March 2014): 117.

Chapter 5

1. Sharita Gruberg, "ICE's Rejection of Its Own Rules Is Placing LGBT Immigrants at Severe Risk of Sexual Abuse," *Center for American Progress*, May 30, 2018. Web. https://www.americanprogress.org/issues/lgbt/news/2018/05/30/451294/ices-rejection-rules-placing-lgbt-immigrants-severe-risk-sexual-abuse/.

2. Nawo C. Crawford, "Prologue: Paris Black Pride 2016," *Decolonizing Sexualities: Transnational Perspectives, Critical Interventions*, eds. Sandeep Bakshi, Suhraiya Jivraj, and Silvia Posocco (UK: Counterpress, 2016), xii.

3. See Kimberle Crenshaw, "Mapping the Margins: Intersectionality, Identity Politics, and Violence against Women of Color," *Stanford Law Review* 43, no. 6 (July 1991): 1241–99.

4. Darren Rosenblum, "Queer Intersectionality and the Failure of Recent Lesbian and Gay 'Victories,'" *Law & Sexuality* 83 (1994). Web. https://digitalcommons.pace.edu/cgi/viewcontent.cgi?referer=https://www.google.com/&httpsredir=1&article=1209&context=lawfaculty.

5. Sokari Ekine, "Beyond Anti-LGBTI Legislation: Criminalization and the Denial of Citizenship," in *Decolonizing Sexualities*, 19.

6. Alisa Solomon, "Trans/Migrant: Christina Madrazo's All-American Story," in *Queer Migrations: Sexuality, U.S. Citizenship, and Border Crossings*, eds. Eithne Luibhéid and Lionel Cantú Jr. (Minneapolis: University of Minnesota Press, 2005), 3.

7. See David A. B. Murray, ed., *Queering Borders: Language, Sexuality, and Migration*, (Amsterdam and Philadelphia: John Benjamins, 2016), 1–2; Eithne Luibhéid and Lionel Cantú Jr., eds., *Queer Migrations: Sexuality, U.S. Citizenship, and Border Crossings* (Minneapolis and London: University of Minnesota Press, 2005); and Jana Evans Braziel, "Queer Diasporas," *Diaspora: An Introduction* (Malden: Blackwell, 2008), 105–27.

8. Binyavanga Wainaina, "I am a Homosexual, Mum," *African Is a Country*, January 19, 2014. Web. http://africasacountry.com/2014/01/i-am-a-homosexual-mum/.

9. Diriye Osman, *Fairytales for Lost Children* (UK: Team Angelica, 2013), 3.

10. Nurrudin Farah, *Hiding in Plain Sight* (New York: Riverhead Books, 2014), 244.

Chapter 6

1. Antony Wild notes that "by the 1620s [the British East India Company] were actively trading coffee from Yemen throughout the Arabian Sea." Antony Wild, *Coffee: A Dark History* (New York: W.W. Norton, 2005), 69.

2. This is perhaps why the novel references the rupee as currency in Aden instead of the pound. *Black Mamba Boy*, 45.

3. "Violence of dispersal" is Nadifa Mohamed's phrase. Reading, September 25, 2012, the Graduate Center, CUNY.

4. Ashley Dawson, "Surplus City: Structural Adjustment, Self-Fashioning, and Urban Insurrection in Chris Abani's Graceland," *Interventions: A Journal of Postcolonial Studies* 11(1) (2009): 16–34, 17.

5. See Mike Davis's influential *Planet of Slums* (New York: Verso, 2006).

6. Claude McKay, *A Long Way From Home: An Autobiography* (New York: Harvest Books, 1937), 4.

7. Senghor, *On African Socialism*, 92.

8. Michela Wrong, *I Didn't Do It for You: How the World Betrayed a Small African Nation* (New York: Harper Perennial, 2005), 5.

9. See Uday Mehta, *Liberalism and Empire: A Study in Nineteenth-Century British Liberal Thought* (Chicago: University of Chicago Press, 1999).

10. Frantz Fanon, *The Wretched of the Earth*, trans. Constance Farrington (New York: Grove Press, 1963), 37.

11. Al Jazeera America, Oct. 31, 2013, http://america.aljazeera.com/articles/2013/10/30/bodies-of-87-migrantsfoundinnigerdesert.html .

12. I refer to Gayatri Spivak's famous formulation of "strategic essentialism." See *Selected Subaltern Studies*, eds. Ranajit Guha and Gayatri Spivak (New York: Oxford University Press, 1988), 13.

13. See James Ferguson, *Global Shadows: Africa in the Neoliberal World Order* (Durham: Duke University Press, 2007), 155.

14. See Teju Cole's 2014 twitter poem "A Piece of the Wall," https://twitter.com/tejucole/timelines/444262126954110977?lang=en. Accessed May 26, 2017.

15. "Being-in-the-world" is Heidegger's term used to theorize what all humans have/are ontologically, marking a departure from Cartesian metaphysics. Martin Heidegger, *Being and Time*, trans. John Macquarrie and Edward Robinson (San Francisco: Harper, 1962).

16. Brent Hayes Edwards, *The Practice of Diaspora: Literature, Translation, and the Rise of Black Internationalism* (Cambridge, MA, and London: Harvard University Press, 2003), 15.

17. Nuruddin Farah, *Maps* (New York: Random House, 1986), 126.

18. *Banjo*, 19. "Aframerican" is McKay's term. *Banjo*, 12. The banjo instrument itself is pan-African, originally West African but developed by slaves on West Indian and American plantations. The instrument is symbolic of migritude in the following ways: it moves or migrates from Africa during the slave trade to the Caribbean and the American South. It is diasporic, then, but it also necessarily interrogates the conditions that catalyze its movement—the slave trade and the plantation economy, where it is initially surreptitiously developed by slaves. Its history also calls into question its use in minstrelsy by a racist white public. It is then recast by Banjo in *Banjo* as inextricable from himself—"mahself"—as a black agential subject as well as representative of radical black transnational networks guided by the saxophone jazzing and music of the ditch.

19. Olaudah Equiano, *The African: The Interesting Narrative of the Life of Olaudah Equiano* (1789; London: Black Classics, 1998), 15.

20. Nuruddin Farah, *Links* (New York: Penguin, 2004), 124.

21. For more on McKay's important term, see Christopher Ian Foster, "Home to Hargeisa: Migritude, Pan-Africanism, and the Politics of Movement from *Banjo* to *Black Mamba Boy*," *Ufahamu: A Journal of African Studies* 38, no. 2 (Spring 2015).

22. Ioan Lewis, *Understanding Somalia and Somaliland* (London: C. Hurst, 2008), 56.

23. G. H. Moore, "Nomads and Feminists: The Novels of Nuruddin Farah," in *Emerging Perspectives on Nuruddin Farah*, ed. Derek Wright (New Jersey: Africa World Press, 2002), 155.

24. Ali Jimale Ahmed, *When Donkeys Give Birth to Calves: Totems, Wars, Horizons, Diasporas* (Trenton: Red Sea Press, 2012), 9.

25. The poem "Gabay" by late nineteenth-century Somali political and religious leader Xasan reads: "Now you depart, and though your way may lead / Through airless forests thick with hagar trees, / Places steeped in heat, stifling and dry, / Where breath comes hard, and no fresh breeze can reach— / Yet may God place a shield of coolest air / Between your body and the assailant sun." And the excerpt from late nineteenth-century Bengali polymath Tagore's poem "Stray Birds" reads: "O troupe of little vagrants of the world, leave your footprints in my words." See the epigraphs in *Black Mamba Boy*.

26. Ashley Dawson, *Extinction: A Radical History* (New York: O/R Books, 2016).

BIBLIOGRAPHY

18 Ius Soli. Dir. Fred Kuwornu. Rome and New York: Struggle Filmworks, 2011. Film.

Achebe, Chinua. "An Image of Africa." *Research in African Literatures* 9, no. 1, Special Issue on Literary Criticism (Spring 1978).

Achebe, Chinua. *Things Fall Apart*. New York: Anchor Books, 1994.

Adepoju, Aderanti. "Rethinking the Dynamics of Migration Within, from, and to Africa." In *International Migration: Within, To, And From Africa*, ed. Aderanti Adepoju. Lagon, Ghana: Subsaharan Publishers, 2009.

Adesanmi, Pius. "Redefining Transmodernity," in *Paris, Capital of the Black Atlantic: Literature, Modernity, and Diaspora*. Baltimore: Johns Hopkins University Press, 2013.

Ahmed, Ali Jimale. *When Donkeys Give Birth to Calves: Totems, Wars, Horizons, Diasporas*. Trenton: Red Sea Press, 2012.

Ahmed, Sara. *Queer Phenomenology: Orientations, Objects, Others*. Durham and London: Duke University Press, 2006.

Alenuma-Nimoh, Sidonia Jessia, and Loramy Christine Gerstbauer. "Gendered Globalization: A Re-examination of the Changing Roles of Women in Africa." In *Critical Perspectives on Neoliberal Globalization*, ed. Dip Kapoor. Rotterdam: Sense Publishers, 2011.

Apter, Emily. *Against World Literature: On the Politics of Untranslatability*. New York: Verso, 2013.

Asad, Talal. "Reflections on Violence, Law, and Humanitarianism," *Critical Inquiry* 41 no. 2 (Winter 2015).

Axel, Brian Keith. "The Diasporic Imaginary." *Public Culture* 14, no. 2 (Spring 2002): 411–28.

Balibar, Étienne, and Immanuel Wallerstein. *Race, Nation, Class*. Trans. Chris Turner. London and New York: Verso, 1991.

Balibar, Étienne, and Immanuel Wallerstein. "Toward a Diasporic Citizen? From Internationalism to Cosmopolitics." In *The Creolization of Theory*, ed. Francoise Lionnet and Shu-Mei Shih. Durham and London: Duke University Press, 2011.

Benchouiha, Lucie. "Hybrid Identities?: Immigrant Women's Writing in Italy." *Italian Studies* 61, no. 2 (Autumn 2006).

Blyden, Edward Wilmot. *Christianity, Islam, and the Negro Race.* Baltimore: Black Classic Press, 1994.

Braddock, Jeremy, and Jonathan P. Eburne, ed. *Paris, Capital of the Black Atlantic: Literature, Modernity, and Diaspora.* Baltimore: Johns Hopkins University Press, 2013.

Brathwaite, Kamau Edward. *Contradictory Omens: Cultural Diversity and Integration in the Caribbean.* Kingston: Savacou Publications, 1974.

Braziel, Jana Evans. "Queer Diasporas," in *Diaspora: An Introduction.* Malden: Blackwell, 2008.

Buck-Morss, Susan. *Hegel, Haiti, and Universal History.* Pittsburgh: University of Pittsburgh Press, 2009.

Butler, Judith. "What's Wrong with 'All Lives Matter'? an Interview with George Yancy." The Opinionator (blog), *New York Times*, January 12, 2015. http://opinionator.blogs.nytimes .com/2015/01/12/whats-wrong-with-all-lives-matter/?_r=0.

Butler, Judith. "Academic Freedom and the ASA's Boycott of Israel: A Response to Michelle Goldberg." *The Nation*, December 8, 2013. Web. https://www.thenation.com/article/ academic-freedom-and-asas-boycott-israel-response-michelle-goldberg/.

Caplan, Marc. "*Nos Ancestres, les Diallobés*: Cheikh Hamidou Kane's *Ambiguous Adventure* and the Paradoxes of Islamic Négritude." In *Paris, Capital of the Black Atlantic: Literature, Modernity, and Diaspora*, ed. Jeremy Braddock and Jonathan P. Eburne. Baltimore: Johns Hopkins University Press, 2013.

Camiscioli, Elisa. *Reproducing the French Race: Immigration, Intimacy, and Embodiment in the Early Twentieth Century.* Durham and London: Duke University Press, 2009.

Carmichael, Stokely, and Charles V. Hamilton. *Black Power: The Politics of Liberation.* New York: Vintage Books, 1967.

Carter, Donald. "Navigating Diaspora: The Precarious Depths of the Italian Immigration Crisis," in *African Migrations: Patterns and Perspectives*, eds. Abdoulaye Kane and Todd H. Leedy. Bloomington: Indiana University Press, 2013.

Césaire, Aimé. *Discourse on Colonialism.* Trans. Joan Pinkham. New York: Monthly Review Press, 1955.

Césaire, Aimé. *Notebook of a Return to the Native Land.* Trans. Clayton Eshleman and Annette Smith. Middletown: Wesleyan University Press, 2001.

Charef, Mehdi. *Tea in the Harem.* Trans. Ed Emery. UK: Serpent's Tail, 1989.

Chomsky, Aviva. *"They Take Our Jobs!" and 20 Other Myths about Immigration.* Boston: Beacon Press, 2007.

Chomsky, Noam. *Year 501: The Conquest Continues.* Chicago: Haymarket Books, 2015.

Chossudovsky, Michel. *The Globalization of Poverty: Impacts of IMF and World Bank Reforms.* London: Zed Books, 1997.

Coly, Ayo A. *Pull of Postcolonial Nationhood: Gender and Migration in Francophone African Literature.* Pennsylvania: Rowan & Littlefield, 2010.

Condé, Maryse. "Order, Disorder, Freedom, and the West Indian Writer." *Yale French Studies* 97, 50 Years of Yale French Studies: A Commemorative Anthology. Part 2: 1980–1998 (2000).

Conway, Cecilia. *African Banjo Echoes in Appalachia: A Study of Folk Traditions.* Knoxville: University of Tennessee Press, 1995.

Crawford, Nawo C. "Prologue: Paris Black Pride 2016/" In *Decolonizing Sexualities: Transnational Perspectives, Critical Interventions*, ed. Sandeep Bakshi, Suhraiya Jivraj, and Silvia Posocco, xix–xxii. UK: Counterpress, 2016.

Crenshaw, Kimberle. "Mapping the Margins: Intersectionality, Identity Politics, and Violence against Women of Color." *Stanford Law Review* 43, no. 6 (July 1991): 1241–99.

Dadie, Bernard Binlin. *One Way: Bernard Dadie Observes America*. Trans. Jo Patterson. Urbana and Chicago: University of Illinois Press, 1994.

Dal Lago, Alessandro. *Non-Persons: The Exclusion of Migrants in a Global Society*. Trans. Marie Orton. Italy: IPOC Press, 2009.

Damas, Léon-Gontran. *Pigments*. Trans. Alexandra Lillehei. Middletown: Wesleyan University Press, 2011 (1937).

Damrosch, David. "Frames for World Literature." In *Grenzen der Literatur: Zu Begriff und Phänomen des Literarischen*, ed. Simone Winko, Fotis Jannidis, and Gerhard Lauer. Berlin and New York: Walter de Gruyter, 2009.Dawson, Ashley. *Extinction: A Radical History*. New York: O/R Books, 2016.

Dawson, Ashley. *Mongrel Nation*. Ann Arbor: University of Michigan Press, 2007.

Dawson, Ashley. "Surplus City: Structural Adjustment, Self-Fashioning, and Urban Insurrection in Chris Abani's Graceland." *Interventions: A Journal of Postcolonial Studies* 11(1) (2009): 16–34.

Diamond, Stanley. *In Search of the Primitive: A Critique of Civilization*. New Jersey: Transaction, 1974.

Di Maio, Alessandra. "Black Italia: Contemporary Migrant Writers from Africa." In *Black Europe and the African Diaspora*, ed. Darlene Clark Hine, Tricia Danielle Keaton, and Stephen Small. Urbana and Chicago: University of Illinois Press, 2009.

Di Maio, Alessandra, "Introduction: Pearls in Motion." In Cristina Ali Farah, *Little Mother*, trans. Giovanna Bellesia-Contuzzi and Victoria Offredi Poletto. Bloomington and Indianapolis: Indiana University Press, 2011.

Diagne, Souleymane Bachir. *African Art as Philosophy: Senghor, Bergson, and the Idea of Negritude*. Trans. Chike Jeffers. London: Seagull Books, 2011.

Diawara, Manthia, "Toward a Regional Imaginary in Africa." In *The Cultures of Globalization*, ed. Frederic Jameson and Masao Miyoshi. Durham and London: Duke University Press, 1998.

Diome, Fatou. *The Belly of the Atlantic*. Trans. Lulu Norman and Ros Schwartz. London: Serpent's Tail, 2006.

Dongala, Emmanuel. "From Négritude to Migritude: The African Writer in Exile." Presentation, Exil: mode(s) d'emploi—Experiencing Exile in Literature and the Arts Conference, University of California Los Angeles, 2005.

Dougnon, Isaie. "Migration as Coping with Risk and State Barriers: Malian Migrants' Conception of Being Far from Home," trans. Helene Gagliardi. In *African Migrations: Patterns and Perspectives*, eds. Abdoulaye Kane and Todd H. Leedy (Bloomington: Indiana University Press, 2013).

Dubois, Laurent. Lecture, Black Banjo Conference, Chicago, 2006.

Du Bois, W. E. B. *Black Reconstruction in America 1860–1880*. New York: Free Press, 1935.

Echenberg, Myron. *Colonial Conscripts: The* Tirailleurs Sénégalais *in French West Africa 1857–1960*. Portsmouth: Heinemann, 1991.

Edwards, Brent Hayes. *The Practice of Diaspora: Literature, Translation, and the Rise of Black Internationalism*. Durham and Cambridge: Duke University Press, 2003.

Ekine, Sokari. "Beyond Anti-LGBTI Legislation: Criminalization and the Denial of Citizenship." In *Decolonizing Sexualities: Transnational Perspectives, Critical Interventions*, ed. Sandeep Bakshi, Suhraiya Jivraj, and Silvia Posocco, 19–31. UK: Counterpress, 2016.

Emeagwali, Gloria. "The Neo-Liberal Agenda and the IMF/World Bank Structural Adjustment Programs with Reference to Africa." In Dip Kapoor, ed., *Critical Perspectives on Neoliberal Globalization, Development and Education in Africa and Asia*. Rotterdam: Sense Publishers, 2011.

Eng, David. *The Feeling of Kinship: Queer Liberalism and the Racialization of Intimacy*. Durham and London: Duke University Press, 2010.

Equiano, Olaudah. *The African: The Interesting Narrative of the Life of Olaudah Equiano*. London: *Black Classics*, 1998 (1789).

Fabre, Michel. *From Harlem to Paris: Black American Writers in France, 1840–1980*. Chicago: University of Illinois Press, 1991.

Fanon, Frantz. *Black Skin White Masks*. Trans. Charles Lam Markmann. New York: Grove Press, 1967.

Fanon, Frantz. *The Wretched of the Earth*. Trans. Constance Farrington. New York: Grove Press, 1963.

Farah, Cristina Ali. *Little Mother*. Trans. Giovanna Bellesia-Contuzzi and Victoria Offredi Poletto. Bloomington and Indianapolis: Indiana University Press, 2011.

Farah, Nuruddin. *Hiding in Plain Sight*. New York: Riverhead Books, 2014.

Farah, Nuruddin. *Links*. New York: Penguin, 2004.

Farah, Nuruddin. *Maps*. New York: Random House, 1986.

Farah, Nuruddin. *Yesterday, Tomorrow: Voices from the Somali Diaspora*. London: Cassell, 2000.

Ferguson, James. *Global Shadows: Africa in the Neoliberal World Order*. Durham: Duke University Press, 2007.

Ferguson, James. "Seeing Like an Oil Company: Space, Security, and Global Capital in Neoliberal Africa." *American Anthropologist* 107, no. 3 (2005).

Foster, Christopher Ian. "Home to Hargeisa: Migritude, Pan-Africanism, and the Politics of Movement from *Banjo* to *Black Mamba Boy*." *Ufahamu: A Journal of African Studies* 38, no. 2 (Spring 2015).

Foster, Christopher Ian. "The Queer Politics of Crossing in Maryse Condé's *Crossing the Mangrove*." *Small Axe* 43 (March 2014).

Foster, Christopher Ian. "Toward a Caribbean Migritude? Immigration, Sexuality, and the Gendered Caribbean Body." *Small Axe Salon* 18, no. 46 (February 2015).

Foucault, Michel. *The History of Sexuality Vol. 1: An Introduction*. Trans. Robert Hurley. New York: Random House, 1978.

Foucault, Michel. *Security, Territory, Population*. Ed. Michel Senellart .Trans. Graham Burchell. New York: Palgrave, 2007.

Gaines, Kevin K. *American Africans in Ghana: Black Expatriates and the Civil Rights Era.* Chapel Hill: University of North Carolina Press, 2006.

Gairola, Rahul K. "Capitalist Houses, Queer Homes: Identity Politics of Sexuality and Belonging in Stephen Frears and Hanif Kureishi's *My Beautiful Laundrette* (1985)." Conference presentation, University of British Columbia, August 17, 2007.

Gairola, Rahul K. "A Critique of Thatcherism and the Queering of Home in *Sammy and Rosie Get Laid.*" *South Asian Review* 32, no. 3 (2011).

Gairola, Rahul K. *Homelandings: Postcolonial Diasporas and Transatlantic Belonging.* London: Rowman & Littlefield International, 2016.

Gantz, Lauren. "On the Feeling of Kinship." *E3W Review of Books* 11 (Spring 2010).

Garelli, Glenda, and Martina Tazzioli, ed. *Tunisia as a Revolutionized Space of Migration.* London: Palgrave Macmillan, 2017.

Gilroy, Paul. *The Black Atlantic: Modernity and Double Consciousness.* United Kingdom: Verso, 1993.

Gilroy, Paul. *There Ain't No Black in the Union Jack: The Cultural Politics of Race and Nation.* Chicago: University of Chicago Press, 1987.

Guéne, Faiza. *Kiffe Kiffe Tomorrow: A Novel.* Trans. Sarah Adams. Orlando: Harcourt, 2006.

Hailu, Gebreyesus. *The Conscript: A Novel of Libya's Anticolonial War.* Trans. Ghirmai Negash. Athens: Ohio University Press, 2013.

Hall, Stuart, Chas Critcher, Tony Jefferson, John Clarke, and Brian Roberts. *Policing the Crisis: Mugging, the State, and Law and Order.* London: Macmillan, 1978.

Hargreaves, Alec. "Banlieue Blues." In *The Cambridge Companion to the Literature of Paris,* ed. Anna-Louise Milne. Cambridge: Cambridge University Press, 2014.

Heidegger, Martin. *Being and Time.* Trans. John Macquarrie and Edward Robinson. San Francisco: Harper, 1962.

Heidegger, Martin *The Fundamental Concepts of Metaphysics.* Trans. William McNeill and Nicholas Walker. Bloomington: Indiana University Press, 1995.

Heidegger, Martin. "The Origin of the Work of Art." In *Poetry, Language, Thought.* Trans. Albert Hofstadter. New York: Harper & Row, 1971.

Hoad, Neville. *African Intimacies: Race, Homosexuality, and Globalization.* Minneapolis: University of Minnesota Press, 2007.

Hobsbawm, Eric J. *The Age of Empire: 1875–1914.* New York: Vintage Books, 1989.

Hobsbawm, Eric J. *Nations and Nationalism since 1780.* Cambridge: Cambridge University Press, 1990.

Husserl, Edmund. *The Essential Husserl: Basic Writings in Transcendental Phenomenology,* ed. Donn Welton. Bloomington and Indianapolis: Indiana University Press, 1999.

Husserl, Edmund. *Ideas: General Introduction to Pure Phenomenology.* Trans. W. R. Boyce Gibson. London: Collier, 1956.

Iyun, Folasade. "The Impact of Structural Adjustment on Maternal and Child Health in Nigeria." In *Women Pay the Price: Structural Adjustment in Africa and the Caribbean,* ed. Gloria T. Emeagwali. New Jersey: Africa World Press, 1995.

Jayawardane, Neelika, and Ainehi Edoro. "Gay Sexuality and African Writers." *Africa Is a Country,* July 31, 2015. Web. http://africasacountry.com/2015/07/gay-sexuality-and -african-writers-adichie-osman/.

Jayawardane, Neelika, and Ainehi Edoro. "Diriye Osman on being Gay, Muslim and African." *Africa Is a Country*, December 8, 2014. Web. http://africasacountry.com/ somali-british-writer-diriye-osmans-fairytales-for-lost-children/.

Kane, Abdoulaye, and Todd H. Leedy. "African Patterns of Migration in a Global Era: New Perspectives." *African Migrations: Patterns and Perspectives*, eds. Abdoulaye Kane and Todd H. Leedy (Bloomington: Indiana University Press, 2013).

Kane, Cheikh Hamidou. *Ambiguous Adventure*. Trans. Katherine Woods. Oxford: Heinemann, 1963.

Kasse, Tidiane. "Africa and its diaspora in migration dynamics." *Pambazuka News: Pan-African Voices for Freedom and Justice* 684, June 26, 2014.

Keith, Brian Axel. "The Diasporic Imaginary." *Public Culture* 14, no. 2 (Spring 2002) 411–28.

Kesteloot, Lilyan. *Black Writers in French: A Literary History of Negritude*. Trans. Ellen Conroy Kennedy. Washington, DC: Howard University Press, 1991.

Khouma, Pap. *I Was an Elephant Salesman*. Trans. Rebecca Hopkins. Bloomington and Indianapolis: Indiana University Press, 2010.

Koller, Christian. "Colonial Military Participation in Europe (Africa)." *International Encyclopedia of the First World War*, 1–2. Web: https://encyclopedia.1914–1918-online .net/home/.

Lemma, Solome. "Against the Gospel of 'Africa Rising.'" *Africa Is a Country*, November 6, 2013, May, 2013. Web. http://allafrica.com/stories/201305310461.html.

Lettevall, Rebecca, and Kristian Petrov. *Critique of Cosmopolitan Reason: Timing and Spacing the Concept of World Citizenship*. Oxford: Peter Lang, 2014.

Lewis, Ioan. *Understanding Somalia and Somaliland*. London: C. Hurst, 2008.

Lewis, Shireen K. *Race, Culture, and Identity: Francophone West African and Caribbean Literature and Theory from Négritude to Créolité*. Oxford: Lexington Books, 2006.

Loingsigh, Aedin Ni. *Postcolonial Eyes: Intercontinental Travel in Francophone African Literature*. Liverpool: Liverpool University Press, 2009.

Lorde, Audre. *Apartheid U.S.A.* New York: Kitchen Table/Woman of Color Press, 1985.

Lorde, Audre, *Zami: A New Spelling of My Name*. USA: Persephone Press, 1982.

Lowe, Lisa. *The Intimacies of Four Continents*. Durham and London: Duke University Press, 2015.

Loyd, Jena, Matt Mitchelson, and Andrew Burridge. "Borders, Prisons, and Abolitionist Visions." In *Beyond Walls and Cages: Prisons, Borders, and Global Crises*, eds. Jenna Loyd, Matt Mitchelson, and Andrew Burridge. Athens: University of Georgia Press, 2012.

Luibhéid, Eithne. *Entry Denied: Controlling Sexuality at the Border*. Minneapolis and London: University of Minnesota Press, 2002.

Luibhéid, Eithne, and Lionel Cantú Jr., eds. *Queer Migrations: Sexuality, U.S. Citizenship, and Border Crossings*. Minneapolis and London: University of Minnesota Press, 2005.

Luraschi, Moira. "Beyond Words: Mirroring Identities of Italian Postcolonial Women Writers." *Enquire* 3 (June 2009).

Mabanckou, Alain. *Black Bazaar*. Trans. Sarah Ardizzone. London: Serpent's Tail, 2012.

Mabanckou, Alain. *Blue White Red*. Trans. Alison Dundy. Bloomington and Indianapolis: Indiana University Press, 2013.

Mamdani, Mahmood. *Citizen and Subject: Contemporary Africa and the Legacy of Late Colonialism*. Princeton: Princeton University Press, 1996.

Mamdani, Mahmood, *Define and Rule: Native as Political Identity*. Cambridge: Harvard University Press, 2012.

Marczewski, Amy, and Julie Nack Ngue. "Exil: mode(s) d' emploi: New readings, new endings." *Paroles gelées* 22(1) (2006). http://escholarship.org/uc/item/14f349×5.

Marx, Karl. *Dispatches for the New York Tribune: Selected Journalism of Karl Marx*. Ed. James Ledbetter. New York: Penguin Classics, 2007.

Mattar, Karim, and David Fieni. "The Global Checkpoint: 'Rights' of Passage, Performance of Sovereignty." Seminar, American Comparative Literature Association Conference, March 29–April 1, 2012, Brown University, Providence, RI.

Mbembe, Achille. "Africa and the Future: An Interview with Achille Mbembe." Thomas M. Blaser, *Africa Is a Country*. November 20, 2013. Web. http://africasacountry.com/africa-and-the-future-an-interview-with-achille-mbembe/.

Mbembe, Achille. *Critique of Black Reason*. Trans. Laurent Dubois. Durham and London: Duke University Press, 2017.

McKay, Claude. *Banjo: A Story Without a Plot*. New York: Harper & Brothers, 1929.

McKay, Claude. *A Long Way from Home: An Autobiography*. New York: Harvest Books, 1937.

McKay, Claude. *The Negroes in America*. Trans. Robert J. Winter. London: Kennikat Press, 1979.

Mehta, Uday. *Liberalism and Empire: A Study in Nineteenth-Century British Liberal Thought*. Chicago: University of Chicago Press, 1999.

Mezlekia, Nega. *Notes From the Hyena's Belly: An Ethiopian Boyhood*. New York: Picador USA, 2000.

Miano, Leonora. *Ecrits pour la parole*. Trans. *Régine Jean-Charles*. (French and European Publications, 2012).

Mohamed, Nadifa. *Black Mamba Boy*. New York: Farrar, Straus and Giroux, 2010.

Mohamed, Nadifa. "Black Mamba Boy: Reading and discussion with Nadifa Mohamed." Reading, September 25, 2012, Graduate Center, CUNY.

Moore, G. H. "Nomads and Feminists: The Novels of Nuruddin Farah." In *Emerging Perspectives on Nuruddin Farah*, ed. Derek Wright. New Jersey: Africa World Press, 2002.

Murray, David A. B., ed. *Queering Borders: Language, Sexuality, and Migration*. Amsterdam and Philadelphia: John Benjamins, 2016.

Murray, Stephen O., and Will Roscoe, ed. *Boy-wives and Female Husbands: Studies in African Homosexualities*. New York: Palgrave, 1998.

Nancy, Jean-Luc. *Being Singular Plural*. Trans. Robert D. Richardson and Anne E. O'Byrne. Stanford: Stanford University Press, 2000.

Nardal, Paulette. "In Exile." In T. Denean Sharpley-Whiting, *Negritude Women*. Minneapolis and London: University of Minnesota Press, 2002.

O'Okwemba, Khainga. "Kenya: Migritude—a Revelation of Migrant Mysticism." *AllAfrica*, May 2013. Web. http://allafrica.com/stories/201305310461.html.

Osman, Diriye. *Fairytales for Lost Children*. UK: Team Angelica, 2013.

Parati, Graziella. "Introduction." In *I Was an Elephant Salesman*, by Pap Khouma. Trans. Rebecca Hopkins. Bloomington and Indianapolis: Indiana University Press, 2010.

Parati, Graziella. *Migration Italy: The Art of Talking Back in a Destination Culture*. Toronto: University of Toronto Press, 2014.

Patel, Shailja. *Migritude*. New York: Kaya Press, 2010.

Patterson, Orlando. "Freedom, Slavery, and the Modern Construction of Rights." In *The Cultural Values of Europe*, ed. Hans Joas and Klaus Wiegandt. Liverpool: Liverpool University Press, 2008.

Paynter, Eleanor. "The Spaces of Citizenship: Mapping Personal and Colonial Histories in Contemporary Italy in Igiaba Scego's *La Mia Casa È Dove Sono (My Home is Where I Am)*." *European Journal of Life Writing* [S.1.], v. 6 (July 2017): 135–53.

Perera, Sonali. *No Country: Working-Class Writing in the Age of Globalization*. New York: Columbia University Press, 2014.

Peters, Jonathan A. *A Dance of Masks: Senghor, Achebe, Soyinka*. Boulder: Three Continents Press, 1978.

Prashad, Vijay. "Speaking of Saris." In Shailja Patel, *Migritude*. New York: Kaya Press 2010.

Puar, Jasbir K. *Terrorist Assemblages: Homonationalism in Queer Times*. Durham and London: Duke University Press, 2007.

"Race and Immigration: A New Kind of Ghetto." *The Economist*, November 9, 2013. http://www.economist.com/news/special-report/21589230-britain-no-longer-has-serious-race-problem-trouble-isolation-new-kind.

Reddy, Vanita. *Fashioning Diaspora: Beauty, Femininity, and South Asian American Culture*. Philadelphia: Temple University Press, 2016.

Reid-Pharr, Robert. "Alas Poor Jimmy." In *Once You Go Black: Choice, Desire, and the Black American Intellectual*. New York and London: New York University Press, 2007.

Renan, Ernest. "What Is a Nation?" Presentation delivered at the Sorbonne, March 11, 1882. In Ernest Renan, *Qu'est-ce qu'une nation?* Trans. Ethan Rundell. Paris: Presses-Pocket, 1992.

Robinson, Cedric. *Black Marxism: The Making of the Black Radical Tradition*. Chapel Hill and London: University of North Carolina Press, 1983.

Rodney, Walter. *How Europe Underdeveloped Africa*. Washington, DC: Howard University Press, 1972.

Rono, Joseph Kipkemboi. "The Impact of Structural Adjustment Programmes on Kenyan Society." *Journal of Social Development in Africa* 17, no. 1 (January 2002).

Rosenblum, Darren. "Queer Intersectionality and the Failure of Recent Lesbian and Gay 'Victories.'" *Law & Sexuality* 83 (1994). Web. https://digitalcommons.pace.edu/cgi/viewcontent.cgi?referer=https://www.google.com/&httpsredir=1&article=1209&context=lawfaculty.

Rosenshaft, Eve, and Robbie Aitken, ed. *Africa in Europe: Studies in Transnational Practice in the Long Twentieth Century*. Liverpool: Liverpool University Press, 2013.

Ross, Eliot, and Sean Jacobs. "The Banana that Revealed Europe's Persistent Racism." Al Jazeera America, April 30, 2014. Web.

Rushdie, Salman. "The New Empire Within Britain." In *Imaginary Homelands: Essays and Criticism 1981–1991*. London: Granta Books, 1991.

Said, Edward. *Culture and Imperialism*. New York: Vintage Books, 1994.

Sandten, Cecile. "Contemporary Nomads, or Can the Slum-Dweller Speak?" In *Narrating Nomadism: Tales of Recovery and Resistance*, ed. G. N. Devy, Geoffrey V. Davis, and K. K. Chakravarty. New York: Routledge, 2013.

Santana, Stephanie Bosch. "Exorcizing Afropolitanism: Binyavanga Wainaina explains why 'I am a Pan-Africanist, not an Afropolitan' at ASAUK 2012." *Africa in Words* (blog), February 8, 2013. https://africainwords.com/2013/02/08/exorcizing-afropolitanism-binyavanga-wainaina -explains-why-i-am-a-pan-africanist-not-an-afropolitan-at-asauk-2012/.

Sartre, Jean-Paul. "Black Orpheus." *What Is Literature? and other Essays*. Trans. John MacCombie. (Cambridge: Harvard University Press, 1988).

Sassen, Saskia. *Guests and Aliens*. New York: New Press, 1999.

Schwartz, Mattathias. "The Anchor: Letter from Lampedusa." *New Yorker*, April 21, 2014.

Scott, David. "Colonial Governmentality." *Social Text* 43 (Autumn 1995): 191–220.

Sembene, Ousmane. *Le Noir de*. France and Senegal: Filmi Domirev and Les Actualités Françaises, 1966. Film.

Senghor, Léopold Sédar. "In Memoriam." In *Léopold Sédar Senghor: Prose and Poetry*. Trans. John Reed and Clive Wake. London: Oxford University Press, 1965.

Senghor, Léopold Sédar. "Negritude: A Humanism of the Twentieth Century." In *Colonial Discourse and Post-colonial Theory: A Reader*, ed. Patrick Williams and Laura Chrisman. New York: Columbia University Press, 1994.

Senghor, Léopold Sédar. "Night of Sine." In *The Negritude Poets: An Anthology of Translations from the French,* ed. Ellen Conroy Kennedy. New York: Thunder's Mouth Press, 1975.

Senghor, Léopold Sédar. *On African Socialism*. Trans. Mercer Cook. New York: Fredrick A. Prager, 1964.

Senghor, Léopold Sédar. "La Poesie Negro-Americaine." Lecture, 1950. Cited in Robert Philipson, "The Harlem Renaissance as a Postcolonial Phenomenon." *African American Review* 40, no. 1 (Spring 2006).

Senghor, Léopold Sédar. *Prose and Poetry*. Oxford: Oxford University Press, 1965.

Sharpley-Whiting, T. Denean. *Negritude Women*. Minneapolis and London: University of Minnesota Press, 2002.

Shringarpure, Bhakti, ed. *Mediterranean*. Connecticut: Warscapes Magazine, 2018.

Singh, Nikhil Pal. *Black Is a Country*. Cambridge: Cambridge University Press, 2004.

Slobodian, Quinn. *Globalists: The End of Empire and the Birth of Neoliberalism*. Cambridge, MA: Harvard University Press, 2018.

Solomon, Alisa. "Trans/Migrant: Christina Madrazo's All-American Story." In *Queer Migrations: Sexuality, U.S. Citizenship, and Border Crossings*, ed. Eithne Luibhéid and Lionel Cantú Jr., 3–29. Minneapolis: University of Minnesota Press, 2005.

Solomos, John. *Race and Racism in Britain*. Gordonsville: Palgrave MacMillan, 2003.

Spivak, Gayatri Chakravorty. "Subaltern Studies: Deconstructing Historiography." In *Selected Subaltern Studies*, eds. Ranajit Guha and Gayatri Spivak (New York: Oxford University Press, 1988).

Stoler, Ann, ed. *Imperial Debris: On Ruins and Ruination.* Durham and London: Duke University Press, 2013.

Talani, Leila Simona, ed. *Globalisation, Migration, and the Future of Europe: Insiders and Outsiders.* London and New York: Routledge, 2012.

Thiong'o, Ngũgĩ Wa. *Decolonizing the Mind: The Politics of Language in African Literature.* Portsmouth: Heinemann, 1986.

Thomas, Dominic. *Africa and France: Postcolonial Cultures, Migration, and Racism.* Bloomington and Indianapolis: Indiana University Press, 2013.

Thomas, Dominic. *Black France: Colonialism, Immigration, and Transnationalism.* Bloomington and Indianapolis: Indiana University Press, 2007.

Torpey, John. *The Invention of the Passport: Surveillance, Citizenship, and the State.* Cambridge: Cambridge University Press, 2000.

Tyson, Lois. *Critical Theory Today: A User-Friendly Guide.* London and New York: Routledge, 2015.

Waberi, Abdourahman A. "Les Enfants de la Postcolonie: Esquisse d'une Nouvelle Génération d'écrivains Francophones d'Afrique Noire." *Notre Librairie* 135 (1998): 8–15. Print.

Waberi, Abdourahman A. *Transit: A Novel.* Trans. David Ball and Nicole Ball. Bloomington and Indianapolis: Indiana University Press, 2012.

Wainaina, Binyavanga. "I am a Homosexual, Mum." *African Is a Country*, January 19, 2014. Web. http://africasacountry.com/2014/01/i-am-a-homosexual-mum/.

Walters, Wendy W. *At Home in Diaspora: Black International Writing.* Minneapolis: University of Minnesota Press, 2005.

Weinbaum, Alys Eve. *Wayward Reproductions: Genealogies of Race and Nation in Transatlantic Modern Thought.* Durham: Duke University Press, 2004.

Westengard, Laura. *Gothic Queer Culture: Marginalized Communities and the Ghosts of Insidious Trauma.* Lincoln: University of Nebraska Press, 2019.

Wild, Antony. *Coffee: A Dark History.* New York: W.W. Norton, 2005.

Wilder, Gary. *Freedom Time: Negritude, Decolonization, and the Future of the World.* Durham and London: Duke University Press, 2015.

Wilder, Gary. *The French Imperial Nation-State: Negritude and Colonial Humanism Between the Two World Wars.* Chicago: University of Chicago Press, 2005.

Williams, Eric. *Capitalism and Slavery.* Chapel Hill and London: University of North Carolina Press, 1994.

Wolfreys, Jim. "Making Racism Respectable: Islamophobia in Sarkozy's France." *Global Social Justice Journal* 1, no. 1. Published by the Centre for International Studies at Cape Breton University, 2013.

Wright, Michelle M. "Pale by Comparison: Black Liberal Humanism and the Postwar Era in the African Diaspora." In *Black Europe and the African Diaspora*, ed. Darlene Clark Hine, Trica Danielle Keaton, and Stephen Small. Urbana and Chicago: University of Illinois Press, 2009.

Wright, Richard. *Black Power: Three Books from Exile: Black Power; The Color Curtain; and White Man, Listen!* New York: Harper Perennial, 2008.

Wrong, Michela. *I Didn't Do It for You: How the World Betrayed a Small African Nation.* New York: Harper Perennial, 2005.

INDEX

Photographer Credit: Charles A. Smith, Photographer, Jackson State University

ABOUT THE AUTHOR

Dr. Christopher Ian Foster is assistant professor of English at Jackson State University. He received his PhD in English literature from the Graduate Center of the City University of New York (CUNY) and has published widely in postcolonial, African, and Caribbean literary studies. He teaches at both the undergraduate and graduate levels in literature, writing, and black Atlantic and diaspora studies.

CPSIA information can be obtained
at www.ICGtesting.com
Printed in the USA
BVHW030419230719
554122BV00003B/9/P